VENEZUELAN ANARCHISM

THE HISTORY OF A MOVEMENT
1811–1998

RODOLFO MONTES DE OCA

TRANSLATED BY
CHAZ BUFE

For information contact:

    See Sharp Press
    P.O. Box 1731
    Tucson, AZ 85702

    www.seesharppress.com

Montes de Oca, Rodolfo.
    Venezuelan Anarchism : the history of a movement / by Rodolfo
Montes de Oca ; Introduction by Daniel Barret ; translated by Charles Bufe.–
Tucson, Ariz.: See Sharp Press, 2019.
Includes bibliographical references.
ISBN 9781937276980

Contents: Map of Venezuela -- Introduction -- Preface -- Foreword -- Transla-
tor's Note -- List of Acronyms -- Chapter 1. The Historical Background -- Chapter 2. Origins and Prehistory -- Chapter 3. Clandestinity, Combat, and Tyranny
-- 4. Resistance and the Spanish Exile -- 5. The Seditious Resurgence of
Anarchism.

1. Venezuela -- Politics and government -- 1811-1998. 2. Venezuela --
Economic conditions -- 19th and 20th centuries. 4. Petroleum industry and
trade -- Political aspects. 5. Petroleum industry and trade -- Venezuela.
6. Anarchism -- Venezuela -- History. 7. Anarchists -- Venezuela -- History.
8. Labor movement -- Venezuela -- History. 9. Syndicalism -- Venezuela --
History. 9. Trade-unions -- Venezuela -- History. 10. Trade-unions and
communism -- Venezuela -- History. I. Title.

CONTENTS

To my family

Aníbal, Yari, Valeria, and Ariel

And to

Emilio Tesoro
a social rebel

Outline map of Venezuelan states courtesy of d-maps.com

INTRODUCTION

To reclaim yesterday, to build tomorrow

The anarchist movement in Latin America has recovered the fighting and pioneering spirit of its best years. Nonetheless, despite its demonstrable expansion and ostensible rejuvenation of the groups of which it's composed, and some renovation of the practices that distinguish it, it's still a minority movement having much to think about, to say, and to do. An array of opportunities faces this rejuvenated movement, an array in which it can provide simultaneously a body of critical thought, a glimpse of utopia, and a day-in-day-out combative, rebellious stance that will play out in a thousand unforeseen ways.

The way forward will benefit from reclaiming our past and our historical antecedents. It's no accident, therefore, that much current Latin American anarchist study concerns the rich history that precedes us.

The reappearance of this historiagraphic, investigational approach can arbitrarily be placed in the years before the current libertarian reawakening. *El anarquismo en América Latina* (1990), compiled and edited by Carlos Rama and Ángel Capppellitti, is without doubt the as-yet-unsurpassed history of Latin American anarchism—an inspired work that at the time it was published seemed to some skeptics a requiem mass, but that today can be seen as an overture to what's to come.

After that book came a raft of other more narrowly focused books—so many that it's impossible to definitively inventory all of them—including the works of Rubén Trejo, Chantal López and Omar Cortés in Mexico; Fernando López Trujillo, Verónica Díaz, and Pablo Pérez in Argentina; Juan Carlos Mechoso in Uruguay; Frank Fernández in Miami, on Cuba; Óscar Ortiz, Andrés Pérez González, Felipe del Solar, Alejandra Pinto, Adriana Palomera, and Darío Covarrubias in Chile; Margareth Rago in Brazil; Luis Alfonso Fajardo Sánchez in Colombia; Norma Valle in Puerto Rico, and a great many others, including books that deal with forgotten feminist pioneers, books that deal with individuals, books that attempt to decipher vast collective undertakings, and others that go back to libertarian origins in centuries past or that deal with the latest trends. These in conjunction serve to reclaim and highlight a historical presence that obscurantists and authoritarians of different stripes have attempted to hide or deride.

This present work by Ricardo Montes de Oca has abundant traces of this copious production, and this in a work that deals with an anarchist movement in a land where anarchism has always appeared peripheral to the driving and loudly trumpeted nationalist movements. In this context he's unearthed an unknown history, a history that raises questioning looks, even among his countrymen. This unveiling reveals unknown sprouts from the familiar trunk of anarchism, unknown shoots that will seem strange if one considers anarchism monolithic. In addition to revealing the unknown, Rodolfo's project also shows the arc of Venezuelan anarchism from its most distant antecedents to the contemporary. It's an ambitious examination that can only be compared, given the period covered, to Frank Fernández's *Cuban Anarchism: The History of a Movement*.

The examination Rafael provides runs from the initial intuitions of Coto Paul near the beginning of the 19th century, through the later though not distant Proudhonist writings of Fermín Toro and Rafael María Baralt, through the influence José Bradford (an acquaintance of Proudhon) exerted upon Ezequiel Zamora. This stretch of time, which he refers to as "prehistory," is not lacking in audacious concepts, which later investigations will confirm or refute.

Beginning there, Rodolfo outlines the adventures and vicissitudes of a movement that unfolded more slowly and with less energy than other similar movements in the region, a movement that was severely impeded by the dictatorships of Cipriano Castro and, for a great deal of time, Juan Vicente Gómez. A movement that existed despite inadequate cohesion, and that was later ignored by partisan historians. A movement that despite major obstacles still produced major figures and that established principles and practices that were utilized in the 20th century, in events such as the emblematic railroad strike of 1918.

Without neglecting the significance of these past events, of the continuities and discontinuities that Rafael outlines in his first chapters, perhaps the most important thing, the most significant, is what Foucault calls going back to the past to write the history of the present. Because the most outstanding thing about this text is not its recounting of the ancient past—an objective and professional recounting—but that it reveals the roots of the present crisis.

The merit of Rodolfo's book consists then not in presenting us with a wax museum, but in introducing us to an indispensable historical account of the wild dance of a movement alive in the present day, an account that considers that movement's possibilities and its limits, that keenly reclaims yesterday and that gives us the tools, the understanding to build tomorrow.

—Daniel Barret, Montevideo, Uruguay

PREFACE

*"The victors write history, and to cover themselves with glory
they cover the vanquished with neglect."*
—Elisee Reclus

In the 19th and 20th centuries the anarchist movement was a revolutionary expression of labor, student, and cultural struggles, designed to lead to a more just, more egalitarian world; it was designed to lead to a world without the state, and without capitalism. The anarchist political current was influential in lands such as Mexico, Cuba, Argentina, Uruguay, Chile, the United States, Russia, France, Greece, Spain, and Italy. But in Venezuela, that bucolic, religious, conservative strong man-oriented country, it's difficult to see how it could have been influential.

But it arose, and in the long history of the republic libertarian ideas were mentioned over and over in many places and venues, and were influential in the times and struggles that gave birth to this tropical enclave known as Venezuela.

And then one must ask, "What is history?" One might explain it as defining (or redefining) the past of a country and the development of its people. This matter is urgent when it comes to Venezuela, not only because of its turbulent present, but also because of the uncertainty of its future. The purpose of this book is to revive the history of the Venezuelan anarchist movement, which has largely been forgotten, and when not forgotten, vilified; it's intended to provide a basis for future antiauthoritarian generations of Venezuelans, a basis that will help them realize their aspirations.

Our area of study runs from 1811 to 1998. The lack of historical attention to the anarchist movement in this period is due to the early nature of most of its contributions.

The first chapter begins with the secession (from Spain) movement in 1811, initiated by the Junta Patriótica, and will consider the figure of Coto Paúl and the movement's similarities to the Guerra Popular of 1814 (which led to Venezuela's independence). It will also look at the figures of Simón Bolívar and

Ezequile Zamora, and the myths surrounding them as egalitarian revolutionaries. The chapter will conclude with a look at the influence of anarchism in Venezuela's rural areas at the time.

The second chapter begins with the arrival of the Andeans in the government of Cipriano Castro, and covers the participation of Biófilo Panclasta in the Revolución Liberal Restaurada (revolution of liberal restoration) march, the participation of José MaríaVargas Vila in the "little corporal's" (Cipriano Castro's) anti-imperialist political movement, the beginnings of the first labor unions, the first labor struggles, and the founding of the workers' press; the chapter will also consider the approach of the "generation of 1928" to anarchist principles at the time the country was beginning to open itself to petroleum exploitation.

The third and fourth chapters will deal with anarchist ideas in the period of the Liberal Democratic Republic (1945-1998), the affinity of anarchism and anarchist elements with Acción Democrática [a social democratic leftist political party]; the arrival, actions, and influence of Spanish anarchist exiles following the end of the Spanish Civil War in 1939, during the corporatist dictatorship of Marcos Pérez Jiménez (1952–1958); the participation of anarchists in the Caracazo [wave of unrest in Caracas in 1989]; and the participation of anarchists during the institutional breakdown in the final decade of the 20th century.

Finally, I should emphasize that this book would not have been possible without the help of those who generously donated their time. Special thanks to Frank Fernández, Daniel Barret, Rafael Uzcátgui, the Méndez Vivas family, Johnny Castro, Javier Torres, Any Alárcon, Lexys Rendon, María Julia Cidras, Eduardo de la Mano, and Antonio Serrano, all of whom went through the manuscript and contributed corrections. But above all I should thank my family, Aníbal, Ariel, Valeria, and Yaritza, the pillars of my life, beautiful and loving souls, my companions on this voyage through life.

—Rodolfo Montes de Oca, Caracas

FOREWORD

Before going on to the body of this book, a history of the anarchist movement in Venezuela, it's first necessary to understand what anarchism is and what it isn't. First, what it isn't.

Anarchism is not terrorism. An overwhelming majority of anarchists have always rejected terrorism, because they've been intelligent enough to realize that means determine ends, that terrorism is inherently vanguardist, and that even when "successful" it almost always leads to bad results. The anonymous authors of *You Can't Blow Up a Social Relationship: The Anarchist Case Against Terrorism* put it like this:

> You can't blow up a social relationship. The total collapse of this society would provide no guarantee about what replaced it. Unless a majority of people had the ideas and organization sufficient for the creation of an alternative society, we would see the old world reassert itself because it is what people would be used to, what they believed in, what existed unchallenged in their own personalities.
>
> Proponents of terrorism and guerrillaism are to be opposed because their actions are vanguardist and authoritarian, because their ideas, to the extent that they are substantial, are wrong or unrelated to the results of their actions (especially when they call themselves libertarians or anarchists), because their killing cannot be justified, and finally because their actions produce either repression with nothing in return, or an authoritarian regime.[2]

Decades of government and corporate slander cannot alter this reality: the overwhelming majority of anarchists reject terrorism for both practical and ethical reasons. In the late 1990s, *Time* magazine called Ted Kaczynski, the Unabomber, "the king of the anarchists"; but that doesn't make it so. *Time's* words were just another typical, perhaps deliberately dishonest, attempt to tar all anarchists with the terrorist brush.

This is not to say that armed resistance is never appropriate. Clearly there are situations in which one has little choice, as when facing a dictatorship that suppresses civil liberties and prevents one from acting openly—which has happened repeatedly in many countries, including Venezuela. Even then, armed resistance should be undertaken reluctantly and as a last resort, because violence is inherently undesirable due to the suffering it causes; because it provides repressive regimes excuses for further repression; because it provides them with the opportunity to commit atrocities against civilians and to blame those atrocities on their "terrorist" opponents; and because, as history has shown, the chances of success are very low.

Even though armed resistance may sometimes be called for in repressive situations, it's a far different matter to succumb to the romance of the gun and to engage in guerrilla warfare in relatively open societies in which civil liberties are largely intact and in which one does not have mass popular support at the start of one's violent campaign. Violence in such situations does little but drive the public into the "protective" arms of the government; narrow political dialogue (tending to polarize the populace into pro- and anti-guerrilla factions); turn politics into a spectator sport for the vast majority of people[3]; provide the government with an excuse to suppress civil liberties; and induce the onset of repressive regimes "better" able to handle the "terrorist" problem than their more tolerant predecessors. It's also worth noting that the chances of success of such violent, vanguardist campaigns are microscopic. They are simply arrogant, ill-thought-out roads to disaster.[4]

Anarchism is not primitivism. In recent decades, groups of quasi-religious mystics have begun equating the primitivism they advocate (rejection of science, rationality, and technology—often lumped together under the blanket term, "technology") with anarchism.[5] In reality, the two have nothing to do with each other, as we'll see when we consider what anarchism actually is—a set of philosophical/ethical precepts and organizational principles designed to maximize human freedom. For now, suffice it to say that the elimination of technology advocated by primitivist groups would inevitably entail the deaths of literally billions of human beings in a world utterly dependent upon interlocking technologies for everything from food production/delivery to communications to medical treatment. Primitivists' fervently desired outcome, the elimination of technology, could only come about through means which are the absolute antithesis of anarchism: the use of coercion and violence on a mass scale, as it's inconceivable that a majority of human beings would voluntarily give up such things as running water, sewer systems, modern medicine, electric lights, and warm houses in the winter.[6]

Anarchism is not chaos. Anarchism is not rejection of organization. The idea that anarchism equals rejection of organization is repeated *ad nauseam* by the mass media and by anarchism's political foes, especially marxists, who sometimes know better. Even a brief look at the works of anarchism's leading theoreticians confirms that this belief is in error. Over and over in the writings of Proudhon, Bakunin, Kropotkin, Rocker, Ward, Bookchin, et al., one finds not a rejection of organization, but rather a preoccupation with it—a preoccupation with how society should be organized in accord with the anarchist principles of individual freedom and social justice. For over a century and a half, anarchists have been arguing that coercive, hierarchical organization (as embodied in government and corporations) is not equivalent to organization *per se* (which they regard as necessary), and that coercive organization should be replaced by decentralized, nonhierarchical organization based on voluntary cooperation and mutual aid. This is hardly a rejection of organization.

Anarchism is not amoral egoism. As does any avant garde social movement, anarchism attracts more than its share of flakes, parasites, and outright sociopaths, persons simply looking for a glamorous label to cover their often pathological selfishness, their disregard for the rights and dignity of others, and their pathetic desire to be the center of attention. These individuals tend to give anarchism a bad name, because even though they have very little in common with actual anarchists—that is, persons concerned with ethical behavior, social justice, and the rights of both themselves *and others*—they're often quite exhibitionistic, and their disreputable actions sometimes come into the public eye. To make matters worse, these exhibitionists sometimes publish their self-glorifying views and deliberately misidentify those views as "anarchist." (This is more of a problem in the United States than in Venezuela or probably anywhere else in the world.) Amoral egoists may (mis)use the label, but they're no more anarchists than the now-defunct German Democratic Republic (East Germany) was democratic or a republic.

The full absurdity of identifying amoral egoism—essentially "I'll do what I damn well please and fuck everybody else"—with anarchism will become apparent in short order when we'll consider what anarchism actually is.

Anarchism is not "Libertarianism." Until relatively recently, the very useful term "libertarian" was used worldwide as a synonym for "anarchist." Indeed, it was used exclusively in this sense until the 1970s when, in the United States, it was appropriated by the grossly misnamed Libertarian Party.

This party has almost nothing to do with anarchist concepts of liberty, especially the concepts of equal freedom and positive freedom—that is, equal access to the resources necessary to the freedom to act. (Equal freedom and positive freedom are discussed in the following section of this foreword.) Instead, this "libertarian" party concerns itself exclusively with the negative freedoms, pretending that liberty exists only in the negative sense, freedom from restraint, while it simultaneously revels in the denial of equal positive freedom to the vast majority of the world's people.

These "libertarians" not only glorify capitalism, the mechanism that denies both equal freedom and positive freedom to the vast majority, but they also wish to retain the coercive apparatus of the state while eliminating its social welfare functions—hence widening the rift between rich and poor, and increasing the freedom of the rich by diminishing that of the poor (while keeping the boot of the state firmly on their necks). Thus, in the United States, the once exceedingly useful term "libertarian" has been hijacked by egotists who are in fact enemies of liberty in the full sense of the word, and who have very little in common with anarchists.

This is what anarchism isn't.

What Anarchism Is

In its narrowest sense, anarchism is simply the rejection of the state, the rejection of coercive government. Under this very narrow definition, even such apparent absurdities as "anarcho-capitalism" and religious anarchism are possible.[7]

But most anarchists use the term "anarchism" in a much broader sense, defining it as the rejection of coercion and domination in all forms. So, most anarchists reject not only coercive government, but also religion and capitalism, which they see as other forms of the twin evils, domination and coercion. They reject religion because they see it as the ultimate form of domination, in which a supposedly all-powerful god hands down "thou shalts" and "thou shalt nots" to its "flock."

Anarchists likewise reject capitalism because it's designed to produce rich and poor, and because it's designed to produce a system of domination in which some give orders and others have little choice but to take them. For similar reasons, on a personal level almost all anarchists reject sexism, racism, misogyny, and homophobia—all of which produce artificial inequality, and thus domination.

To put this another way, anarchists believe in freedom in both its negative and positive senses. In this country, freedom is routinely presented only in its negative sense, that of being free from restraint. Hence most people equate freedom only with such things as freedom of speech, freedom of association, and freedom of (or from) religion. But there's also a positive aspect of freedom, an aspect which anarchists almost alone insist on.[8]

That positive aspect is what Emma Goldman called "the freedom to." And that freedom, the freedom of action, the freedom to enjoy or use, is highly dependent upon access to the world's resources. Because of this the rich are in a very real sense free to a much greater degree than the rest of us. To cite an example in the area of free speech, Bill Gates could easily buy dozens of daily newspapers or television stations to propagate his views and influence public opinion. How many working people could do the same? How many working people could afford to buy a single daily newspaper or a single television station? The answer is obvious. Working people cannot do such things; instead, we're reduced to putting up blogs ot posts on social media in our relatively few hours of free time.

Examples of the greater freedom of the rich abound in daily life. To put this in general terms, because they do not have to work, the rich not only have far more money (that is, access to resources) but also far more time to pursue their interests, pleasures, and desires than do the rest of us.

To cite a concrete example, the rich are free to send their children to the best colleges employing the best instructors, which the rest of us simply can't afford to do; if we can afford college at all, we make do with community and state colleges employing slave-labor "adjunct faculty" and overworked, underpaid graduate teaching assistants. Once in college, the children of the rich are entirely free to pursue their studies, while most other students must work at least part time to support themselves, which deprives them of many hours which could be devoted to study. If you think about it, you can easily find additional examples of the greater freedom of the rich in the areas of medical care, housing, nutrition, travel, etc., etc.—in fact, in virtually every area of life.

This greater freedom of action for the rich comes at the expense of everyone else, through the diminishment of everyone else's freedom of action. There is no way around this, given that freedom of action is to a great extent determined by access to finite resources. Anatole France well illustrated the differences between the restrictions placed upon the rich and the poor when he wrote, "The law, in its majestic equality, forbids the rich as well as the poor to sleep under bridges, to beg in the streets, and to steal bread."

Because the primary goal of anarchism is the greatest possible amount of freedom for all, anarchists insist on equal freedom in both its negative and positive aspects—that, in the negative sense, individuals be free to do whatever they wish as long as they do not harm or directly intrude upon others; and, in the positive sense, that all individuals have equal freedom to act, that they have equal access to the world's resources.

Anarchists recognize that absolute freedom is an impossibility, that amoral egotism ignoring the rights of others would quickly devolve into a war of all against all. What we argue for is that everyone have equal freedom from restraint (limited only by respect for the rights of others) and that everyone have as nearly as possible equal access to resources, thus ensuring equal (or near-equal) freedom to act.

This is anarchism in its theoretical sense.

In Spain, Argentina, Cuba, and a few other countries, including Venezuela, there have been serious attempts to make this theory reality through the movement known as anarcho-syndicalism. The primary purpose of anarcho-syndicalism is the replacement of coercive government by voluntary cooperation in the form of worker-controlled unions coordinating the entire economy. This would not only eliminate the primary restraint on the negative freedoms (government), but would also be a huge step toward achieving positive freedom. The nearest this vision came to fruition was in the Spanish Revolution, 1936–1939, when huge areas of Spain, including its most heavily industrialized region, came under the control of the anarcho-syndicalist Confederación Nacional del Trabajo (National Workers Confederation). George Orwell describes this achievement in *Homage to Catalonia*:

> The anarchists were still in virtual control of Catalonia and the revolution was in full swing. . . . the aspect of Barcelona was something startling and overwhelming. It was the first time that I had ever been in a town where the working class was in the saddle. Practically every building of any size had been seized by the workers and was draped with red flags or with the red and black flag of the anarchists; . . . Every shop and café had an inscription saying it had been collectivized; even the bootblacks had been collectivized and their boxes painted red and black. Waiters and shop-workers looked you in the face and treated you as an equal. Servile and even ceremonial forms of speech had temporarily disappeared. . . . The revolutionary posters were everywhere, flaming from the walls in clean reds and blues that made the few remaining advertisements look like daubs of mud. . . . All this was queer and moving. There was much in it that I did not understand, in some ways I did not even like it, but I recognized it immediately as a state of affairs worth fighting for.

This is anarchism. And Orwell was right—it is worth fighting for.[9]

1. *Bourgeois Influences on Anarchism*, by Luigi Fabbri. Tucson, AZ: See Sharp Press, 2001, p. 16.

2. *You Can't Blow Up a Social Relationship*. Tucson, AZ: See Sharp Press, 1998, p. 20.

3. It may be that now due to apathy, but in violent/repressive situations other options are cut off for almost everyone not directly involved in armed resistance.

4. For further discussion of this matter, see *You Can't Blow Up a Social Relationship: The Anarchist Case Against Terrorism* and *Bourgeois Influences on Anarchism*.

5. Ted Kaczynski is in some ways quite typical of this breed of romantic. He differs from most of them in that he acted on his beliefs (albeit in a cowardly, violent manner) and that he actually lived a relatively primitive existence in the backwoods of Montana—unlike most of his co-religionists, who live comfortably in urban areas and employ the technologies they profess to loathe.

6. For further discussion of this topic, see *Anarchism vs. Primitivism*, by Brian Oliver Sheppard. Tucson, AZ: See Sharp Press, 2003 (available online at www.libcom.org). See also the "Primitive Thought" appendix to *Listen Anarchist!*, by Chaz Bufe. Tucson, AZ: See Sharp Press, 1998.

7. Indeed, there have been a fairly large number of admirable religious anarchists, individuals such as Leo Tolstoy and Dorothy Day (and the members of her Catholic Worker groups, such as Ammon Hennacy), though to most anarchists advocating freedom on Earth while bowing to a heavenly tyrant, no matter how imaginary, seems an insupportable contradiction. To the best of my knowledge there have been no such shining examples of anarcho-capitalists, with the notable exception of Karl Hess.

8. To be fair, marxists also tend to emphasize positive freedom, but for the most part they're curiously insensitive, and often downright hostile, to "negative" freedom—the freedom from restraint (especially when they have the guns and goons to do the restraining).

9. Of course, this discussion of anarchism is necessarily schematic, given that this foreword is intended as an introductory 10-minute read. For elaboration see the many other books explaining anarchism, especially *Anarchism and Anarcho-Syndicalism*, by Rudolf Rocker; *What Is Communist Anarchism?*, by Alexander Berkman (now published by AK Press as *What Is Anarchism?*); *Fields, Factories and Workshops Tomorrow*, by Peter Kropotkin; and *Anarchy in Action*, by Colin Ward.

TRANSLATOR'S NOTE

Those familiar with the Spanish-language version of this book, *Contracorriente: Historia del Movimiento Anarquista en Venezuela, 1811–1998*, will notice many differences between it and this English-language version. There are a number of reasons for those differences. The first is that the author wrote this book for a Venezuelan audience and assumes that the reader is already familiar with Venezuela. One cannot assume this for North American readers, so, I've added a bit of explanatory information throughout the book.

The second reason that this book differs significantly from the Spanish-language version is that I edited the book as well as translated it, and in the process made many changes. One of those changes was eliminating the footnotes and using endnotes in their place. As well, I eliminated a great many of the notes, in part because in a large number of places I incorporated explanatory information that was in the footnotes into the text.

I've also eliminated many quoted passages within the text, primarily where they merely reinforced information already in the text. In other places, I've shortened quotations to eliminate extraneous matter. Where I've done this, I've inserted ellipses.

As well, I've inserted some additional information in a few places, primarily in the sections dealing with events in Mexico and Russia. Where I've done this, I've put that information in brackets.

Some readers will wonder why the only Spanish words italicized are book, magazine, newspaper, and film titles. The reason is that a large number of such titles appear in the text, as do a great many organizational names, and if all of the Spanish terms in the text were italicized it could easily have led to confusion. As for the titles themselves, I've included English translations where their meanings would not be immediately apparent to English-speakers, but have skipped them elsewhere, espeically in lists of periodicals and books mentioned in passing.

One point of political clarification is that there are numerous references in the text to "libertarians" and to *El Libertario* (The Libertarian), Venezuela's long-running anarchist periodical. Readers should understand that "libertarian" has a very different meaning in the U.S. than in the rest of the world. There, the term is used as a synonym for "anarchist," one who believes in equal freedom and therefore rejects all forms of coercion and domination.

In contrast, here in the U.S. the term was hijacked by right-wing, *laissez-faire* capitalists in the 1960s and 1970s. "Libertarian" now refers, in the U.S., to a supporter of capitalism who is liberal on social issues, such as legalization of drugs and prostitution, but who wants to do away with all social welfare functions of the state (social security, medicare, unemployment benefits, etc.) while retaining its repressive functions (the police, military, prisons, etc.). Unfortunately, this grotesque redefinition of this formerly useful term appears to be a permanent part of the American political landscape.

Please keep this in mind while reading Rodolfo's enlightening book.

—Chaz Bufe, Tucson, Arizona

ACRONYMS

ACAT – Asociación Continental Americana de Trabajadores

AD – Acción Democrática

AIT – Asociación Internacional de los Trabajadores (same as IWA)

ALC – Asociación Libertaria Cubana

BR – Bandera Roja

CAL – Colectivo de Autogestión Libertaria

CEJAP – Comando Especial de Contrainsurgencia José Antonio Páez

CGT – Confederation Generale du Travail (France)

CGT – Confederación General del Trabajo

CNT – Confederación Nacional del Trabajo (Spain)

CNT-V – Confederación Nacional del Trabajo de Venezuela

COPEI – Comité Organizado Para Elecciones Independientes

CRA – Comité de Relaciones Anarquistas

CRA-AIT – Comité de Relaciones Anarquistas- AIT (see also AIT)

CTV – Confederación de Trabajadores de Venezuela

DIM – División de Inteligencia Militar

DRIL – Directorio Revolucionario Ibérico de Liberacíon

EBR-200 – Ejército Bolivariano Revolucionario

FAI – Federación Anarquista Iberica

FALN – Fuerzas Armadas de Liberación Nacional

FIJL – Federación Ibérica de Juventudes Libertarias

FND – Frente Nacional Democrático

GEA – Grupo de Editores Alternativos

GCR – Grupos de Comando Revolucionario

IMF – International Monetary Fund

IWA – International Workers Association (same as AIT)

IWW – Industrial Workers of the World

JDN – Juventud Democrática Nicaraguense

LS – Liga Socialista

M26J – Movimiento 26 de Julio

MAS – Movimiento Al Socialismo

MBR-200 – Movimiento Bolivariano Revolucionario

MEP – Movimiento Electoral del Pueblo

MIR – Movimiento de Izquierda Revolucionaria

MJEZ – Movimiento Juvenil Ezequiel Zamora

ML-CNT – Movimiento Libertario-Confederación Nacional del Trabajo

MLCE – Movimiento Libertario Cubano en el Exilio

MONCA – Movimiento Nacional Campesino Revolucionario

OR – Organización de Revolucionarios

PDN – Partido Democrática Nacional

PCC – Partido Comunista de Cuba

PCV – Partido Comunista de Venezuela

PRV – Partido de la Revolución Venezolana—Ruptura

PPT – Pátria Para Todos

PSOE – Partido Socialista Obrero Español

PTJ – Cuerpo Técnico de Policia Judicial

RECADI – Régimen de Cambio Diferencial

SAMOP – Sociedad de Auxilio Mutuo de Obreros Petroleros

UCV – Universidad Central de Venezuela

UGT – Unión General de Trabajadores (Spain)

UJR – Unión de Jóvenes Revolucionarios

UMP – Unión Militar Patriótica

UNE – Unión Nacional de Estudiantes

URD – Unión Democrática Republicana

VENAMI – Venezolanos Amigos de América

VENAMICUBA – Venezolanos Amigos de Cuba

CHAPTER 1
The Historical Background

Christopher Columbus (1451–1506) "discovered" Venezuela in 1498 during his third voyage to the Americas. He explored Venezuela's coastal region from the 4th to the 12th of August in that year, and found the Gulf of Paria and the Isla de Margarita. Later, other Spanish colonizers would return. The first was Alonso de Ojeda (1468–1515) in 1499, who was accompanied by the Florentine cartographer Amerigo Vespucci (1451–1512), who in turn led expeditions in 1499 and 1502, with the purpose of finding mineral resources to exploit.

The word "Venezuela" itself comes from Vespucci, who upon seeing the huts on poles in which native people lived in Lake Maracaibo, dubbed the land "Venezziola," that is, "little Venice." In a letter from his first voyage, Vespucci said:

> Near the Gulf [of Maracaibo] we found a large population who had their houses built over the water, as in Venice. We wanted to see them, and naturally the inhabitants resisted our entrance. They fled upon feeling the points of our swords, and we found houses filled with the finest cotton.[1]

Another version of the origin story of "Venezuela" is that it's an indigenous word derived from the terms "Vene" and "Zuela," which the natives used to designate the areas in which they lived, "big waters" or "great waters."

Regarding this, the cleric Antonio Vásquez de Espinosa wrote in his *Compendium and Description of the West Indies*, "Venezuela in the native language of that region means 'great waters,' the great lake of Maracaibo."[2]

But it wasn't until 1500 that the Cantabrian [Cantabria—a province in northern Spain adjacent to the Basque region] cartographer Juan de la Cosa (1450–1509) created a world map that, for the first time, designated the region as Venezuela.

The expedition of Alonso de Ojeda in 1499 marks the beginnings of the commercial exploitation of Venezuela and the enslavement of its native peoples; in other words, that expedition marks the beginnings of the imposition of mercantilism, slavery, the state, taxation, monotheism, the concepts of caste and class, and the systematic use of force and violence in human affairs.

Some Venezuelan natives were sent back to Spain as booty, and others were forced to work as manual labor in the Greater Antilles, where the native peoples had been all but exterminated in less than two decades, which was the result of infectious diseases that the conquistadors brought to the islands, as well as their use of extreme violence.

But it wasn't until 1510 that the first extraction industry appeared in Venezuela, in the form of mass collection of pearls along the coast, especially around the island of Cubagua, where the Spaniards created a settlement, Nueva Cadiz de Cubagua, expressly for the purpose of pearl collection. The settlement remained until 1541, when it was destroyed, supposedly by natural disasters.

* * *

Lamentably, the contributions and historical significance of all of these native peoples haven't been sufficiently studied nor valued by social scientists. On the contrary, the genocidal violence of the conquest and colonization, the deformation of native cultures produced by the European invasion, contributed greatly, for a very long time, to the image of native peoples as savages, the barbaric and irrational aspect of human beings, when in reality the native inhabitants of these lands had forms of organization that were in some ways libertarian, and they also practiced to an extent collectivism and self-management. Lamentably, gunpowder, the sword, and the cross nearly put an end to the indigenous peoples and their communalist practices.

Nonetheless, there still exist vestiges which suggest similarities between the practices of the original peoples and those of the much later anarchist movement. One of these is provided by the indigenous, Amazonian Wotjuja people (spellings vary), described by anthropologists David Graeber[3] and Joanna Overing as anarchistic in certain ways.

According to them, the Wotjuja place great value upon the autonomy and liberty of individuals, and are aware of the importance of assuring that no one has to take orders from anyone else. They're also concerned that no one seize control of physical resources, which would limit the freedom of others in the community. It's because of this that hierarchy among the Wotjuja is minimal, despite all of the leaders being men, even though Graber and Overing doubt whether male dominance is what it appears to be.

Citing Luis Arango[4] and Enrique Sanchez, we can add that another Wotjuja characteristic that can be considered anarchist is the absolute rejection of violence, both physical and verbal. The Wotjuja are very self-controlled (when there aren't disturbing factors, such as alcohol), and are horrified when individuals can't control their emotions. They tend to flee from the dangers of uncontrolled emotional displays. Among them, homicide is unknown, because they believe that murderers will die almost immediately under horrible circumstances.

These qualities combine to create a way of life in the Wotjuja's dispersed, semi-nomadic settlements. Economically and technologically, the Wotjuja still use a simple technology largely reliant on traditional tools in a subsistence economy, in which there are a myriad of small exchanges among individuals and a web of commerce between communities, all of which makes for a notable existing indigenous people and a way of life that is antiauthoritarian, libertarian.

Another example of anarchistic tendencies among Amazonian native peoples is provided by the Yanomami, who are descendants of the Tupinambá people who lived in Brazil prior to colonization by the Portuguese, who libeled them as "cannibals." Of them, Montaigne wrote:

> It's a nation, I would say to Plato, where there's no commerce, no written language, no knowledge of arithmetic, no judges or politicians, no vassalage, no rich or poor, no contracts, no inheritance, no commercial dealings, no occupation other than idleness, no knowledge of ancestors other than the community, no clothes, no agriculture, no metal, no wine or wheat. No words for lies, betrayal, deception, avarice, envy, distraction, forgiveness. These words are never heard! How far is this perfection from the republic you imagine![5]

The Yanomami are descendants of the peoples "recently delivered from the hand of God," who Montaigne, paraphrasing Seneca, described as uncontaminated by the West, living a communitarian life in shacks, with a gift economy and subsistence agriculture, where "command" is only that of a spokesman, and where rest, laziness, and enjoyment is the daily routine.

* * *

In March 1528, the Welsers, a powerful German banking family, signed a contract with Carlos I (1500–1558), king of Castille, assigning them the right to exploit and settle Venezuela. Ambrosio Alfinger (1500–1533) was named governor and captain-general of the new province, thus creating the beginnings of the state in Venezuela.

An early example of what was to come, an orgy of rebellion and murder, occurred in 1561. It was conducted by the conquistador Lope de Aguirre, who through lies and betrayal took command of an expedition called "the cashew gatherers" (Los Marañones). He besieged and sacked the settlements of Margarita, Borburata, Valencia, and Barquisimeto before he was killed by his own troops. Following his death, the crown declared him guilty of lese majeste.

There has been a lot of speculation about the motivations for Aguirre's disobedience, for the acts of rebellion that scandalized the monarchy and left as their legacy a trail of senseless destruction. This tormented man, who not only rebelled against the crown, but assigned himself the title "Prince of Liberty of Terra Firma and the Province of Chile," was a perfidious, nearly perfect example of individual liberty and autonomy carried to such an extreme that they become their opposite: amoral egoism.

In the following century, an especially convulsive period occurred between 1666 and 1680, when Venezuelan coastal regions and especially the cities of Maracaibo and Puerto Cabello were besieged and sacked by pirates, the incursions of Jean David Nau (1666), Henry Morgan (1669), and Michel de Grandmont (1680) are the most notable, because of the bloody outrages committed by the corsairs.

Even though during the heyday of the Caribbean pirates there were distinct libertarian and egalitarian traits, as exemplified by the Guild of Brothers of the Island of Tortuga (Haiti), and off Africa by the pirate community of Libertatia on the coast of Madagascar, those traits were entirely absent in the Venezuelan region. This was the stomping ground of freebooters and pirates who solely wanted to augment their coffers. This type of piracy inhibited the development of cities in Venezuela, and it also served to strengthen the hold of the Spanish military through the construction of castles and fortresses, but above all it helped to channel the development of commerce in the coastal region.

This gave rise to the creation of the Guipuzcoana Company in 1728, whose purpose was to monopolize trade between the colony and Spain. One of its goals toward that end was to protect the coastal regions of Venezuela against raids by pirates and freebooters.

The other purposes of the Guipuzcoana Company included the sending of fruit to Spain, the regulation and augmentation of cacao and tobacco exports to that country, and in this manner to lower the costs of such commerce. The company managed to reduce if not stop smuggling by pursuing the foreign commercial interests engaging in this illegal activity.

Indigenous resistance to this monopolization of commerce diminished over the years, while at the same time the colonizers strengthened their settlements. The great majority of the original inhabitants ended up being subjugated and, along with slaves brought from Africa, were integrated into the new Spanish colonies.

Diverse estimates of the population of Venezuela at the end of the 18th and beginning of the 19th century place that population at no more than one million, with the inhabitants concentrated on the coast and in the mountainous areas. The peoples of Venezuela were markedly divided and stratified along ethnic lines, even though these lines were not totally rigid. The civil and Catholic Church authorities furthered this segregation through laws, decrees, and customs designed to produce good Christian living.

During this epoch the most numerous group were free mestizos, who were the result of interbreeding between the Spaniards, indigenous people, and African slaves. The second largest group were the white Europeans (Spaniards) and their descendants; the third group was comprised of enslaved Africans and mulatos. The mestizos were the ascendant group, owing not only to their involvement in agricultural, artisanal, and mechanical activities, but also to their participation in the Spanish militia.

The discriminatory treatment of slaves and others considered beneath them by the Spaniards was the detonator for a number of uprisings and movements during the period, some with markedly egalitarian traits. Among these we should mention the uprising, inspired by the French Revolution and its Liberty, Equality, Fraternity watchwords, led by José Leonardo Chirinos in the Sierra de Coro on the haciendas in the mountainous region in the west of the country that ended in a massacre of rebels in the city of Coro. There was also the Comuna del Negro Miguel (Black Michael Commune) in Barquisimeto in approximately 1553 where slaves established a collectivist system.

The type of collectivist system embodied in that commune exemplified the clandestinely organized communities known as "cimarrones" (wild or untamed places) established by fugitive slaves. [Such communities also existed in Colombia and Brazil.] It's necessary to point out, though, that these collectivist systems were hierarchically organized, had leaders, and had patriarchal, pyramidal power structures.

The revolutionary ideas provided by the French Revolution arrived in Venezuela through Portuguese merchants and the native white Spanish descendants who went to Europe for their educations. The most outstanding of these ideas were self-government and refusal to pay onerous taxes to the Spanish crown. Thus began a series of republican plots and attempts such as the failed conspiracy of Juan Bautista Picornell (1759–1825), Manuel Gual (1759–1800), and José María España in the port of Guaira in 1797, and the expeditions of Francisco de Miranda (1750–1816) in the Vela de Coro in 1806.

This all ended on April 19, 1810 when Vicente Amparan, Captain-General of Venezuela, under popular pressure, renounced his position as the representative of the Spanish crown in favor of an organizing junta which led to the declaration of independence on July 5, 1811.

From then on republican life held sway in Venezuela, and with it the presence of anarchist thought.

CHAPTER 2
Origins and Prehistory

The word "anarchy" was used in Venezuela as early as 1811, when the Sociedad Patriótica (Patriotic Society) discussed the political direction the nascent republic should take, in a session presided over by Francisco De Miranda, and which Simón Bolivar (1783–1830) attended. Antonio Muñoz Tébar (1792–1814) advocated that the new state should take a conservative, centralized form. The attorney, War of Independence veteran, and member of the Sociedad Patriótica, Francisco Antonio "Coto" Paúl (1773–1821), answered moments later as follows:

> Anarchy! It's liberty, when you flee from tyranny, when you unbind it and let your hair fly in the wind! Anarchy! The god of the weak when they're cursed by dread and uncertainty; I fall on my knees before it. Sirs: Anarchy, the torch of the furies in the hands of humanity, let it guide us in this congress, let its vapors enrapture the rebels against order, and let it lead us through the streets and plazas crying "Liberty!"[6]

Regarding this meeting, the historian Caracciola Parra Pérez would add that "Francisco Antonio Paúl . . . launched in a stentorian voice his famous aphorisms . . .'salvatory anarchy' that enraptures the rebels against order and would 'reanimate the dead sea of the congress.'"[7]

During the First Republic Coto Paúl was one of the most advanced figures. He was a well known orator, and also, along with Guillermo Pelaron y Garcia, was co-editor of the republican periodical *El Publicista Venezolana*. Caracciolo Parra describe Paúl as "Dantonian," in honor of the French revolutionary George-Jacques Danton (1759–1794).

Regarding Paúl, the historian Domingo Alberto Rangel notes:

> Paúl was very radical, and the moderates of 1810 harassed him saying that extremism would lead, in the long run, to political reaction. Paúl rejected such manufactured fears, as one might suppose, and advocated sticking to reality.

We are, said Paúl, at the summit of the sacred mountain of anarchy and that's our best guarantee [of what's to come]. Nobody before or after Coto Paúl has called anarchy 'sacred.' As one should note, anarchy has the rare quality of being attacked from both the left and the right.[8]

But we should point out that when Coto Paúl expressed himself, with all of the flowery rhetoric characteristic of the era, Pierre Joseph Proudhon was only one year old, and Mikahil Bakunin wouldn't even be born for another four years. It's likely that Paúl had read William Godwin's *An Enquiry Concerning Political Justice*; otherwise it's difficult to explain how he could have been familiar with the ideas later identified as anarchist.

Another of the figures often cited as having libertarian traits is the revolutionary caudillo Simón Bolivar. To illustrate, we'll take a passage from the book by Juan Uslar Pietri, *History of the Popular Rebellion of 1814*:

Bolivar was resolved to achieve the independence of the country at any cost. He gathered around him all the people of Venezuela, imposing the equality of classes in his ranks. He raised up black people, such as Pedro Camejo, who deserved to be called heroes. And he eliminated the unnecessary courtesans and aristocrats from the national leadership.

[But] behind the image of the tough guerrilla leader one could glimpse a man used to the good life, the gilded salons, the exemplar of a society of which he was the most outstanding exponent. . . . He wore a helmet the color of snapdragon, a blue smock with red braids and three rows of buttons, with a black sash on which one could see a skull and crossbones with the slogan "Liberty or Death."[9]

As we can appreciate, this description of Bolivar bears some resemblance to the Ukrainian anarchist guerrilla leader Nestor Makhno (1889–1934), whose guerrilla army combated not only the czarists but also the Bolsheviks. The Makhnovist partisans used the black banner of anarchy inscribed with the skull and crossbones and the words "Liberty or Death."

With the exception of this coincidental resemblance, Bolivar has nothing to do with anarchism. There is not a trace of antiauthoritarianism in Bolivar. On the contrary, he was a conservative, high-handed and autocratic, a figure who should be considered as antagonistic to anarchism, not one with any affinity for it.

There are factions within the Venezuelan marxist movement who have wanted, in vain, to see in Bolivar certain libertarian traits that would serve to show coincidence between anarchism and the Bolivarian movement. [This refers to the modern-day Chavista {Hugo Chavez} movement, which calls it-self the "Bolivarian movement."]

Here it's necessary to remind ourselves that Bolivar had no clear ideolog-ical concepts, and that he employed the word "anarchy" as a synonym for "chaos," a very common, confused misuse.

The writer Jorge Mier Hoffman provides the following illustrative quota-tions from Bolivar:

> The anarchists destroy and divide themselves, totally contrary to the virtuous
> . . . I see how it's possible to establish political and social stability in this country.
> If weak laws are established, such as those issued by a very liberal government,
> we would become a country without a government, because it's a constant that
> the strength of the government should be in proportion to the extent of its
> enemies. . . . Our principal problem is the anarchy of our politicians, our army,
> our church, our businessmen, and even with our people themselves. Everyone
> believes he has the solution and wants to be a leader from day one . . .[10]

As can be seen, Bolivar had a negative opinion about anarchy as a social system, more through ignorance than from understanding it. He put anarchy on the same plane as the disorder afflicting Venezuelan society.

A further example of the apprehensions of Bolivar about anarchy can be found in the following passage by the historian Manuel Caballero about the Congress of Angostura [which produced the Venezuelan Constitution of 1819]:

> In sum, the Bolivarian project awoke reservations in the hearts of the illustrious
> participants who, in articles in the *Correo de Orinoco* (Orinoco Mail) expressed
> their differences. [The Bolivarian program] was not then imposed without dis-
> cussion, without resistance: at bottom, there were still present the tradition-
> al tensions between centralism, a synonym for efficiency, and of course very
> popular within the military sector, and federation, which among the illustrious
> civilians was a synonym for participation, even for democracy, and in any event
> for liberty—but also for frightful anarchy.[11]

In fact, the rhetoric used by Bolivar throughout his life demonstrated an animadversion to anarchy [which was exemplified in] the phrase he used in several ministerial dispatches: "Union! Union! Or anarchy will devour us!" The only liberty recognized by the illustrious Caracan was that delivered by a governmental legislative body and its chief executive. (Bolivar's rhetoric was compiled in great measure by the marxist academic José Rafael Núñez Teno-rio in his work, *Reencarnar el espíritu de Bolívar: El problema de la libertad no sólo lo concibió Bolívar en oposición a la tiranía, sino también en conflicto con la anarquía* (Reincarnating the Spirit of Bolivar: The problem of liberty not only as Bolivar conceived it in opposition to tyranny, but also in conflict with anarchy).

As we can see Simon Bolivar, revolutionary general and in large part the architect of the Republic of Venezuela, had little in common with the anarchist ideal. Bolivar and the Patriotic Junta looked with skepticism and misconfidence upon liberal figures such as Coto Paúl. As the historian Tomas Straka wrote, "They interpreted revolutionary fervor as fanaticism."

Another early patriot tied to anarchism was José Félix Ribas (1775–1815), who during the Battle of Victoria, when 800 university students clashed with 8,000 "cowboys" ("llaneros") under the control of the caudillo José Tomás Boves (1782–1814). According to Hoffman:

> The enemy unleashed its fury upon the plaza, valiantly defended by the students. The cannons roared, vomiting shot, and an immense hail of balls crossed the plaza with an ominous whistle, turning the plaza into a circle of fire, and covering the ground with dead and dying bodies, while Boves contemplated the slaughter with insensate jubilation. . . . Ribas, covered in blood and surrounded by cadavers and the moans, cries and curses of the wounded that shook the skies, impetuously rose and called on the anarchy carried within every Venezuelan, calling on every student in their little trench to unleash their own battle . . . Now Boves didn't have a single battle, but hundreds of small battles carried out by the individual students, who with fearlessness and ferocity defeated Boves' army of thugs, who fled terrified with the same urgency with which they'd tried to take Victoria.[12]

Another of the early independence advocates sometimes tied to anarchism is Bolivar's teacher, Simón Rodríguez (1771–1854), who in his later days advanced the concept of "toparquia" (or "government of locale") as a model of collective organization. He would write, in the letter he sent to Anselmo Pineda on February 2, 1847:

> The true utility in the creation of a republic is that its inhabitants have an interest in the prosperity of the land . . . Thus are destroyed provincial [parochial] interests . . . Would that each place become a local sovereignty, because then we would have a federation of local sovereignties.[13]

These comments of Rodríguez are a response to the disastrous results of the establishment of Greater Colombia, the hegemony of Simon Bolivar, and the separatist movements of the various provinces of Greater Colombia. Even though these remarks can be seen as a forceful declaration in favor of libertarian communalism and federation, concepts held by some anarchist currents, these comments led to no further developments during the process of republican consolidation, which we'll treat later.

The Social Conflict of 1814

Another of the emblematic figures of the independence struggle, José Tomás Boves [the same as mentioned above], was an Asturian who raised on the Venezuelan plains a vast army of mestizo and black troops, with which he overthrew the Second Republic.

Notorious for his pitilessness against his adversaries and for declaring war to the death with Bolivar, he has been in general vilified as "bloody and cruel," and has largely been written out of Venezuelan history. However, he was the first to declare social warfare in Venezuela. The writer Francisco Herrera Luque has this to say about him:

> Boves was anti-Bolivar, not because they had confronted each other during the war, not because he would have embraced the banner of the king while Bolivar embraced the banner of the republic, not because one was uncultured while the other was cultured, not because one was creole and the other Spanish, not because one was poor and the other rich, but because Bolivar thought in terms of society and creating a state, while the other [Boves] thought in terms of the masses, with the masses being at war with the society of which they were a part.
>
> . . .
>
> [That the] masses rebelled in Venezuela . . . was because . . . before the rebellion of the masses those who benefited were a minority who maintained through blood and iron an intolerable social system, that didn't allow the smallest change. . . . The offensive power of the Venezuelan masses of 1813 was proportional to the resentments they had been accumulating during the entire colonial period.(13)

Boves and his followers didn't respect religion, age, or gender; the only thing they considered was whether or not people were white colonialists, who they killed brutally. Even though the history books classify Boves as a royalist, the truth is that he was an uncontrollable who didn't obey the Spanish crown, much less the Catholic Church. He didn't recognize the royal representative, Don Juan Manuel de Carbijal, and proclaimed himself the only authority sustained by the arms of his 20,000 men, a situation that lasted until his death.

His military program was to arm the slaves against the masters, with the confessed aim of disposing with a gang of thieves.

According to various chroniclers of the epoch, such as Juan Uslar and Juan Bosch, the army of Boves, known as the "Infernal Legions," was organized in a democratic manner, even though it had a unified military chain of command under Boves. The historian Aristedes Rojas writes:

> In contrast to the "royalists" and patriotic [nationalist] leaders, Boves had the people on his side. Within his army he permitted all types of liberties, liberties that in an uncultured group equaled lack of discipline and anarchy [chaos]. When soldiers didn't want to obey the orders of an officer, they would ask Boves to dismiss the officer. Boves, to keep the peace and acting as an expression of the will of the people, would dismiss them and name a new officer more to the liking of these fierce warriors.[14]

In order to understand the Boves phenomenon, it's necessary to return to the original pre-independence movements. The insurgency of the "negros de Coro" and the attentat of Francisco Javier Pirela (1770–1799) in Maracaibo surged from the breasts of the working classes of those epochs. Their leaders were generally black, creole, or mestizo, or at least citizens dedicated to the creation of a regime dedicated to the liberty and equality of all. And these movements resonated within the community because they corresponded with the sentiments of the majority.

The exact contrary occurred after April 9, 1810 with the war of "patriotic" independence. The masses sensed the oligarchic nature of the movement instituted in Caracas. The slaves, the creoles, the campesinos heard their bosses, the great land owners, and the upper classes of the cities speaking of a republic and liberty, and they didn't understand them, because there was no connection between their words and existing reality. This gave rise to the dispossessed uniting around the "royalist" cause, not because they felt any loyalty to the Spanish crown, but because they wanted to fight their historical oppressors. Boves undoubtedly took advantage of this sentiment.

The "royalist" reaction of 1811 allows us to take note of the character of the social war that devastated Venezuela. In Valencia, the creoles rebelled against the whites. The same happened with the uprisings of blacks in Barlovento and the Valleys of Tuy that were so ferocious and exhibited such blinding hate that the perpetrators became terrified by their own works and fled toward Caracas, which was smothering in fear of the approaching hoards.

Thus was formed the avalanche directed by José Tomás Boves, whose burning hatred of the republican cause led him to foment class war, "dividing the goods and lands of the dead and those who had fled among the creoles, giving them titles [to the land]."[15] The Asturian Boves had set in motion a movement to create a nation of creoles and blacks on the plains of Venezuela, whose peoples would be the same colors as his soldiers, who inspired or revived the desires for the common well-being that would be taken from the whites, their women, and their property.

Boves' popularity as a leader stemmed from his humility and the way he treated the blacks, slaves, and mulattoes who had been exploited by the Spaniards. Juan Uslar states that "Boves carried his role as democratic caudillo past the point that former leaders considered harmful. He led the life of a simple soldier, spoke with them in their language, slept among them, and took his recreation with them." His army had humble roots, counting in its files a wide range of fugitives and social outcasts. The majority of them were slaves, peddlers, smugglers, thugs, gang bosses, and former prisoners. Uslar Prieti adds:

> The uprising in Venezuela in 1814 was not simply a local affair, something to be expected given the area. It was the most wide ranging event in the history of social emancipation in the Americas. . . . In Venezuela, and this is the question at the heart of the matter, there was in addition to a War of Independence a revolution, structurally speaking, against the [ruling class] patriots who formed the independence movement. A revolution that had nothing to do with the king of Spain nor with the king's partisans, but which on the contrary had democratic and egalitarian characteristics. . . . Anyone who has observed these Venezuelans, democratic to their marrow, can't but affirm that they couldn't be partisans of the king and the privileged. Those insurrectionist fighters who were sacking estates and killing the whites, who were committing sacrileges in the churches and defiling altars, could simply not be royalists, could simply not be partisans of religion and order . . . They rose because of their class hatred, in order to realize their longing for social liberty.[16]

Despite his egalitarian leanings, Boves was the boss, and he took advantage of popular resentment to promote his political objectives. He would pass into history as the most fratricidal and devastating figure of the war for independence. According to Bolivar, more than 80,000 people died in Boves' campaigns.

Nonetheless, Boves placed in the public arena and in the agenda of the independence leaders the "social question," which had not previously been taken up by the Patriotic Society. Two years after the 1814 uprising, Simón Bolivar, on July 6, 1816, at his headquarters at Ocumare de la Costa, proclaimed social equality: "Nature, justice, and politics [political reality] demand the emancipation of the slaves; from here on there will be only one class of people in Venezuela, citizens." In January 1817 he repeated the order in the Valleys of Tuy: "There will be no slaves in Venezuela." [Nonetheless, slavery wasn't formally abolished in Venezuela until 1854.]

Concerning this, the historian Federico Brito Figueroa writes:

> In the framework of class war, the most advanced of the patriotic leaders, from the viewpoint of being democratic-revolutionary, understood that in the end the freedom of the slaves was one of the cornerstones of national liberation. They understood the very important matter that the exploited masses, fighting in one band or another, or taking independent action, had been fighting for their own goals, that is for their own social liberation, symbolized under the circumstances by Jose Tomas Boves.[17]

The death of Boves dissipated the uprising of the dispossessed, which later was led by José Antonio Páez (1790–1873); addressing the needs of the downtrodden would later help to swell the patriotic ranks when that movement started to promote social benefits for the excluded. Among these benefits was the Law of Redistribution of the National Goods, which went into effect on October 10, 1817, and which regulated the distribution of lands seized as "booty of war" to the soldiers in the patriotic ranks.

Another event that throws into relief the authoritarian disposition of Bolivar and his contradictory roles as politician and military leader, was the shooting of the General in Chief of the Guayana region, Manuel Piar Gómez. He was a dark-skinned Curazaoan [Curacao, an island off Venezuela's northwest coast] who was popular in the lower classes that had supported the revolution, and who had clashed with Bolivar over the class nature the war had taken.

The peak of the friction occurred on May 8, 1817 when the Congress of Cariaco urged the elimination of the unified headquarters of the liberation forces, and Piar said he supported the proposal. As a consequence of this, Bolivar removed Piar from his command. Because of this, Piar asked to retire from the army with the rank of General in Chief, a request which was granted on June 30, 1817.

Shortly thereafter, Piar was imprisoned in Arugura de Maturin on September 28, 1817, accused of going among the troops to turn them against the white leadership from the upland regions. He was subsequently taken to the general headquarters in Angostura, where he was put on trial. On October 15, the Council of War sentenced him to death for sedition, insubordination, desertion, and conspiracy. Simón Bolivar approved the sentence, without mitigating it. The following day Piar was shot by a firing squad against the western wall of the Cathedral of Angostura, and then buried in the El Cardonal cemetery.

The rebellious nature of Piar, his constant push for equality of the classes, his advocacy of freedom for the Indians, blacks, and mestizos, and his struggles to democratize the command structure of the insurrectionary army gained him the enmity of the ruling class leadership within the republican ranks. The charges against him didn't mention his attempt to foment and strengthen the lower class movement in the social war, the class war, the cause championed by Jose Tomás Boves years before.

In 1830, the republican forces realized their intentions to create a new nation after 19 years of war that had left the emerging nation submerged in ruin and misery. In that moment of the downfall of Spanish colonialism, when the creole latifundistas became the governors of the republic, they took on the mission of consolidating the socio-economic system in waiting [in place of colonialism]: the rule of the landowners.

The republican constitution guaranteed centralization, the privileged role of the conservative sectors, and maintenance of the parasitic, tribute-collecting system of taxation on the mercantile and productive classes as well as on communications and transport activities,

The government stores remained; the taxes, the tributes, the transit taxes, the import taxes, the tolls—[it all remained] including the servitude of the indigenous peoples and Venezuela's blacks.

An example of all this is provided by the Italian geographer and explorer Agustín Codazzi (1793–1859) in *The Physical and Political Atlas of the Republic of Venezuela*, in which he says that in 1834 the country had a population of 994,348 inhabitants, of which only 9,125 were hacienda [plantation] owners taking up more that half of the cultivable land in the country.

In agreement with this, the historian José Luis Salcedo Bastardo, in his *Fundamental History of Venezuela*, wrote:

> The war of liberation, that was so cruel and prolonged, unhinged the Venezuelan economy. It produced a near stoppage of agricultural production, which is illustrated by the fall in cacao production from 110,000 bushels prior to the outbreak of the war to 25,000 in 1816 in Guaíra. The production of indigo fell a spectacular 98%.[18]

Despite the economic system inherited from colonialism, with its slavery, haciendas, and difficulties in commercial transactions and communications, modern capitalist production was slowly developing in Venezuela. This early stage capitalism began to develop through the impact of more advanced forms of technology and organization via foreign investment, and its slow adoption by domestic producers.

In 1834, an electoral process began from which the physician José María Vargas (1786–1854) emerged as the first civilian to hold the post of chief magistrate. Until then the leading political role had been taken by the military chiefs who had taken part in the independence movement in Venezuela and the other Andean countries.

Therefore, certain sectors of Venezuelan society which had observed with distrust the political ambitions of the generals, tried to bolster the power of Vargas. But he was thrown out in short order by the self-proclaimed "Revolution of the Reforms," which was neither revolutionary nor reformist. It was a military reaction directed by the old caudillo Santiago Mariño (1788-1854). Vargas was sent to the island of St. Thomas, but he was later restored as chief magistrate by José Antonio Páez, who had in turn thrown out the "reformist" rebels and assumed the presidency in 1836. (This wouldn't be the first time that the military, to preserve their hegemony, would seize state power.)

Anarchism After Independence

The ideas of Pierre Joseph Proudhon were known in Venezuela starting with Sería Fermín Toro (1806–1865), who the writer Roberto J. Lovera considers "the first [Venezuelan] socialist," and of whom he writes:

> The unknown Toro was the first socialist among us, but of course a utopian socialist. He had been a diplomat in London and had seen the conditions of the working class there; he revisited his experiences there in his novel *The Martyrs* (1842), which anticipated the work of Engels on the same topic by five years.[19]

Fermín Toro, one of the most critical voices against the oligarchy, considered liberty to be on a contract or use basis. In this respect, in his emblematic work, *Reflections on the Law of April 1834*, he wrote:

> Liberty is not the goal of society and that as means it should be subordinated to necessary equality, that is the principle object of association, since through it, in the category of rights, everyone should be able to possess their moral dignity and physical existence.[20]

So, Toro was among to first to explain that liberty without equality of opportunity is as pernicious as equality without liberty. Nonetheless, Toro was one of the strongest advocates of federalism/centralism in the National Congress, controlling a national organization that in 1858 established a strong central government that allowed a certain amount of decentralization in the provinces, something that remains until this day and that has little in common with libertarianism.

There are repeated references to Proudhon in the works of Rafael María Baralt (1810–1860). Beyond that, Baralt knew Proudhon personally. The magazine *Antología Español*, which Baralt founded with the journalist Memesio Fernández, published works on liberty and the Paris Commune, and also polemics with Francois Guizet (notable for his interpretation of the Communist Manifesto). As well, on September 18, 1852, an article by an anonymous author appeared in the *Correo de Caracas* (Caracas Mail) titled "Analysis of socialism and a clear, methodical, impartial exposition of socialist principles ancient and modern, especially those of Saint Simon, Fourier, Owen, F. Leroux, and Proudhon." The article claimed to be a synthesis of the modern socialist doctrines designed to inform the Latin American public about philosophical discussions in the previous decades in Europe, especially in France. Nevertheless, it's important to point out that with this publication the Venezuelan reader gained access for the first time to a more or less systematic exposition of the social philosophy of Proudhon [one of the first anarchists].

This article appears to have raised fears and adverse reactions in the property-owning classes, and there were a number of replies in the press. Three years later a defender of Western society and Christianity, Ramón Ramírez, attacked the socialist theories of Proudhon as destructive of private property in a work titled *El cristianismo y la libertad—Ensayo sobre la civilización Americana* (Christianity and liberty—an essay about American civilization.)

From 1842 until 1846, popular discontent reached unprecedented levels; it was a product of the collective state of ill-being in Venezuela, from its marked social inequality, to its early stage capitalism, and above all to its rural latifundista system exploiting the campesinos.

Beginning in 1842, an economic crisis brought on the pauperization of small and medium-sized landowners, many of whom saw themselves dispossessed of their lands because of their growing debts; so, they decided to rise up. This situation was a part of the reason for the popular uprisings of 1846 and 1848 known as the Revolución Popular (Popular or People's Revolution.)

Juan Vicente González, a well known defender of the conservative oligarchy and an able romanticist, says of these events:

The slave asked for liberty, and the proletarians asked for the land promised to it. Governors! You heard and tolerated the promise that doubtlessly made us appear as criminals. What did you give to the slave and proletarian? Day after day they continue to work, [you're] perpetually struggling to stop, to contain the aspirations [of the slaves and proletarians]—so much ambition, so much vileness threatens our lives and properties . . . Never has a more frightening revolution threatened any people; poison has flowed through the veins of Venezuela . . . In the shadows of the night, the proletarian, the bum, the poor [those without credit], have come to unite against the bosses, against the prosperous and the rich, resolving to kill them.[21]

In this situation, the uneasiness of the oligarchs grew. The Spaniard Ángel Quinteros (1802–1866) wrote of his fear to a friend in Puerto Rico: "The social revolution that grows day by day on the plains and prairies, with ideas of communism and a commonwealth of goods, threatens more danger than that of the calamitous year 1846. The anger is growing more intense."[22]

In the campesino insurrection of 1846, a young peddler from Cúa, Ezequiel Zamora, took part. He would later become one of the principle protagonists in the second most important social convulsion of the 19th century in Venezuela. [Zamora received at least some of his revolutionary ideas] from his English friend José Bradford, who introduced Zamora to utopian socialist ideas. In a letter he wrote to Zamora on November 2, 1846, Bradford said:

I've received some very interesting papers . . . from Trinidad, from M. Lassabe, an artillery officer in the army of Napoleon, to whom I gave some lessons [presumably lessons in English] . . . He says that there are revolutionaries in Europe, who in France use the color red as a banner . . . They speak of a proletarian revolution as inevitable—as expounded by a revolutionary named Blanqui—and of the existence of a society or league that wants to hold all goods in common, as well as the earth. . . . I'm sending you copies of these papers, material for books or bullets, whatever may come.[23]

This revolution of 1846 was the first uprising fomented by the Partido Liberal Venezolano, which was founded in 1840 by Leocadio Guzmán (1801–1884), via an article in his publication, El Venezolano (The Venezuelan). Guzmán, along with Zamora, Juan Antonio Paúl (son of Coto Paúl) participated in the rebellion.

As a result of this, the above-mentioned Juan Vicente González, who came to be a council member in the Canton of Caracas, accused these federalists of being "anarchists, communists, and enemies of society."

One example of the reaction of the conservative sectors was the publication of the *Manifiesto de 1846*, edited by the ex-president of the republic, José Antonio Páez, in which he qualified as "anarchy" all attempts at social, economic, and political improvement, attempts provoked by the weariness with the promises and demagoguery of the new bosses and by the hopelessness of the struggle for the most elemental necessities of life.

Abolition of Slavery

On March 24, 1854, slavery was abolished in Venezuela by decree of President José Gregorio Monagas (1795–1858). This was a blow to capitalist production, as it eliminated nearly free labor for the haciendas, merchants, manufacturers, and all the rest. At the same time, the latifundistas and hacendados retained all of the power in a colonial [economic] structure, while foreign capitalists cornered the market [on manufactured goods]. In this epoch Venezuela, despite appearances, wasn't even an important provider of raw materials to the capitalist powers.

The dominant domestic classes managed to raise protectionist barriers in order to foster the growth of local industry, and with it came an incipient proletariat. In this precarious stage of capitalist development, Venezuelan capitalists turned to foreign investment from Germany, Britain, and U.S. firms for loans and credit. In the same year, the National Congress passed a law under which it authorized the executive to give privileges to persons or companies that introduced to Venezuela new industries or discoveries. The law conceded to those given such privileges the right to import raw materials tax free so long as their privileges were in force.

Meanwhile, the freed slaves were still exploited as "free workers" in jobs such as brick layer, carpenter, barber, metal worker, etc.; to put it another way, they continued to do manual labor. As a result of this, the publication *El Artesano* appeared in Caracas in 1856 as the organ of the Sociedad de Artesanos y Amigos del Progreso (Society of Artisans and Friends of Progress), with the "preoccupation with and necessity of the artisans to organize themselves and to confront the inclemencies of life."

Other freed slaves, due to their age or infirmities, or because they had no marketable skills, couldn't work and continued as domestic servants or found themselves out on the streets.

The painter who became radicalized in the face of injustice

In 1852, the flyer "Egalitarian Credo" circulated in Victoria and other population centers, and in the same year the impressionist painter Camille Pissarro (1833–1903) arrived in Venezuela, along with his Danish teacher, Fritz Melbye (1826–1869). Both of these artists spent two years in the cities of Caracas and Guaira, where they dedicated themselves to producing paintings portraying the customs of the inhabitants, above all those of the campesinos on the margins of the coastal zones. In reference to the awakening social conscience of Pissarro, which was bolstered in Venezuela, Ralph Shikes, in his work, *The Political Philosophy of Pissarro and His Art*, writes:

> From the first stages of his artistic career, Pissarro displayed the empathy and solidarity with the most humble members of society. In Saint Thomas, where he was born in 1830, and in Venezuela, he painted many pictures of agricultural laborers, laborers on the bottom of the social scale, such as mestizos, Indians and black people.[24]

We can infer from this that the social inequity Pissarro saw in daily life in Venezuela contributed in a decisive manner to his later affinity for anarchism. The writer and doctor Julio Ptenziani Bigelli writes:

> Without doubt, these concepts were apparent in the early adulthood of Pissarro, when he was in Saint Thomas and saw the social subjugation involved in colonialism, and in Venezuela where he saw a society dominated by military strongmen, nepotism, and corruption on every level.[25]

Pissarro became acquainted with the writings of Proudhon a few years after his arrival in Paris in 1855. He socialized with Proudhon and other anarchists such as Peter Kropotkin, Jean Grave (1854–1939), and Elisée Reclus (1830–1905). He was a subscriber and contributor to magazines such as *La Révolte* and *Les Temps Nouveaux* (New Times). Pissarro was also on the government's list of known anarchists, and his letters were intercepted and censored by the police. Nonetheless, despite the very real danger of arrest and detention for his political opinions, he remained dedicated to libertarian ideals, as evidenced by how he lived and what he painted until his death in Paris.

Even though Pissarro was not an anarchist activist in Venezuela, and his adherence to the cause came after his visit, it was in these lands where the painter developed his political commitment against the injustices that he saw that were impelling the famished masses to take up arms to set aflame the lands that he painted.

The Unbounded Liberty of the Cattle Rustlers

It was during these years of the 1850s that an old phenomenon reappeared, though with fresh virulence due to the precarious conditions of life: banditry. Bands of outlaw horsemen dedicated themselves to cattle rustling and robbery in order to survive.

Banditry of course is ancient and universal; it's appeared wherever misery and injustice have reigned, where members of the poor have taken up smuggling, robbery, and other types of crime, producing in more or less collective form a type of organized crime. A less romantic view sees in bandits bums, evildoers, criminals, fugitives, and upper class men who have ruined themselves through gambling or other vices.

But the bandit groups not only lived outside of "law and order," they lived communally and democratically in most cases, rejecting the concept of private property; their primary slogan was "Death to money!"

In Venezuela, the bandit phenomenon was common on the plains, the poorest region of the republic. To the writer Robert Paul Mathews, the plains were a stew pot where this type of conduct could develop, owing to the nature of the plains people:

> Their mode of life, characterized by their liberty of spirit and antiauthoritarianism, was a direct expression of the socioeconomic conditions in which they lived. The plains people usually didn't belong to any particular group of bandits or rustlers; living at the margins of the law, they simply weren't fenced in.[26]

Matthews added:

> It was rare for the bandits to be in groups of 30 or more, and they weren't into any type of planned conspiracy, but were in a more general state of illegality. To the measure in which the authorities impeded their activities, they opposed the government. Products of the 1840s and 1850s, the plains bandits often declared themselves rebels and attacked the local authorities. In addition, the illegal groups often joined futile rebellions and major insurrections. So, it was generally difficult to distinguish between bandits and rebels, since they existed in a precarious symbiosis."[27]

An anonymous writer in the conservative paper *Opúsculo* (Tract) gave his personal impression of the bandits:

> This class loves liberty without limits, without social restrictions, in short, free will. Thus they comprehend political liberty. They hate by instinct with a tenacious rancor the government or any authority that opposes their insane and savage beliefs . . . This licentious liberty that they love, this inexhaustible spring moves them because in it lie all of their ambitions and well-being, and it's their unique way of rebelling against power.[28]

This spurning of authority and private property by the bandits, summed up in a rudimentary collectivism, brought them near to a primitive form of anarchism. However the bandit bands, totally lacking in education, acted in the spirit of an instinctual confraternity rather than in the ambitious context of a transformational social experiment. In this respect Robert Matthews writes:

> The comportment of the bandits had its roots in what could be called pre-anarchist attitudes that combined withering disdain for private property with a profound distrust of the authorities. Even though they didn't represent the vanguard of a new order, their movement, nonetheless, had at its heart the necessary elements of social change.[29]

The anarchist theoretician Mikhail Bakunin addressed the question of banditry, and in his writings differed with Karl Marx, for whom only the proletariat could lead a revolution. In contrast, Bakunin shared with the narodniki (populists) a belief in the latent power of the Russian agricultural workers, with their long tradition of uprisings. As in any campesino society, there was a long tradition of banditry, that is to say that there had always been persons who "statesmen consider criminals, but who remain within rural society and are considered by its members as heroes, paladins, avengers, fighters for justice, at times including liberatory leaders, and in all cases as persons to admire, aid, and support."[30]

A less romantic vision than that expounded by Bakunin is that of the British historian Eric Hobsbawm, outlined in his book, *Primitive Rebels*, in which he refers to banditry as follows: "A man turns bandit because he does something that local opinion doesn't see as criminal, but that is seen as criminal in the eyes of the state or by the ruling local groups."

Still another view was offered by the writer Rámon Díaz Sánchez:

> It's as if gangrene eats away at the social fabric and unleashes disorder. The peons of the haciendas and cattle herders of the plains no longer accept the yoke

of discipline from anyone, and don't want to be commanded by anyone. They kill their bosses. The free drag the slaves to the rebellion. The fields and cattle raising are in ruins, and robbery and depredation become the desperate institutions of the anarchistic masses.[31]

The miserable conditions described previously, in addition to the spontaneous formation of the bandit gangs, were the cultural petri dish for a new social revolt of grand dimensions that would bathe the villages and settlements of the plains in blood, as in 1814. This conflict would come to be known as the Federal War or the Long War (1859–1863), which would be one of the most bitter military conflicts in Venezuela, second only to the War of Independence.

The Federal War

The Federal War was a military campaign designed by the Liberal Party to seize power from the conservative government, which was composed of Spanish landowners and the partisans of Páez who had enriched themselves from the booty of the War of Independence.

The Liberal Party platform in the insurrection consisted of demands for more autonomy for the provinces, consolidation of a federal system of control, agrarian reform, as well as demands for equality and equitable sharing of revenues.

The bandit gangs which for years had been waging guerrilla war in the mountains decided to join the forces of the Partido Liberal (Liberal Party), with whom they shared the concept of federation, which for the bandits involved an almost mythical sense of equality and personal autonomy. The historian Lisandro Alvarado says of the bandits, "In reality, they weren't the precursors of the February revolution but the revolution itself."[32]

The Liberal Party forces ranged from the leaders of the Caracas oligarchy, such as Antonio Guzmán Blanco (1829–1899) and Juan Cristómo Falcón (1820–1870), to the bandit gangs from the plains. But what interests us here are the possible libertarian socialist influences which had as the principal actor "the general of the sovereign masses of the people," Ezequiel Zamora.

(We should highlight here that libertarian and socialiast ideas were spread by the welfare and mutual aid societies created by artisan and worker guilds via the pamphlets and periodicals they published, which were occasionally edited by people of humble origin.)

Historians of the Federal War, such as Brito Figueroa and Laureano Vil-
lenilla Lanz, have pointed out the influence of the ideas of Proudhon and the
French-derived socialism in Zamora, which had come via José Bradford and
the attorney Francisco J. Iriarte. The historian Brito Figueroa states:

> Zamora thought that the plains belonged to no one, that they belonged to ev-
> eryone through use and custom, and besides, before the arrival of the Spaniards
> . . . those those lands were held in common, just like the air, sunlight and the
> waters.[33]

Figueroa also stated that "Our hypothesis [is that] radical and utopian socialist political ideas [existed along with] bourgeois democratic ideas in the
Federal War."[34]

The writer Roberto J. Lovera de Solo, who cites several other relevant works
on socialism, says this of the origins of the socialist ideas that circulated in
Venezuela at the time of the Federal War:

> [H]ere in Venezuela, socialist ideas were propounded in 1848 via the transla-
> tion of an article by L. Reybaud about the utopian socialist ideas of Charles
> Fourier, Robert Owen, Saint Simon, and Claude Henri de Rouvroy, who as-
> pired to completely restructure the social order. . . . [And] in 1850 the publisher
> Domingo Salazar, under the imprint de Pedrera a Gorda [literally from Stone
> Quarry to the Weighty], issued the book . . . *Intellectual Anarchy*.[35]

In contrast with Figueroa, the writer Manuel Caballero presents a very different estimation:

> The fact is that the myth of Zamora as a socialist, or at least an agrarian reform-
> er, is a creation of Marxist historiography . . . The first Venezuelan Marxists . . .
> were awakened by the first great revolution of this century [the Russian Revolu-
> tion] and transplanted [interpretations of] historical figures and situations to
> Venezuela. Above all, they desperately searched for an agrarian revolution in
> our history, for a mustachioed Emiliano Zapata and the Plan de Ayala [Zapata's
> agrarian reform plan]; in a feat of ideological prestidigitation, they put [Za-
> pata's] sombrero on Ezequiel Zamora.

The historian Luís Ugalde wrote this on the matter:

> Some have wanted to present this struggle above all . . . as a social revolution
> undertaken to obtain equality and redistribution of the land, as a political ex-
> pression of the desires of the people. But this was not the goal of the leaders of
> the movement nor of Zamora."[36]

Another equally critical historian, Guinara González, commented that "Zamora went no further in his declarations" than echoing the first Proclamation of Coro that said that federation meant 'government by all,' 'government of the free.'"

In contrast, other authors saw in Ezequiel Zamora a continuation of the social program of Boves. The historian Armas Chitty said that "the federation completed the War of Independence," and Laureano Vallneilla Lanz, author of "The Necessary Policeman" thesis would write that one could see the same "egalitarian desires" in the soldiers of the plains who supported Zamora as in those who supported Boves."

And we can do an analysis that establishes the continuity between the popular uprising of 1814 led by José Tomás Boves and that led by Zamora. The writer Juan Vicente González put it this way:

> The war which would tear Venezuela apart would be called the Social War. It wasn't fought because of principles of freedom, nor for popular ideas, nor to replace an abusive government with one that expressed the popular will. Those who fought it did so to destroy the established order, physically altering social relations and creating a chaos from which it would be possible to organize a new order of things with new proprietors, new laws, new customs.[37]

If we take these observations as true, we can conclude that in less than a century Venezuela had experienced two instances of social war, with totally distinct actors but with common causes, which set Venezuela apart from the rest of Latin America.

But was Zamora an anarchist or a proto-anarchist? The answer, according to the evidence, is no. As the historian Adolfo Rodríguez pointed out in his book *The Sacred Fire*, "In 1846 the voracious flames were lit with anarchist ideas. But, we can ask ourselves, 'Anarchist in the sense of political anarchism or anarchist in the sense of chaos?'"[38]

[There's no record of Zamora referring to the first coherent anarchist political works—P.J. Proudhon's *What Is Property* (1840) and, arguably, William Godwin's *An Enquiry Concerning Political Justice* (1793)—let alone having read them.]

There are further indications that Zamora was not an anarchist nor a partisan of anarchist ideas. The fact is that he was a regional caudillo riding on popular social unrest. He wasn't a partisan of libertarian ideas of social organization—quite the contrary. He was a small landowner and a believer in seizing centralized power in order to foster social change, to reform land ownership, and to make upward mobility possible within different strata of society.

As laudable as one might consider this, Zamora had no intention of putting anarchist ideas into practice.

The war of 1846 was the most costly war in Venezuelan history in terms of human lives. It was a brutal affair, and the caudillos who controlled the armed bands acted as feudal rulers; they didn't shrink from destroying entire communities.

The war put a definitive end to the regime of José Antonio Páez. But new regional caudillos emerged who seized the lands. The price for all this was paid by the civil population. Approximately 175,000 people, the majority campesinos, died during the five years of the war—almost 10% of the country's population. In the regions where the war took place, much productive land went out of production, either destroyed by fire or simply abandoned because of labor shortages. This considerably reduced agricultural and cattle production; over 7,000,000 head of cattle died, a number larger than had perished during the War of Independence.

The Federal War destroyed the economy of the country, because it was fought for the most part on the plains, the center of Venezuelan cattle production. Because of this, the Andean zone, which hadn't been directly affected by the war, began to grow in importance because of the development of its coffee production and its communities, from which would grow the new elite of the coming century.

Bohemian Coffee Shop Anarchism

After the events of the Federal War, the ideas of Bakunin arrived in Caracas via the French and Spanish books read by the intellectuals and occasionally workers. Miguel Eduardo Pardo, the Caracan poet and author, in his novel *Todo un Pueblo* (All One People), published in Caracas near the end of the 19th century, included a discussion by young intellectuals with the following dialogue: "Jesus wasn't a demagogue, but rather the first apostle of anarchism. Ravachol, Vaillant, and Pallás [all terrorists] were saints who carried Christ within their bosoms, and the first of these wasn't a vulgar murderer who desecrated corpses, but rather an extraordinary being perhaps greater than Jesus."[39]

In any event, such literary allusions show that there was a certain amount of interest in anarchism among the intellectuals of the time. There were references not only to terrorists such as Auguste Vaillant (1861–1894) and Ravachol (1859–1894), but also to ethical anarchists such as Tolstoy and Kropotkin.

During this time, Carlos Brandt Tortolero was born on October 11, 1875. He was the son of Carlos Augusto Brandt Caramelo and Zoraída Tortolero Ortega, who were descended from German immigrants. In time, Carlos Brandt Tortolero would become of the one of the best libertarian writers in Venezuela. He was the first advocate of anarcho-pacifism and vegetarianism in the region. Oddly, Carlos first became aware of anarchism when his father recited from memory and explained entire sections of the eloquent defense mounted by the lawyer for [the anarchist and terrorist] Vaillant.

Carlos Brandt would later write:

My education began at home, and my father was the most effective of my teachers. He was the most liberal, with the most advanced ideas, and was well versed in social and economic questions. His conversations at the dinner table centered around social matters in order to make me see the injustice of the social system and the hateful exploitation of the workers by the capitalists.[40]

On May 4, 1877, the founding meeting took place in Caracas of the Aociácion de Demócratas Radicales, which was a club consisting of intellectuals and free thinkers who discussed political ideas ranging from socialism to anarchism. On June 2 of the same year in Caracas, the Instituto Venezolano de Ciéncias Sociales appeared. It was part of the College of Santa María, owned by the attorney Avelada. It featured discussion of socialism in the context of Venezuela.

Two years later the newspaper *El Obrero* (The Worker) began to circulate in Caracas. It was the publication of the Artisans Guild of Venezuela, which had been founded in 1864 to provide protection for its members and to advance social demands. The paper had as its motto "The emancipation of the workers should be the task of the workers themselves," which demonstrated a keen understanding of socialist ideas among the Venezuelan workers and which later because the motto of the International Workers Association (IWA/AIT), the anarcho-syndicalist international.

The historian Rodolfo Quintero points out that "in these years . . . [Venezuelan] guild periodicals carried in their pages the historical call, 'Workers of the world unite!,'" which was frequently found in publications of the IWA.

Other relevant works circulating in Venezuelan literary circles of the period included those of the Hungarian writer Max Nordau (1849–1923) and especially of his most important work, *Conventional Lies of Our Civilization*, which appeared in 1883. The "lies" Nordau cited include religion, the aristocracy, politics, economics, marriage, the press, justice, and public opinion.

Even though he wasn't an anarchist, his ideas and critiques found a niche in many antiauthoritarian circles around the world, and did contribute to anarchist thought.

One of Nordau's Venezuelan admirers was Antonio M. Cerranto, the director of the Jáuregui College in Puerto Cabello, who published several articles extolling Nordau's book in the *Diario Comercial* (Daily Commerce). One of Cerranto's students was Carlos Brandt.

In 1884, a cooperative society was founded in Valencia that openly cited its affinity with the works Owen, Cabet, Fourier, and Proudhon. The society published a pamphlet about workers' emancipation, which had been published previously by a similar society in Santa Cruz de Tenerife, Spain.

In 1888, in Valencia, the first workers' paper published in that locale appeared: *El Obrero*, which had the same name as its counterpart in Caracas, though it only published two issues. In an editorial in the first of these, it proclaimed: "We don't want an isolated anarchist guild or to proclaim anarchism amongst ourselves . . . We want to make our guild an active participant in civil struggles and in the social aspirations that fall under the name 'natural rights' guaranteed by the republic."[41] The article speaks for itself, and shows the probable influence of anarchist ideas in Venezuela and within the Venezuelan working class.

Before proceeding further, it's necessary to point out the differences between the publications that appeared under the title *El Obrero*. The historian José Urquijo writes:

> One sign of "workerism" is the appearance of papers with the name *El Obrero*, which honor labor with their name, and which reflect the social unrest and even the socialist tone of the epoch. One should mention *El Obrero* of 1879, a Christian publication; *El Obero* of 1890, an openly socialist periodical . . .; *El Obrero* of 1894 in Caracas and Mérida; *El Obero Católico* in Tovar (1896–1901); *El Obrero* in Caracas (1896); and *El Obrero* in Caracas (1900–1901). In all, fourteen papers appeared under the name.[42]

In 1892, Venezuelan anarchists took part in the struggle for the eight-hour day. In the paper *El Fonógrafo* (The Phonograph), published in Maracaibo, there was an article by Ernesto Álvarez titled, "The first of May for the Anarchists," in which the follower of Bakunin wrote:

> The first of May for the workers is a day which marks the belief that it's necessary to change the situation, change the onerous conditions in which they live, and from there the importance of the revolutionary viewpoint.

Until now amongst the workers we have discussed which measures are most effective in obtaining better conditions, until we arrive at complete emancipation. The socialists, partisans of delegations, parliaments, and civil government, maintain that the only way of achieving the eight-hour day is through legal channels, that is to uproot the power of the people. We, who know perfectly well that the mission of the state is nothing other than safeguarding the interests of the class it represents, will combat this contrary idea and will work with resolve for the revolutionary path.

Our impugners . . . even today attempt to distract once again the workers making them believe that this revolutionary date par excellence [May 1] should become a date for parties, a ruse which won't last long. . . . It's not a stretch to say that before many more May Days have passed the working class will find itself in shape to unleash the final successful battle that will put in its hands that which today the the bourgeoisie have seized.[43]

In the same year of 1892, the celebrated Venezuelan paper *El Cojo Ilustrado* (The Enlightened Gimp—the title can also be translated as The Illustrated Cripple) published information about the European anarchist movement. Unfortunately, this periodical presented the information in a defamatory manner, and ridiculed and attempted to criminalize libertarian ideas. Unfortunately, this attitude continued in the daily press until 1915, and was an obstacle to the spread of libertarian ideas.

The International in Caracas

After the fall of the Paris Commune in 1871, refugees from the following repression, among them Proudhonist anarchists, arrived in Caracas and clandestinely founded the Venezuelan section of the International, which functioned until at least 1893, as evidenced by a letter they sent to the Fourth International Workers Congress in Zurich in that year. In contrast with sections in other countries, the Venezuelan section didn't manage to reach the workers of the country and was comprised of a small circle of French, Swiss, and German members.

On July 25 in that same year, there was an organizing meeting at the Restaurant Café Caracas, at which 14 workers constructing the Caracas-Valencia rail line (completed in 1894) attended. They voted to create a coordinating committee, with Adolf Pickel, H. Willhoft, and Bruno Rossner being elected to it. They also voted to send Franz Schleese as their representative to the upcoming Workers Congress in Europe, the meeting ending with the singing of the Marsellaise.

The Congress took place in Zurich from the 6th of September to the 13th. Another Venezuelan was in attendance beside the delegation from that country: Daniel De Leon (1852–1914), [a leading member of the Socialist Labor Party, which advocated revolutionary syndicalism, and which DeLeon joined in 1890] one of the co-founders of the Industrial Workers of the World, to which we'll return in later chapters. The only other Latin American country represented at the Congress was Brazil.

Under the title "News of Venezuela," dated August 1, 1893, the delegation delivered a report to the Congress, including the following:

> Dear Comrades,
> In the first place, we salute the social-democratic and fraternal clasping of hands by the participants in the 4th Socialist Workers Congress, and hope that the deliberations of those workers will be fruitful for the entire world and that in the near future our efforts will be crowned with deserved success. . . .

> On July 25, 1893, for the first time 14 German-speaking socialists located around Caracas (in the suburbs, such as Palo Grande, etc.), met. . . . Because of the recent dissolution of the Reichstag, they have sent a contribution of 200 Deutschmarks, collected through small donations, with comrade Schleese to help with social-democratic agitation in Germany.

Regarding the situation at the time in Venezluela, Rodolfo Quintero notes:

> Already in the final years of the nineteenth century there were demonstrations and other expressions of resistance by groups of foreign workers with ties to the First International, workers who had been contracted to work on the railroads and major buildings. For example, a good number of the German workers working on the Puerto Cabello railway were partisans of Marx and others partisans of Bakunin.[44]

Labor historian Julio Godio, comments in one of his books, "The only section of the AIT [Asociación Internacional de los Trabajadores—International Workers Association] with a majority of marxists was that founded in Buenos Aires."[45] The Latin American labor historian Carlos Rama adds, "The interest by workers in the ideas of the AIT was facilitated by the previous diffusion of socialist ideas [in the region]. In many cities from Mexico to Bolivia there were San Simonists, Fourierists, and Proudhonists."[46]

This leads to the conclusion that the other Latin American sections of the International, among them the section in Venezuela, were in good measure Proudhonist, that is to say that they had anarchist proclivities.

It's not known what happened to the original members of the International in Venezuela. It's likely that they returned to their countries of origin, and it's also possible that they continued to informally work within Venezuela for justice and equality.

The Revival of Anarchism in Venezuela

The year 1894 was a difficult one for the republic. The situation of the country had worsened due to the failure of the coffee and cocoa harvests and also because of the low international prices for those products. The president, Joaquín Crespo (1841–1898), named the rich businessman David León as finance minister. The condition of public finances was every bit as desperate as that of the economy. The business and commercial sectors, and even the mass of workers demanded the opening of new public works projects. But the lack of resources obliged the state to regulate the economic areas that generated income for the public treasury.

When all this unfolded, there existed in Caracas many guilds: those of the cattle herders, typographers, bakers, tailors, musicians, barbers, laborers. There was also a freethinkers association (Sociedad Central de Libre Pensadores) that proposed celebrating the overthrow of earthly power. At the opening of their of their very well attended party-like event on the Plaza Bolívar de Caracas they had a band play the Marseillese.

In this otherwise tense climate, what we might call the first class-conscious march took place in Venezuela. It consisted of the unemployed or, as some called them, "the poor in spirit." The press (*El Diario de Caracas*, *El Tiempo* and *El Republicano*) reported on the march and denounced it citing the response of the police, who it called "a violation of constitutional rights." The governor, Juan Francisco Castillo said: "We're not dealing with a demonstration, but with a riot. They didn't ask permission, they gave no advance notice to any of the authorities, and the wording of the signs they carried was a clear incitement to riot." He added, "The people know the poor finances of the government," [apparently to excuse the government's inaction in the face of the economic crisis]. He also stated, "This action is a reflection of the socialist wave that's invading the Old World!" A few months later Francisco Castillo was named Minister of Interior Relations.

At the time of this tumult, the writer and poet Rafael Bolívar Coronado was born on June 6, 1896 in the town of Villa de Cura (House of the Priest). He was the son of the legislator and businessman Rafael Bolívar Álvarez, from Aragon, and Emilia Coronado. Later this fortunate son would become a noted anarchist and writer who would be active in the anarchist movement in Catalonia. At about the same time, the Caracas daily paper *El Avisador* (The Messenger) distributed handbills about anarchism, the German workers movement, and the Haymarket martyrs.

A few months after the birth of Bolívar, on October 28, 1896, the First Workers Congress of Venezuela took place in Caracas. The organizers were the attorney Alberto González Briceño and the poet Leopoldo Torres Abandero, who weren't revolutionaries but rather freethinkers preoccupied by the "social question." The attendees did, however, include Spanish anarchists who had emigrated to Venezuela.

The Tailors Union, Carpenters Guild, and the Alliance for Work[ers] took part in the event, and at the time those who used the name "Alliance" were generally anarchist in orientation. The alliance itself had publicly proclaimed its sympathies with the Cooperative of Valencia, which was Proudhonist. To leave no doubt about the libertarian sympathies of some participants in the Congress, an article published in the Caracas daily *El Tiempo* (The Times) stated: "[T]he workers have a dual sentiment not represented by professional politicians: they don't want changes in their workplaces brought about by government bureaucracy, but rather they want to govern themselves and therefore have a disinterest in the electoral process."

But at the same time the orgnizers of the Congress tried to use it to launch their own political party, the Partido Popular ("People's Party"), but the majority of those in attendance showed a total disinterest in the electoral organization, a disinterest reflected in the short life of the party.

In 1898, a peculiar paper appeared in Caracas, *La Unión Social*, under the direction of Alberto González Briceño, one of the organizers of the Congress. In the editorial in its first edition, "Nuestro Rumbo" (Our Course), the paper proclaimed its ideological stance:

> The capitalist who doesn't think of anything but oppressing the working classes is a terrible volcano that destroys the social edifice; he's a profanity that resides in the temple of misery, who laughs about the necessities of life; . . . he's the hangman of humanity . . . Workers! Let's unite to bring about social evolution and let us exclaim, in the words of the poet, "I do not accept tyrants from above or below."

This euphoric exclamation in favor of liberty and against capitalism, autocracy, and inequality shows affinity with libertarian ideas. Unfortunately, the paper lasted only three issues before disappearing.

* * *

At the end of the nineteenth century, Venezuela was a mostly rural and agricultural country submerged in poverty and unemployment, and afflicted by innumerable "revolutions" that were far removed from real social change.

When the First Workers Congress took place, Venezuela only had 96 [large] companies. Its principle industry was agriculture, and it was in the hands of a very few large landowners who kept the campesinos who worked for them in ignorance and misery. This in turn contributed to the slow development of anarchist ideas in the country.

Nonetheless, even though there wasn't much industrialization in the country, there was a proletariat that wanted to break free of class limitations, and that was searching for social ideas that offered hope of a better life. So, in that epoch we find discussion in theaters and cultural centers about socialism, anarchism, and communism.

At the same time, around 80% of the population was completely illiterate. The campesinos were the most forlorn and miserable class, the lowest on the social scale. All of the conditions involved in national disintegration afflicted them, especially conscription and economic exploitation by the latifundistas. The same conditions afflicted the fishing workers along the coast.

The historian Luis Salcedo Bastardo summed up the condition of Venezuela at the end of the nineteenth century: "The autocracies mired Venezuela in individualism, and deaf and blind to progress, they kept it there. They even held back reactionary innovations, such as the 'freedom of contract' [the basis of laissez-faire economic relations], which had been inaugurated in England twenty years prior."[47]

As regards the law, the norms in the Venezuelan republic reinforced capitalism. The labor legislation held to the juridical view of liberty, that the state could not protect any of the parties in a dispute, because all of them were equal in theory. Because of this, the state couldn't even act as guarantor that the parties would honor their contractual obligations, as can be seen in the brutal and atrocious working conditions of the time.

Workers, lacking their own means of providing sustenance and the most basic necessities of life, saw themselves obligated to labor under inhumane conditions and to commit to contracts that did nothing but guarantee their misery. The so-called "police codes" didn't protect labor but only existed to preserve "public order" and bourgeois control. They were the judicial tools necessary to prevent any socialist, anarchist, or other progressive uprisings.

The police code of Margarita, in force since 1845, prescribed prison for labor disorder:

> All day laborers or peons who commit to doing work are obligated to do it. If they want to stop doing it, they are required to advise their boss days before and always with justified reasons in the view of a judge. Those who abandon their required work without filling these prerequisites will be jailed for three days.[48]

As we can see in the history of Venezuelan anarchism, from the start it faced obstacles to its full, integrated development. But at the same time the events and social-political participants of the nineteenth century were important precursors of the development of socialism and anarchism in Venezuela, a land which did not have classic capitalist evolution as in Europe.

Soon, what we can call the prehistory of anarchism in Venezuela would be superseded by the formation of a labor movement with a clear orientation toward anarchism.

CHAPTER 3

Clandestinity, Combat, and Andean Tyranny

In 1899, the Colombian anarchist Máximo Lizcano, better known by his pseudonym, Biófilo Panclasta, arrived in Venezuela in search of work opportunities. In the pueblo of Capacho he came to know Eleazar López Contreras (1883–1973), a young man who became his companion in his travels through the Venezuelan Andes. Lizcano wrote:

> López Contreras was my compañero in both work and adventures for a long time. And you know that he and I founded the first public school in Capacho in Tajira state. I arrived in Venezuela after fleeing from a school in Bucaramanga and crossing on foot the wasteland of Mortiño in 1899. I ran out of money in Capacho, and very quickly couldn't cover my most basic expenses. Harried by misery, I talked with the Reverend Contreras, the parish priest, and after telling him about my problems I suggested starting a public school, something the people lacked. . . . The priest was very enthusiastic about the idea and recommended to me one of his nephews, Eleazar López Contreras, who had just arrived from La Grita where he had finished his secondary studies, and so I found myself a bit disoriented not knowing exactly how to proceed. Three months later, Cipriano Castro, inspired by autonomous liberalism and by José María Vargas Vila (1860–1933), organized from Colombia an invasion which would come to be known as la Revolución Liberal Restauradora (The Revolution of Liberal Restoration). Castro, leading a handful of men, crossed the frontier with the the aim of overthrowing the constitutional government of Ignacio Andrade (1839–1925).[49]

Panclasta states, "Avid for adventure, we abandoned the school, took up arms and marched to Caracas under the fluttering, victorious banners of the revolution, becoming overnight aides to General Castro."[50] Panclasta was appointed correspondence secretary for the general.

It was in Venezuela, as with Camille Pissarro, that Panclasta developed his radical politics; despite his position and friendships with the influential, he had to flee to Colombia in 1904, which was the beginning of an astonishing voyage of travel, political agitation, writing and publishing, exile, and prison. He spent time in perhaps 20 countries and time in even more jails.

During the same period, the young Carlos Brandt carried on correspondence with Leo Tolstoy, from which hatched the idea of publishing in Venezuela Tolstoy's book *Church and State*, in which Tolstoy developed his vision of Christian, pacifist anarchism. Of this close relationship between Brandt and Tolstoy, the writer Jon Aizpúrua would write:

> At age 25, Brandt dared to send a letter to Leo Tolstoy, which Tolstoy was happy to receive. He answered, and from that moment on there was an interchange of correspondence, in which Tolstoy asked Brandt to translate *Church and State*, and later to write a prologue for it. The book was published in 1901 in Puerto Cabello.[51]

Another Venezuelan anarchist writer of the time, José María Vargas Vila, wrote about U.S. foreign policy and its insidious effects on Latin America. In 1903, the magazine *Némesis* published his article "Before the Barbarians" (Ante los Bárbaros—published in book form 15 years later) which earned him expulsion from the country. Vargas Vila's anti-imperialist "Propaganda of the Deed?" was also influential.

At the time the government of Castro was facing strong internal and external political opposition. Its arrest of the bankers who refused to collaborate with the state in resolving the financial crisis contributed to the rebellion known as the Revolución Libertadora (Liberating Revolution) which was launched overseas by transnationals such as the New York and Bermuda Company and the Orinoco Steamship Company. Castro faced twenty coup attempts, an assassination attempt, a civil war, and an international conspiracy designed to dispossess Venezuela of a good part of its territory. Between 1899 and 1903, there were 372 battles that left over 20,000 dead.

The failed assassination attempt occurred on February 27, 1900 in the middle of the carnaval festivities. Police agent Andrés Cabrices knocked away the gun, and a multitude rushed to Castro's defense.

An aide of Castro, Eleazar López Contreras, relates what happened:

> On February 27, the Wednesday of the carnaval, on the corner of Socarras, a man named Anselmo López tried to take the life of the Supreme Leader. He arrived [at the carnaval parade] with his wife in a carriage displaying two swans made of roses, which the papers described as pretty. When López pointed his

revolver [at Castro] a policeman grabbed his arm and a hundred arms were raised against the attacker. Castro intervened, and later continued home to the presidential palace."[52]

The would-be assassin, Anselmo López was a baker from Aragua who worked in the center of Caracas. Little is known of his life, not even what his motives were. nor what happened to him after he was arrested, not even whether he died there or spent ten years in custody and was then released. The writer Jesús Sanoja Hernández described him as a "feeble-minded artisan."

Journalist and historian Luis Eduardo Zambrano Velasco wrote:

> Anselmo López. a native of El Pao de Zárate, was the author of the attempted homicide. He was an illiterate firewood tender in the bakery of Francisco Marrero . . . According to the statements made before the criminal court judge, Marrero planned the assassination attempt and induced his employee López to carry it out.[53]

Regarding [the illiterate] Anselmo López, it's impossible to demonstrate an anarchist affiliation. Nonetheless, his actions have passed into the national historiography, with reference to his possibly having been influenced by various anarchist assassinations and engaging in "anti-imperialismo a la venezolana."

Again, of the political or ideological reasons for the attack, little is known. What makes it stand out is its occurrence during the time when some anarchists practiced "propaganda of the deed" [terrorist acts]. These types of actions were known to Venezuelans; an example can be found in the writings of historian Rufino Blanco Fombona (1874–1944), who in his book *La Lámpara de Aladino* (Aladdin's Lamp) celebrated the assassination of U.S. President William McKinley in 1891 by the [supposed] anarchist León Czolgosz (1873–1901).

Fombona was a government official who held several posts including Venezuelan delegate in Amsterdam. He publicly admired the poems and writings of the Spanish anarchist Rafael Barrett (1876–1910), going so far as to publish some of Barrett's works in Spain via the publisher Editorial Americana directed by Peruvian libertarian Manuel González Prada (1844–1918).

The instability in Venezuela, the confrontation of Castro's government with would-be caudillos, and the decrease in the price of agricultural exports obliged Castro to temporarily suspend service on the external debt. As well, foreign powers continued to demand recompense for damage to their citizens who had been caught up in the civil wars.

The principle powers demanded immediate payment of debts owed them, but the government refused to recognize the demands and suspended payment on them. On December 9, 1902, Germany and Great Britain blockaded Venezuela's coasts in response. Italy joined the blockade on December 12, and a little later France, Holland, Belgium, the U.S., Spain, and Mexico demanded the debts owed them be given the same consideration as those owed the blockading countries.

The U.S. managed to end the conflict through mediation, with the signing of the Protocols of Washington on February 13, 1903, in which the powers agreed to the gradual cancellation of the debts owed by Venezuela. During this period, the Venezuelan regime had presented itself as nationalistically confronting foreign powers. This was echoed in the Drago Doctrine elaborated by the Argentine chancellor in which he argued against the illegal, violent collection of debts by the major powers at the expense of the sovereignty, stability, and dignity of weaker states.

Once the blockade crisis had passed, the international policies of the Castro government continued devolving into confrontations and conflicts. The government filed suit against the foreign companies that had participated in the "Liberatory Revolution," including a suit against the New York and Bermúdez Company, in which it demanded an indemnity of 50 million bolivars. It also began proceedings to expropriate the Orinoco Steamship Company. Both of these cases resulted in the breaking of relations between Venezuela and the U.S. in 1908.

But the confrontations were not only with the companies tied to the "Liberatory Revolution." In 1905, Venezuela rescinded its contract with the French Interoceanic Cable Company. Castro ordered the closure of the company's offices and expelled the French charge d'affairs, and in consequence of this Venezuela and France broke off diplomatic relations in 1906. Parallel with this, the regime confronted the German companies and ordered the seizure of ships under the Dutch flag, which in turn led to the rupture of diplomatic relations with Holland.

The anti-imperialist character of Castro was a product of the empty public treasury, though one should also mention the influence of the texts of Vargas Vila.

While all this was going on in Venezuela, the founding congress of the Industrial Workers of the World took place in Chicago in 1905. Venezuelan activist Daniel DeLeón, son of a rich family from Curacao, attended this convention of radical syndicalists, independent radicals, and anarchist groups. DeLeón had graduated with a PhD in political science from Columbia University. He was entrusted with drafting the first manifesto of the IWW, which even today remains active in the U.S. and other parts of the world.

Daniel De León can be considered one of the most important figures within the libertarian ambit of the period, and many writers have considered him as the ideological author of American anarcho-syndicalism. There's nothing surprising in this given that his approach can be encapsulated in the slogan "All power to the industrial socialist unions," and that he denounced without respite the parliamentary opportunism of some socialists.

But Daniel De León represents for many a contradictory figure, and someone who was by no means an anarchist. Cuban anarchist historian, Frank Fernández [author of *Cuban Anarchism: The History of a Movement*], in an interview conducted as part of the research for this book, commented:

> As regards DeLeón, in reality he wasn't a Venezuelan. He studied in Germany and the Netherlands before emigrating to the U.S. in 1874, where he helped found the Socialist Labor Party in 1876. This party split in 1895, and in 1899 DeLeón founded the Socialist Workers Alliance, and after that the American Socialist Party which merged with the IWW in 1905. Finally, DeLeón split from the IWW and organized a rival called the Union of Industrial Workers. He was never an anarchist, though in principle he could be considered a "leading militant." But he was involved in politics and helped to fossilize the American labor movement.

(Here it's necessary to clarify a few things, particularly the references to DeLeón's origins, which were effectively Venezuelan: DeLeón was born in Caracas on December 14, 1852 to a rich family from Curacao. The family returned to Curacao in 1859 shortly before the outbreak of the Federal War in that year. And it's undeniable that De León was active in the struggle for proletarian emancipation, being the primary rival of Big Bill Haywood (1869-1928), who was an advocate of the general strike, the boycott, and sabotage. In the end, Haywood's approach won out in the IWW, and De León and his faction withdrew, founding in 1908 the Union of Industrial Workers.)

In 1908, General Juan Vicente Gómez (1857–1935) snatched power from his compadre Cipriano Castro, taking advantage of Castro's absence from the country due to health reasons. This seizure marked the consolidation of the Venezuelan state, ushering in an era of caesarism and long years of dictatorship.

For his part, Castro undertook a long journey from country to country, paradoxically living for times in Spain and the U.S., from which he was forced to leave in 1913. He died in Santurce, Puerto Rico in 1916, watched by spies from the new regime, and financing assassination plots against Gómez which never came to fruition.

In 1909, a year after the coup, the mutualist, proudhonist book *El Socialismo y las Clases Jornaleras* (Socialism and the Laboring Classes), written by Manuel Vicente Martínez was published in Caracas. In its 171 pages, Martínez exalted the working class and called for the construction of a new society based on horizontal organization and solidarity. In addition to Proudhon, he also referenced Jean Grave, Charles Malato (1857–1938), Peter Kropotkin, and Alfred Naquet (1834–1916). Nothing more is known of the author of this book.

A Tolstoyan in Mérida

A few kilometers from Puerto Cabello and the radius of influence of Carlos Brandt, another wealthy young creole, the writer and attorney Julio Cesar Salas (1870–1933), in 1904 using his own money, began publishing the magazine *Paz y Trabajo* (Peace and Work), which was inspired by the antiauthoritarian Christianity of Leo Tolstoy. Cesar Salas would continue in this work years later with the journal *De Re Indica* (Of Indian Note). In the final edition of the publication, under the title "Leo Tolstóy and His Work," the biographer Francisco Javier Pérez summed up Tolstoy's thought in the epigram, "Neither slaves nor masters," the epigram of a very wealth man who gave freedom to his serfs and divided up his lands among them.

Salas's studies regarding the ethno-linguisitics of native people and his systematic analysis of the impact of Spanish immigration during the colonial period are laid out in his book *Civilización y Barbarie* which was published in Barcelona in 1919 by Talleres Gráficos Lux, and which would lead Salas to correspondence and friendship with the learned Italian-Argentine José Ingenieros (1877–1925).

Salas the ethnographer, professor, and man of letters, with his peaceful, egalitarian morals, never openly declared himself an anarchist, perhaps for fear of a government that on more than one occasion lashed out against critics via the legal process.

A Venezuelan in the 1912 Baja California Uprising

In February 1911 in a hotel in Pasadena, California, Rafael de Nogales Méndez (1879–1936), a Venezuelan adventurer and mercenary, met with the great Mexican anarchist Ricardo Flores Magón (1874–1922), a prolific writer, organizer of the Partido Liberal Mexicano (PLM), [and one of the primary precursors of the 1910 Mexican Revolution]. In his memoirs, Nogales Méndez wrote:

> After having dragged my bones out of the ruins of Nevada, I found myself comfortably installed in the sitting room of the Hotel Green in Pasadena, California, asking myself what I would do next. Being hungry and with no immediate plans, I found myself going to breakfast in the dining room when I tripped over a distinguished Mexican man, who courteously excused himself . . . After breakfast, and having nothing to do, I went again to the sitting room, where the Mexican man greeted me; we exchanged a few pleasantries and then went to the bar. Before the day ended, we understood each other like old friends.
>
> His name was Ricardo Flores Magón, a ranchero [not true—tr.] and revolutionary exiled by [longtime Mexican dictator] Porfirio Díaz. He told me that he had heard stories about my adventures in Cuba, Alaska, and Venezuela. As I was going for a stroll the next day, Flores Magón asked me if I was ready to take part in the approaching great revolution, and I accepted immediately while knowing nothing about this great possibility.[54]

At the start, Nogales Méndez didn't take part in Flores Magón's invasion of Baja. On the contrary, he crossed the frontier to take part in cattle rustling with a band of outlaws in order to later sell the stolen cattle in the U.S. During this incursion the group was detected by Porfirio Díaz's troops and made a daring escape which ended when two of Magóns militia men stopped Méndez. At that moment the Venezuelan joined the anarchist insurgency.

Before continuing this narrative, let's take a few moments to make a historical semblance of this man.

Rafael de Nogales Méndez was born on October 14, 1879 in Venezuela to a well-to-do family. He was educated in Belgium and France, and learned to speak several languages. A military man by profession, he participated in many armed conflicts, including the U.S. war on Spain that resulted in Cuban independence. He was an arms trafficker in Central America and the Caribbean, a cowboy and gold prospector in Nevada, a spy in the 1905 Russian-Japanese War, a participant in the uprising led by Augusto Sandino (1895–1934) in Nicaragua, and a militia man in the Partido Liberal Mexicano.

The PLM uprising in which Nogales pariticipated is known as the Rebellion in Baja California, and it consisted of a [poorly organized, poorly provisioned, small-scale] military invasion propelled by the PLM and in which members of he IWW took part, including Joe Hill, Frank Little, and John Mosby. The intent was to establish a community of cooperatives in the territory occupied by the rebels.

During the Baja uprising, Nogales Méndez commanded a column of one hundred men who operated in northern Mexico in the states of Chihuahua, Durango, and Sonora. Regarding an assault on the town of Sacal, Nogales Méndez wrote:

> Immediately after the assault I went to a typesetter and dictated a proclamation saying "In the name of liberty and justice, we came to liberate people from the oppression of Porfirio Díaz, to give them a good part of the earth which has been fraudulently snatched from them by centuries of despotism and particularly by the Díaz gang."[55]

According to Nogales Méndez, communication with Flores Magón was scanty, so he had to establish a channel of communication with the troops of Francisco Madero (1873–1913), who were fighting in the zone but under a different flag and a different slogan. [The slogan of the PLM was "Land and Liberty."]

Other military actions in which Méndez took part included resisting the three-week assault of Torreón by federal forces directed by Victoriano Huerta (1850–1916) and taking the village of Concepción.

Unfortunately, the militia column led by Nogales Méndez fell into pillaging and acts of vandalism. Regarding this he wrote:

> The men turned into savages, sacking stores and taverns where they sold tequila, robbing citizens, despite all my efforts. I shot three of them myself and had a gun battle with others, two of whom tried to abuse a bar girl. But the inferno continued. . . .

> Our situation became more and more critical. We'd been going without food, and couldn't get near to the pueblos with cattle for fear of falling into an ambush. The rurales [a type of federal troops] were good scouts and terrible enemies. If it hadn't been for our knowledge of the country and my system of advancing by night, we would have ended up with a noose around our necks.[56]

In Baja California, the uprising was smothered by federal troops and the insurgents had to cross the frontier and seek refuge in the United States. The [fiasco] in Baja ended up with the organizing committee of the PLM in prison, and various wobblies, including Frank Little and John Mosby, also in jail. And there was also a series international accusations accusing the rebels of filibusterism and of being agents of U.S. annexation.

Rafael de Nogales didn't fall prey to judicial sanctions, and left for Venezuela. He tried to organize an uprising against Juan Vicente Gómez, but it failed and he had to abandon the country and flee to Turkey, where he offered his services to the Ottoman Empire in 1915, which gave him command of two thousand Turkish soldiers facing thirty-five thousand Caucasian rebels during the revolt in the city of Van, where paradoxically he fought against the partisans of the Armenian Revolutionary Federation, which counted among its members anarchists such as Alexander Atabekian and others influenced by the subversive traditions of the Federation's founder, Khristaphor Mikaelyan. (This uprising was a foreshadow of and an impulse leading to the infamous Aremenian Genocide by the Turks.)

Years later Rafael de Nogales wrote several books about his adventures, including *Memorias* (Memories), *Saqueo de Nicaragua* (The Pillaging of Nicaragua), and *Cuatro años bajo la Media Luna* (Four Years Beneath the Half Moon). After a lifetime full of incredible journeys and experiences, the Andean mercenary died in Panama on July 10, 1936.

Nogales Méndez was not an anarchist, but rather an adventurer who sold his services to the highest bidder. Nonetheless, his participation in the Baja uprising merits coverage in this book about Venezuelan anarchism.

In the Infamous Dungeons

In 1912, the young Rafael Bolívar Coronado arrived in Caracas from Villa de Cura, and began working as an editor of the papers *El Nuevo Diario*, *El Impulso*, *El Universal*, and *El Cojo Ilustrado*, and the magazines *Horizontes* (Horizons) and *Atenas* (Athens). Thus his name began to be talked about in the city of red roofs, and it eventually arrived at the ears of the strong man Juan Vicente Gómez.

In the following year, on July 13, 1913, Carlos Brandt was arrested without cause in Puerto Cabello. He suspected that his arrest was due to his closeness to the writer Rafael Arévalo González, the editor of the daily *El Pregonero* (The Town Crier), who had launched the presidential campaign of Dr. Félix Montes. Regarding the reasons for his imprisonment, Brandt would state in his book, *La época de terror en el pais de Gómez*:

> It could have been for any of the following reasons: my friendship with Arévalo González, for whose paper *El Pregonero* I worked for a time as a collaborator and agent; having refused to take part in a famous smuggling scheme involving high customs officials [while I worked as a customs official]; not having attended a dance I'd been invited to thrown by Carabobo State governor Martines Méndez . . .

One day at the beginning of 1913 I was ordered to call on General Rafael María Velasco—who for a long time had been my immediate superior in the customs agency in Puerto Cabello—and who told me in a friendly manner that [officials] had noticed in Maracay that my name was always absent from the interminable columns of congratulations [presumably to Gómez] in the official daily papers *El Nuevo Diario* and *El Universal*. I won't deny that this news frightened me greatly. I apologized saying that I would gladly add my name if given the opportunity. That opportunity didn't arrive, and Gómez had me arrested.[57]

During his imprisonment, Brandt went on a hunger strike. He would say later that he "believed he was the first Venezuelan to engage in this form of slow-motion suicide" as a form of protest.

On February 13, 1914, thanks to the intervention of two men close to Gómez's inner circle, José Gil Fortoul (1861–1943) and José Felipe Arcay, Brandt was released after spending six months in jail without charges. After his release, he left Venezuela for the United States and Europe, where he had a lengthy writing career.

Later in 1914, on September 19, the light opera *El Alma Llanera* (The Soul of the Plains), with lyrics written by Rafael Bolívar Coronado and music by Pedro Elías Gutiérrez (1870–1954) had its premiere at the Municipal Theater of Caracas. This work had a deep impact on Venezuelan society, being considered by many as a "second national anthem." It was an immediate success, and its sudden fame prompted the Gómez administration to give Bolívar Coronado an award that allowed him to go to Spain to study. The first thing the author did after the ship left the dock and was heading out to sea was to go on deck and yell, "Death to the tyrant Gómez! I'm an anarchist, Bolshevik, and [partisan of our] race!" Thus Bolívar Coronado entered the annals of antiauthoritarian history.

That same year, Biófilo Panclasta returned to Venezuela after having participated in the anarchist movements in Europe and Argentina, among other things having been the delegate of the FORA (Federación Obrera Regional Argentina) to a workers congress in Amsterdam.

Once back in Venezuela, in the city of Valencia, he was arrested a few days after the start of World War I supposedly for making a speech in a public square cheering on France in its fight against imperial Germany. The real reason was that his arrest had been ordered by Juan Vicente Gómez's partisans, who knew of Panclasta's friendship with Cipriano Castro. Panclasta never had a trial on any charges, and there was never an official explanation of his detention.

During the first years of his imprisonment, Beófilo suffered hardships and nearly starved. He shared those years in prison with political prisoners of all stripes, many of whom died while in custody.

In 1921, under the guardianship of a warden named by the new governor of Carabobo state, José Antonio Baldó, Biófilo was transferred to the colonial-era fort, Castillo Libertador, where he was treated more humanely and was liberated after a few months. After his release, he left for Mexico where he continued his seditious activities and also polished his reputation as a world traveler.

His prison experiences in Venezuela led to the work *Siete años enterrado vivo en las mazmorras de Gomezuela*, (Seven Years Buried Alive in the Dungeons of Gomezuela), which was one of the first works of literature about prisons and prisoners in the Gómez period. It was printed in Columbia by the publisher Águila Negra (Black Eagle) in 1931.

Intellectual Property

In 1916, Rafael Bolívar Coronado arrived in Madrid. Once in the epicenter of the land of La Mancha, the first thing he did was to get in touch with the poet Francisco Villaespesa (1877–1936), the manager of the literary magazine *Cervantes*, who gave Bolívar Coronado a job as his secretary. At the same time, he contacted the famous Venezuelan writer and editor Rufino Blanco Fombona, who managed the publishing house Editorial América, where Bolívar Coronado transcribed several obscure works.

His time at this publisher coincided with one of the most prolific periods in the publishing of anecdotal books about Latin America. The books published included *La Gran Florida y Nueva Umbria: conquista y colonización de este reino* by Maestre Juan de Ocampo, *Los Chiapas* by F. Salcedo y Ordóñez, *Los Desiertos de Achaguas*, by Diego Albéniz de la Cerrada, *Los Caciques Heroicos: Nicoraguan,* by Fray Nemesio de la Concepción Zapata, *Misiones de Rosa Blanca* and *San Juan de las Galdonas en 1656* by Mateo Montalvo de Jarama, *El Llanero*, by Daniel Mendoza, *Letras Españolas*, by Rafael Maria Baralt, and *Obras Científicas,* by Agustín Codazzi. Some of these works became true icons in the history of Venezuela, notably *El Llanero* (The Plainsman).

These works were sold by Bolívar Coronado to Blanco Fombona as part of a series of "lost manuscripts" that he had found in the public libraries of Spain. What the buyer didn't know was that these "lost manuscripts" never existed and that they were compilations put together through the ingenuity of the writer, Bólivar Coronado, using false names for the authors or assigning works to well known [but dead] authors.

Years later the sly author would write the leitmotiv for these acts of intellectual pillaging: "Because I didn't have a name in the republic of letters, so I had to use the names of famous authors. I couldn't afford the luxury of spinning [literary] spiderwebs."[58]

When the fraud was discovered by Blanco Fombona, Bólivar Coronado took flight to Barcelona, where he came in contact with the libertarian currents in the city. In revenge, his defrauded publisher published Bolívar Coronado's *Memorias de un semibárbaro* (Memories of a Semi-Barbarian) without signing a contract with him or paying him any royalties.

Following this episode, Bolívar Coronado, commonly wrote under pseudonyms.

The Anarcho-Syndicalists Arrive

Getting away from these anecdotes about individual anarchists, a rigorously clandestine workers movement with clear anarcho-syndicalist influences was taking root in the country during and after World War I. It arose in disparate, sometimes contradictory form, laboring beneath the burden of clandestinity and the repression of all forms of labor organizing by the Gómez regime. Nonetheless, it was influential in awakening working class consciousness.

During this epoch, the first well, Zumaque I, in Lake Maracaibo, gushed oil on July 31, 1914 setting off the petroleum boom in Venezuela, which would generate huge amounts of revenue for the government of Juan Vicente Gómez and the state coffers.

Exploitation of petroleum was (and is) so important in the history of Venezuela that by 1926 one in four Venezuelan workers was an oil worker. Campesinos poured in from the countryside, forming a new type of working class that would be of vital significance to the spread of anarchist ideas. This spread was rooted in the exploitation they all suffered, living for the first time in crowded urban areas, suffering pauperization and horrible living conditions. There they became ever more organized in response to foreign oppression and the Gómez tyranny.

That government and the foreign companies played up the "blessings" Venezuela was enjoying in contrast with the deteriorating conditions in Europe during the war. Those "blessings" did, however, facilitate migration to Venezuela by skilled foreign workers to work in the factories, railroad facilities, ports, and petroleum industry.

Among these workers, primarily from Spain and Italy, there were experienced men from the anarchist tradition who spurred workplace struggles, using direct action in their workplaces. The syndicalist Celestino Mata, in his book *Historia Sindical de Venezuela* mentions:

> Juan Vicente Gómez decided to build up Maracay, a city that could compete advantageously with Caracas, undertaking a series of construction projects in the Aragueña capital, and trying to deal with the lack of qualified labor in the country. To overcome this inconvenience, he made easy the immigration of experienced construction workers from the Old World. Among them were militants from anarchist organizations.[59]

The historian Rodolfo Quintero adds that "The Spaniards and Italians, almost in their entirety, belonged to the anarchist federation; [they were] anarcho-syndicalists and organizers of clandestine groups, and [participated in workplace] struggles and even strikes."[60] In another text, Quintero mentions:

> The Hotel Las Delicias was constructed by Gómez for foreign workers, but these weren't Germans as was the case with the railways; these were in the majority Catalan construction workers, that is to say, all brought from Spain, and they introduced a frankly anarcho-syndicalist current which in my judgment spread through and characterized a good part of the workers movement until 1936.[61]

Domingo Alberto Rangel adds:

> Gómez himself contributed, in an indirect manner and without suspecting it, to the adoption among the workers of the most advanced ideas. To rebuild the National Pantheon to commemorate the centenary of Bolívar's death, and to construct the housing in Maracay . . . the government brought in Catalan masons. Some of them were anarchists and active members of the CNT [Confederación Nacional del Trabajo—the anarchist union federation]. They sowed the seeds of the anarchist or libertarian ideology in many strata of the working class until well into the 1960s.[62]

Antonio Serrano, a militant Iberian anarchist who lived for years in Venezuela, comments:

> These Catalans were in the great majority anarchists or had had contact with [anarchist] ideas. Upon arriving in Maracay, they had a meeting with one of Gómez's overseers, who told them what the working conditions would be.

At the end of the meeting, the workers convened [immediately] to organize a union, without realizing that the overseer overheard them through a closed door. The overseer then informed Gómez of what was happening, and Gómez said, "I'll grab these Catalans and toss them on the first ship going to Spain."[63]

Juan Vicente Gómez was conscious of the slow penetration of libertarian ideas in Veneuela, and because of it a message presented to the National Congress by Victorino Márquez Bustillo (1858–1941), provisional president of the republic, proposed an immigration law that would regulate the admission and residency of foreigners in the country. In his address Márquez said:

It's of manifest necessity to legislate in regard to this matter, because . . . [World War I] has left in its wake in some parts of Europe the scourge of anarchy, which even though transitory given the narrowly focused repression of it by the victorious nations, stirs in monstrous spasms and tends to survive by spreading its lethal germs among the vital youths of the people who, [even] if they don't suffer the tyranny of Capital in their work nor the ailment of poverty, are more susceptible than the adults of the nations, or they confuse liberty with license . . .

Let us defend ourselves from this contagion which you will find amidst the mob of bums, of the vicious, of some foreign adventurers already rooted in the country . . . We must exercise what I would call moral prophylaxis in the same manner as [we] watch over the physical health of the people, guarding them against the evils they can acquire through habit and indolence. It is in our vital interest to import vigorous and healthy elements into the national organism.[64]

The historian, Adela Pellegrino, in her book, *Historia de la inmigración en Venezuela, siglos XIX y XX*, outlines other elements in the fear that the Gómez regime had of the progressive ideas that were slowly germinating in Venezuelan soil:

With the passage of time, Gomecista policies regarding immigration became ever more cautious. The wave of revolutionary movements that shook Europe at the end of World War I and the influence of socialist and anarchist ideas among the working masses and peasants created an atmosphere of fear and uncertainty among those in power who had formerly considered [foreign workers] "ideal workers."[65]

The Venezuelan government was hardly alone in this anti-immigrant approach. During this period, many governments used immigration laws as mechanisms to repress anarchist immigrants, two examples being the Law of

Residency in Argentina and the Immigration Act of 1917 in the United States. Even though immigration restrictions weren't applied with equal stringency in Venezuela, it's likely that they did contribute to suppressing the spread of anarchist ideas in the country.

Anarcho-syndicalism, as a concept contrary to parliamentarianism, and to political parties, proposes the tactics of spontaneous action and the revolutionary general strike, as well as the organization of decentralized unions. It was the most important political tendency in the awakening of the Venezuelan labor movement.

The Bolivar Railway Company Strike

What we could well term the first industrial strike in Venezuela started on July 3, 1918. Aroa, capital of the Bolivar District in Yaracuy State, was the site of the general headquarters of the English company, The Bolivar Railway Company Limited. The company employed, according to Julio Godio, 1,500 workers, the majority of whom were office workers, and its net worth was 350,000 pounds sterling.

When it started, the strike paralyzed all of the train traffic at the Aroa station, and also maritime transport between Tucacas and Puerto Cabello, the ports from which Venezuela's primary products, the coffee and cocoa produced in the west-central part of the country, were exported. This also stopped the ship traffic between the port of Tucacas and the Antilles.

Godio quotes another writer, Carlos Eduardo Febres, as saying that the strike was caused by low pay and bad working conditions specified under the ompany's "Internal rules of English railways in South America," and that the company designated its director, the Englishman Charles A Hutehing and its Dutch traffic chief, Jhon C. Prince, as the representatives of the firm during the strike. Febres also said that the strike paralyzed the company's activities in Aroa, Tucaca, and Duaca, as well as the extraction and processing activities of the South American Cooper Syndicate Limited company.[66]

The workers named Simón Aular, Juan Lazo, Manuel Segovia, J.E. Ponce, Andrés Eduarte, Domingo Sánchez, P. Izquierdo León, Etilio Bonaguro, Ramón Aular, José Bavaresco, Cheito La Rosa, Gonzalo Arias, and Roberto Ramírez Urquiola to direct the strike.

In Caracas, when General Gómez learned of the outbreak of the strike, he sent a commissioner from the Ministry of Public Works to bring a swift solution to the conflict. Despite the presence of the commissioner and the police forces commanded by General José Cornelio Pérez, the strikers persisted in their demands and derailed freight trains on the El Hacha-Cayure (Lara state) and Alambique-Palma Sola (Falcón state) routes.

As to the worsening of the conflict and its unfolding, historian Godio wrote:

> The gravity of the conflict obliged the company and the commissioner to arbitrate a solution that would raise salaries. . . . The strike leaders were divided, with some, including Simón Aular Torres, Juan Lazo and Manuel Segovia, refusing the offer saying it was insufficient. Taking advantage of the confusion, General Cornelio Pérez intervened and arrested the strike leaders and sent them to the Castillo Libertador prison where they were held for six months.[67]

Anarchists played a leading role in this strike, including Venezuelans Manuel Segovia, Andrés Yllas Eduarte, Simón Aular Torres, Juan Lazo, and P. Izquierdo León, almost all of whom were imprisoned as a result of the strike. There was also the Italian anarchist Vicenzo Cusati, who was entrusted with organizing, for the first time in Venezuela, a workers group to confront scabs. Cusati was, according to Febres, the first one arrested because he was so "incendiary."

The Idea Takes Root in Caracas

Another current radiated out from the city of Caracas, in an atmosphere of great militancy, and which was impelled by the influence of Spanish anarchists. The mouthpiece for this tendency was the magazine *El Obrero*, directed by Luis Armando García, Rafael Villasana, and Emilio Lovera; its manager and owner was Cándido De Armas. It [appeared during World War I] and published daily in 1919 and 1920. It featured Luis Amitesarove, Medardo Medina, and Gustavo Parodi as national correspondents, and José Jerique as correspondent in Madrid. The paper's major foreign concerns were the occupation of the Ruhr in Germany, the rise of fascism in Italy, and the dangers of war in Europe, and it was sympathetic to the October Revolution in Russia in 1917. It also featured discussions contrasting the [revolutionary] syndicalism expounded by George Sorel with anarchist ideas. As well, the páper was of vital importance in the organization of the first railway unions following the strike against the Bolivar Railway Company.

Anarchist militants were also active in other union movements, including Juan C. Cignoni, Carlos Moreno, A.R. Risquez Blanco, and Adolfo Montero in the graphic arts union; in the Asociación General del Trabajo (General

Workers Association) Ezequiel Marín and Rafael Oyarzabal; in the dock-workers union Francisco González Blanco and Ladislao Yañez; and among the shoemakers José Tostón, Pérez Padilla, Nicasio Páez, and Carlos Graner. Leonardo Rodríguez, historian of the working class during the epoch of Gómez, states:

> The anarchists, revolutionary syndicalists, trade unionists were the activists within the Venezuelan Labor Confederation (Confederación del Trabajo de Venezuela—CTV). Through their talks and their articles in *El Obrero* these ideological currents confronted the socialist [current], rejecting the [electoral] political struggle and advocating the general strike as the fundamental revolutionary tactic. Nonetheless, the CTV after 1922 entered into a dormant period, because of repression by the dictatorship, that lasted until the CTV's revival in 1936.[68]

In the heat of the [early] struggle, the Spanish anarchists Ezequiel Marín and Rafael Oyarzabal, who were the president and the secretary of the Asociación General del Trabajo, invited several bodies of workers to join together, "all of one will to unite in the broadest base possible to confront any emergency that poses an obstacle to us."[69] Their goal was the construction of the CTV.

Initially this aspiration had been broached in the pages of *El Obrero*, whose slogan had been "Labor y Progreso," and the inspiration for it had been the French General Confederation of Workers (CGT—Confederation Generale du Travail), a syndicalist organization founded on September 23, 1895 in Limoges, France. Originally apolitical, but in practice near to anarcho-syndicalist, it promoted voluntary organization of society through the unions. (Later, the CGT's positions would change greatly.)

The CTV's stated purpose was to advocate the need for confederation, to hold conferences (meetings), and, to publish papers within the workers groups in the following companies: Tranvias Eléctricos de Caracas (Caracas Electric Streetcars), Ferrocarril Central (Central Railroad), Gran Ferrocaril de Venezuela, Venezuela Electric Light Co., Teléfonos de Caracas, Casa Sucre Paredes, Centro de Ebanistas y Carpinteros (Cabinet-Makers and Carpenters Center), and in the Ferrocarril Caracas-La Guaira.

The other locus of activism was among the shoemakers. Celestino Mata says that, "The shoemaker José Tostón, a cripple and a shoemaker, founded the Gremio de Zapateros (Union of Shoemakers), assigning himself the task of editing a little periodical. The Gremio launched its first strike [on July 16, 1919] against the Casa de Boccardo, and it won."[70]

Casa Boccardo was an industrial shoe manufacturer that was very important in Venezuela. The Venezuelan historian Gerardo Lucas states that the firm was the largest and oldest shoe manufacturer in the country, founded in 1860 by Geronimo Astengo, initially with 40 workers. By 1898, it employed 4,000 workers.

Regarding anarchist influence within the shoemakers union and its future leadership, Rodolfo Quintero comments that those taking part in the early struggles included González Navarro (later president of the CTV), Augusto Malavé Villalba (founder of the workers wing of Acción Democrática, the Democratic Action Party), and others who became Democratic Action deputies in the national assembly. He also says that many Spaniards took part in these struggles, including anarcho-syndicalists.[71]

Even Fernando Key Sánchez, founder of the Partido Comunista de Venezuela (PCV), acknowledged the importance of the anarchists in these early struggles, stating: "The artisanal workers movement, despite the dictatorship of Gómez, had a certain level of development and had important leaders, principally Spanish anarcho-syndicalists including José Toston, Claudio Hernández, and Ramos Abad among others."[72]

(Claudio Hernández and Ramos Abad would later abandon anarchism; they actively participated in the organizing of the PCV and took part in its founding conference on August 8, 1937.)

In an interview in the paper *Compañero*, an old union official commented on anarchist influence in the early union movement, saying that the early unions, such as the railway workers, masons, and graphic arts workers, were "born under the star of anarcho-syndicalism." He added, "I remember a comrade named Antón, who was a shoemaker, who would meet clandestinely with anyone with ties to the workers movement. From him we learned the first notions of what a union was and what was its purpose. The anarcho-syndicalists were those who taught the intellectuals the first things about unions."[73]

As you might have guessed, Antón was the pseudonym used by José Tostón.

As for things to come, on September 21, 1919, one of the most colorful and unusual figures in Venezuelan anarchism, Salom Mesa Espinoza, was born to a campesino family in Guarebe in the state of Miranda. We'll have more to say about him later.

Twelve years earlier, Mesa Espinoza's inseparable compañero in ideas and action, Francisco Olivo, was born on June 2, 1907 to the hard-line syndicalists Francisco Tosta Pérez and Virginia Olivo Martínez.

We'll have more to say about Olivo, too.

A Venezuelan who agitated for Sacco and Vanzetti

On May 5, 1920, the Italian anarchists Nicola Sacco (1891–1927) and Bartolomeo Vanzetti (1888–1927) were arrested and charged with the April 20 armed robbery of $15,776.51 from the Slater-Morrill Show Company in South Braintree, Massachusetts, and of having murdered Frederick Parmenter, the holder of the funds, and the security guard Alessandro Berardelli,

The two arrested men were close to the Piedmont (Italy) orator and propagandist Luigi Galleani (1861–1931) who was well known for his odes to revolutionary violence and for being the central figure in a group of militant anarchists of Italian origin operating on North American soil, and who would come to be known as the Galleanists.

The arrest of the two immigrants led to a strong solidarity campaign by the IWW and American Federation of Labor, which both took part in the defense committees composed of workers and anarchists. The controversial trial triggered a virulent anti-Italian, anti-immigrant, and anti-anarchist reaction in the middle and upper classes of the Anglo-Saxon-dominated nation.

The trial of Sacco and Vanzetti was a judicial abomination, and their execution on January 2, 1927, in the midst of popular protests, became a day of remembrance for anarchists around the world.

Some time after their execution, several investigators showed the robbery and murders were carried out by mafiosi in the gang of Joe Morelli, and that the anarchists were condemned and murdered for their beliefs and militancy. Historians, including Howard Zinn, have concluded that the persecution and judicial murder of Sacco and Vanzetti displayed open contempt for civil liberties. In 1997, then-Massachusetts governor Michael Dukakis issued a declaration stating that Sacco and Vanzetti were unjustly, tried, convicted, and sentenced, and that whatever ill beliefs about them persist should forever be uncoupled from their names.

While this tragic chapter in American history unfolded, the defense committees' agitation involved the mobilization of thousands of workers in large American cities and in urban centers abroad including London, Amsterdam, and Tokyo. There were bombings in response to the trial and verdict, in both Buenos Aires and Montevideo, and there were violent disturbances in Paris, Geneva, Germany, and Johannesburg. There were also coordinated solidarity actions from labor federations in several countries attempting to stop the executions.

One participant in these actions demanding freedom for Sacco and Vanzetti was the Venezuelan Valmore Rodríguez (1900–1955), who arrived in New York on June 9, 1919 in search of work and a new start in the busiest city in the world. During his stay in the city, he fraternized with various unions and above all participated in the Sacco-Vanzetti defense committee.

Concerning Rodríguez' activities in the U.S., the writer Domingo Alberto Rangel, who participated in militant activities with Rodríguez in Venezuela, says, "He was a conscious, incorruptible proletarian. . . . [In] the [early] 1920s, he was an activist in the most militant unions, those which were the cradles of protest against the judicial murder of Sacco and Vanzetti."[74]

The native of Falcón State returned to Venezuela in 1921, where he participated in the formation and development of several unions and rose to some prominence in the worlds of letter and politics, though little is known of any further anarchist activism or contacts.

Wobblies in the Petroleum Fields

By 1922, Venezuelan anarcho-syndicalism was undergoing changes. In Caracas, anarcho-syndicalists continued to have a tight connection with the working masses, participating actively in labor organizations and strikes, while opposing participation in politics and advocating direct action as a means of achieving proletarian demands.

In the petroleum-producing areas of the country (Zulia State), the presence of Central American workers, especially Guatemalans and Nicaraguans, brought new influences; the character of the struggles there seemed to dictate an anarcho-syndicalist approach, which in turn centered around the Industrial Workers of the World (IWW). The writer and professor Domingo Alberto Rangel would write:

> Other proletarians from other parts of the world arrived and quickly brought the light to their Venezuelan brothers. When imperial capitalism made a qualitative leap in Venezuela, from the ports and railroads to the petroleum fields, there came along with the ships to muddy Lake Maracaibo "the [salt] of the earth" . . . Many of the sailors who came on those ships were Americans who were or had been members of the IWW, which constituted the fiercest vanguard of the North American proletariat. In the brothels of Ambrosio, in the garrets of Cabima, and in the workplaces, the sailors spread the seeds of revolutionary unrest among the oil field workers.[75]

The anarcho-syndicalists managed to coordinate efforts of the first class-struggle projects in the petroleum zone. One example of this was the Bandera Roja (Red Flag) barbershop in the city of Maracaibo, which served as a meeting place for marxists, socialists, and wobbly sailors, and in which they exchanged opinions and radical printed materials. The Red Flag was similar to the Peluquería del Pueblo (The Hair Salon of the People) which operated in Santiago de Chile [in the nation of Chile], and whose proprietors were the anarchists Teodoro Brown and Manuel Garrido, militants of the Sociedad de Resistencia de Oficios group and also contributors to the anarchist papers *La Batalla* and *Verba Roja*.

It's not known how long the Red Flag barbershop lasted, but there was a police notice on January 24, 1929 that Hilario Montenegro, a member of the October 28 Society, was killed by 18 knife wounds apparently at the hands of Gómez' security apparatus for being involved in the marxist PRV's (Partido Revolucionario Venezolana)—at the time controlled by Venezuelans in exile and directed by Delfín Pérez—bizarre invasion plan which ended in disaster in June 1929.

On June 8 of that year, 39 badly armed PRV members assaulted the Amsterdam fort in Curacao, took hostage the governor, Leonardo Alberto Fruytier, and appropriated a small ship named Maracaibo, in which they traveled to Puerto La Bela de Coro de Falcón. But the landing ended in failure, as the large majority of their fellow PRV members didn't support the invaders, and the invaders' leaders had to flee on foot to Colombia.

Anarchists participating in the petroleum-field struggles included José Pío Tamayo (1898–1935), who while in jail a few months before his death was still teaching young anti-Gomez activists about the socialism of Bakunin and Marx—and it is necessary to underline that Tamayo was an active promoter of the the the ideas of both Bakunin and Marx. He was a poet and one of the principle advocates of radical leftism in the country; he participated the discussion group Tonel de Diógenes (Diogenes' Cask) and was the organizer of the Union of Venezuelan Workers in Barranquilla, Colombia and also the Tenants' Strike in Panama. He was also a contributor to many periodicals, including *Venezuela Libre*, *Avispas* (Wasps), and *Nueva Prensa*. He was jailed following the students' uprising in 1928, and was imprisoned for the rest of his life.

During that epoch, Venezuela was a melting pot of ideas and movements in all spheres, cultural, political, and social, and politically active people for the most part didn't make clear distinctions between anarchist and marxist ideas. So, Venezuela was largely spared the interminable disputes between advocates of the different approaches.

Regardomg the ideological pastiche that was very common in the unions and political culture of the region, Bernardo Pérez Salinas put it like this: "There were people with socialist ideas, people with communist ideas, and people with anarchist ideas. At the time, none of them predominated."[76]

But basic disagreements remained. Rodolfo Quintero states: "[The anarcho-syndicalists] were fighters who didn't want conciliation between classes. Among other things, the anarchists said that the marxists did want class conciliation. The [anarchists] fought against the state, and they left behind a legacy that I would say was ninety percent positive, as they formed the first expression of unions here."[77]

As regards the plethora of ideas, Rafael Elías Rodríguez, a member of the Digoenes' Cask group, said in a letter to the writer Raúl Agudo Freites:

What did we read? . . . History, literature, philosophy, poetry. Anatole France, (Guy de) Maupessant, Beaudelaire and (Paul) Verlaine, Darwin . . . And Tolstoy, the great Tolstoy with the white beard and Christian passion. . . . In 1917, I recall that a a program of the Mexican Revolution [probably the program of Ricardo Flores Magón's Partido Liberal Mexicano] fell into our hands. It arrived by mail and without being censored. We spent entire nights discussing its points. . . . Another time I clearly remember Pio bringing back a book by Kropotkin from Barquisimeto about private property. As was usual, we all read it, but no one was interested in it except me and Pio, and we discussed it exhaustively."[78]

The anarchists were the principal organizers of the first proletarian organizations in the oil fields. An old worker, Raúl Henríquez Estrella, recalled having heard of anarchist ideas in 1930: "My political and union activities unfolded more or less like this: The Spaniard José Fernández, a lathe operator in a machine shop and a marxist/anarcho-syndicalist in Spain, won me over with his ideas about class."[79]

Here, it's necessary to emphasize that the petroleum fields were the places where systemic injustice and social inequality, produced by the North American investors and their henchmen, were most evident. The reporter and unionist Jesús Prieto Soto wrote: "The desire of the blond-haired bosses was to produce petroleum, petroleum, and more petroleum. Anything that didn't have to do with petroleum wasn't important to them."[80]

Bernardo Pérez Salinas wrote of the time and place:

In their disdain toward the Venezuelan, in their ostentatious displays of racial superiority, it all came to a point many recorded times when a creole sailor's knife met the guts of a despotic and insolent invader. . . . The jodhpurs, the pipe, the pith helmet . . . and with the offensive epithet on the lips "hijo de perra" (son of a bitch). In the papers there were often notices such as the following from April 1, 1936: "In one of 13 stabbings, a German died in Lagunillas."[81]

Nonetheless, many of the gringos stimulated the formation of the first petroleum workers unions. Regarding one of them, "Mister Roberto," Rodolfo Quintero states, in regard to contacts with workers from the Antilles and progressive North Americans:

> "Mister Roberto" was the most resolute one . . . [There were] clandestine meetings in the Corito barrio, or disguised as drinking sessions at night where they resolved to create an organization of struggle to present a list of demands to the companies.[82]

Various authors including Ángel Cappelletti confirm that in the clandestine petroleum workers union, Sociedad de Auxilio Mutuo de Obreros Petroleros (SAMOP—Petroleum Workers Mutual Aid Society) anarchist tendencies predominated. SAMOP was organized by Rodolfo Quintero and had 5,000 members. Quintero and Leonardo Rodríguez, the first the organizer and the second a journalist, comment on SAMOP and its functioning:

> In a clandestine manner, the protagonists of the society, employees of the Venezuela Oil Concessions in Cabimas, formed an organization to press demands. . . . They created committees within each of the companies and subcommittees within their different departments. (Later they created a similar association in Lagunillas.) Weeks after the foundation of SAMOP, with the participation of workers from Venezuela Oil Concessions, Lago Petroleum Company, and Venezuela Gula Company, the directors of SAMOP secretly prepared to deliver their demands after creating a base for resistance and strike preparation. But the expulsion of workers from the petroleum companies and the imprisonment of Quintero after the companies raised the alarm of violent insurrection, crushed the movement.[83]

(It is, though, necessary to state that SAMOP was not an anarcho-syndicalist organization: it was hierarchical, a pyramidal group. But there were many anarchist individuals working within it, as the group's founder Rodolfo Quintero said himself.)

In the aftermath of the crackdown, many Spanish anarcho-syndicalists and socialists fled to other countries in the Caribbean.

The Educational Work of Brandt

At the same time as anarcho-syndicalism began to influence the labor struggles in Venezuela, in the literary world the writer Carlos Brandt collaborated in exile with the Spanish libertarian journals *Estudios, Tiempos Nuevos,* and *Generación Consciente.*

After his expulsion from Venezuela in 1914, Brandt lived in Spain, Italy, Belgium, the Netherlands, and the United States over a period of almost twenty years. This was the period of his greatest literary output. He wrote books such as the anti-war tome *La paz universal, El sendero de la salud* (The Path to Health); *Filosofía del vegetarianismo; La superstición médica; Vegetarianismo y los enigmas de la ciencia, El fundamento de la moral* (The Basis of Morality); *La clave del misterio* (The Key to the Mystery); and *El camino a la superstición* (The Road to Superstition). In all of these he dealt with the theme of ethics as the model for collective conduct and social conventions. He also wrote *El fanatismo religioso* (Religious Fanaticism), in which he dealt with the virtues of primitive Christianity and its abandonment by the Catholic Church, which he viewed as a coercive apparatus.

The writings of Brandt were influential in naturist circles in Spain, as the Catalan writer Eduard Masjuan Bracons noted, "The writings of Brandt influenced the advent of a naturism that called for a return to nature . . . but at the same time ably advocated organic agriculture."

In the field of organization, while in New York Brandt contributed to the formation of the Vegetarian Society, which was backed internationally by naturist figures such as Margaret Cousins, Ilya Tolstoy, and Herman Schildkraut. Brandt also founded the Sociedad Naturista Hispana, which had a column in the daily paper *The Open Door* in which Brandt wrote about healthy eating and against vivisection. He was so well regarded in the naturist movement that the Instituto Naturista located in San Luís Potosí, Mexico carries the name Dr. Carlos Brandt College.

Things Heat Up in Barcelona

In 1917, Rafael Bolívar Coronado, arrived in Barcelona with his acidic and colorful writing. He quickly became involved in the conflicts in the manufacturing city where the anarcho-syndicalst Confederación Nacional del Trabajo (CNT—National Confederation of Workers) was battling its ideological foes [notably the Union General de Trabajadores—General Union of Workers— which was tied to the Spanish Socialist Workers Party (PSOE)].

Following the arrival of Bolívar Coronado, in 1919 Carlists [conservative royalists] tied to the Ateneo Obrero Legitimista (Legitimist Workers Atheneum) founded the Sindicatos Libres (Free Unions) to counter the class-conscious and insurrectionist politics of the CNT. "The Free," as the Carlist initiative was known, dedicated themselves not only to supplying scabs, seizing space from the anarcho-syndicalists, and calming the boiling waters, but to organizing armed groups supported by the powers that be that were charged with hunting down and murdering anarcho-syndicalist militants.

In response to this viciousness by the ruling class and the resultant climate of terror created by the Carlist thugs, the CNT organized armed groups whose motto was "an eye for an eye," initiating a low-intensity war. The two most prominent victims of this conflict were on the one hand the anarcho-syndicalist Salvador Segui, and on the other the Presidente del Consejo de Ministro de España (President of the Council of Ministers), Eduardo Dato (1856–1921) among the Carlists,

One notable aspect of this war was extrajudicial murder carried out by the police under the Ley de Fuga (Law of Escape). That law allowed the police to shoot those under arrest if they "tried to escape" and refused to stop when ordered to. So, the police would lag behind a detained person until they determined that there was enough distance, and then shoot the arrested person in the back.

Bolívar Coronado found himself in the middle of this pandemonium, and of course rallied to the side of the CNT, becoming an assiduous contributor to the CNT organ *Solidaridad Obrera* (Workers Solidarity).

During these same years the Soviet Union established the apparatus called the Third International. Its purpose was to impel and coordinate actions of radical left organizations and political parties with the purpose of establishing an international union of "soviets." [In reality, organizations subservient to the Bolsheviks. Never mind that immediately upon taking power the Bolsheviks had systematically disempowered and taken over the soviets (directly democratically controlled workplaces). Lenin et al.'s hypocritical slogan was "All power to the soviets!"] To this end, the Soviet Union invited the CNT to send a delegation to their International's congress in 1919.

This occasioned debate within the CNT about whether or not to attend the event. It eventually did send a small delegation consisting of Juan Peiro (1887–1942) and Ángel Pestaña (1886–1937). Peira and Pestaña returned with strong criticisms of the Leninist system, accusing it of being a dictatorship and coming out in support of the anarchist prisoners held in the dungeons of the Cheka [later the NKVD; after that the KGB; and now the FSB. During Lenin's time in power, the Cheka murdered over 100,000 political prisoners, including many anarchists.] The CNT, and other anarchist unions and groups, later affiliated with the revived International Workers Association/ Asociación Internacional de los Trabajadores (IWA/AIT) at its founding congress in Berlin in 1922.

At the start of all this, several anarchists asked Bolívar Coronado to write about what was going on in Russia, and in January 1919, six months before the congress of the Third International attended by Peira and Pestaña, his pro-Bolshevik book, *Las grandes figuras del bolcheviquismo. Lenine. El sindicalismo en acción* (The Great Figures of Bolshevism, Lenin, Syndicalism in Action), appeared. In this work, the Venezuelan agitator not only drew a favorable portrait of Lenin, but also used it to attack the dictatorships of Juan Vicente Gómez in Venezuela and Manuel Estrada Cabrera (1857–1924) in Guatemala, in scathing terms, saying, "It's necessary to kill Gómez and make Venezuela into a Bolshevik country."[84]

It's not known what Bolívar Coronado made of the condemnatory reports by the CNT's representatives to the congress, but what is known is that in his subsequent writings he never again wrote about occurrences in the Soviet Union, nor did he ever publicly criticize it.

Even though today it might seem strange that an anarchist would be attracted to Bolshevism, it's necessary to understand the times in which this took place. The Russian Revolution was celebrated and closely followed by the revolutionary and socialist forces of the world, and the anarchists were no exception to this. So, Bolívar Coronado's attitude was not unusual, and he supported the Bolsheviks despite being clear about the differences between the two ideological currents. In his book, he wrote: "Bolshevism and anarchism have nothing in common beyond their adherence to the general idea of socialism. . . . We shouldn't confuse the two, just as we shouldn't confuse anarchism with nihilism . . . which lacks the economic character that predominates in the other two [anarchism and Bolshevism]."[85]

Getting back to Bolivar Coronado's activities in Barcelona, due to his closeness with the anarchist movement there he was assaulted several times. Concerning one attack, the historian Rafael Ramón Castellanos, citing Bolivar Coronado's compañera María Noguera said, "Rafael was struck in the head with a blunt object one night as he departed a cafe near to the Music Hall Pompeya. He arrived home and said that the reds had done this, specifically a group that had infiltrated the Sindicatos Libres."[86]

On another occasion he survived a theater bombing, of which his widow would later recount that "we inexplicably survived . . . and stumbled out of the place, still shaking from the explosion."

These events caused the Venezuelan to become closer, to make common cause with the victims of the bosses' pisolteros. He wrote articles in the periodical *La Publicidad* under the pseudonyms Pere Peyre, Joan Kopolek, Pedro Pelayo, Tisiano Tepek, Indistor, Rufino Garcia Calderon, Cristos Teques, Esteva Rodao, Celeste Olivar, Reyes Yacidos, Mirinkoff, Josefa Mujia, Augusto Tancretti, Joan Xenius, and six hundred others making him the writer with the most pseudonyms in the history of Venezuela, [perhaps in the history of the world].

The attacks and the bombing didn't frighten Bolívar Coronado. He hadn't forgotten his homeland, and he also published two works, under pseudonyms, about Venezuela. The first concerned the creation of a *Movimiento de Liberación Venezolano* and the second was titled *Sindicatos Unidos de Venezuela*, and proposed creation of such a union federation. It's unknown what influence these texts had in Venezuela.

What is known is that the first time Bolívar Coronado was imprisoned in Spain was in 1920, when he was arrested for distributing flyers urging the Catalan proletariat to support the union movement in Venezuela that was trying to do away with the Gómez regime.

At the same time, Rafael Bolívar maintained a heated dispute with the Cónsul General de Venezuela in Barcelona, Alberto Urbaneja, a well known Gómez functionary. Due to the constant stream of anti-Gómez writing Bolívar Coronado produced, Urbaneja made a series of formal complaints to the authorities in Catalonia, seeking Bolívar Coronado's arrest or expulsion from Catalonia back to Venezuela. At the same time, Bolívar Coronado started writing anti-Gómez tracts using variations on Urbaneja's name, such as Mapurite A. Urbaneja and Karroña Urbaneja.

The intrigues and formal diplomatic complaints led to Bolívar Coronado's arrest on July 8; he was released on July 11. Many of the papers in Barcelona celebrated his release and mocked Urbaneja for his clumsy maneuvering.

Bolívar Coronado also wrote in several Catalan periodicals including *El Diluvio, El Impulso, La Publicidad, Resistencia, La Vanguardia, Idea, El Correo Catalán, Savia,* and *Noticiero Universal.* Beyond this, he wrote and published the books *Corazón, memorias de una niña rubia* (Heart, memories of a blonde girl), and *Parnasos Costarricense y Boliviano* (Costa Rican and Bolivian Panassus). He also collaborated on the *Enciclopedia Universal Ilustrada Europeo Americana.*

But the legal troubles and his turbulent life contributed to health problems, particularly pulmonary problems, which he had had since adolescence. Bolívar Coronado died on January 31, 1924, when he was only 39 years old, in the Hospital de la Santa Cruz in Barcelona. Many anarchist friends and workers attended his funeral, giving a colorful farewell salute to this little-known Venezuelan writer and agitator.

A Fugitive from Devil's Island

Another well known anarchist who trod Venezuelan soil, arriving in 1926, was the French libertarian Eugéne Dieudonné (1884–1944) who was accused of being a member of the Bonnot terrorist gang, even though his participation in its violent acts was never proven. Despite this, he was condemned to forced labor at Devil's Island in 1913. [Despite its name, the penal colony called Devil's Island consisted of more than the island: it was also comprised of brutal forced labor camps in Guyana on the South American mainland, which relied on the impenetrable jungle to make escape next to impossible.]

On December 6, 1905, Dieudonné, who had always maintained his innocence, managed to escape the prison colony on a raft fashioned from palm trunks. After 12 days of battling the waves and nearly sinking several times, he finally arrived at the mouth of the Orinoco River in Venezuela, where he continued on foot along the coast, before eventually continuing on to Brazil. Little is known of his activities in Venezuela during his short stay, but his escape from Devil's Island was comparable to that of Henri Charriere, the subject of the book and later the movie *Papillon*. [Translator's note: René Belbenoit's autobiographical and well written *Dry Guillotine* (1937) is quite probably more truthful about escape from Devil's Island than *Papillon*.]

Connections with the Cuban Communist Party?

Two Venezuelans attended the founding meeing of the Partido Comunista de Cuba (PCC) in 1925: Gustavo Machado Mancera (1898–1989) and Salvador de la Plaza (1896–1970). Other founders of the group, which received support from the Third International, included militant marxists such as Julio Antonio Mella and ex-anarchists such as Alejandro Barreiro and Carlos Baliño (1848–1925), [who were the the founders of the Partido Revolucionario Cubano], the anarchist Enrique Roig San Martín, and Enrique Flores Magón (1877–1954), brother of Ricardo Flores Magón and an old militant who attended as the delegate of the Partido Comunista de México, which he had joined after the long struggles he participated in with Ricardo prior to and during the Mexican Revolution.

Frank Fernández, wrote in his book *El Anarquismo en Cuba* (slightly expanded and somewhat differing English version is titled *Cuban Anarchism: The History of a Movement*):

> The militants of the PCC became a disciplined and self-abnegating minority [within the Cuban labor movement] which at first continued to mouth anarchist slogans, but became an obedient tool of the Comintern, which undertook to eradicate all traces of anarcho-syndicalism, which had for decades been the propulsive motor of the Cuban working class.[87]

As we saw in the case of Bolívar Coronado, the strange mix of marxists and ex-anarchists was characteristic of the time. The two Venezuelan participants were Gustavo Machado and Salvador de la Plaza who would become key pieces in the founding of the Partido Comunista de Venezuela (PCV).

The 1928 Generation Learns about Anarchism

In February 1928, the Week of the Student (la Semana del Estudiante) events took place. The Week consisted of a a series of peaceful meetings and recreational activities called by the Federación de Estudiantes de Venezuela to support the rector of the Universidad Central de Venezuela (UCV), Diego Carbonell (1884–1945), even though it should be noted that [some of] the students had beliefs and attitudes considered "communist." During the coronation of the student queen, José Pío Tamayo spoke, and the poem he composed in honor of the queen was considered subversive by the authorities. As well, the speeches of the students Rómulo Betancourt (1908–1981), Jóvito Villalba (1908–1989), and Joaquín Gabaldón Márquez (1906–1984) were judged to be revolutionary. The government reacted with repression, and jailed all of these speakers.

In an act of solidarity with their comrades, a groups of 214 students (a relatively large group at the time) voluntarily surrendered to the police and were taken to the Puerto Cabello castle. They remained there for 12 days, and at the end of that time were released due to the reaction in Caracas. When the students returned to the capital, they were received as heroes. They and others would later be known as the Generation of '28.

Due to the political consequences they'd unleashed, these students had initiated a new type of opposition to the Gómez regime. Later this same Generation, with the return of representative democracy, would become the national political class, and some of them would hold the highest offices. In addition to those mentioned above, others stood out: Jacinto Fombona Pachano (1901–1951), Raúl Leoni (1905–1972), Elías Benarroch, Miguel Otero Silva (1908–1985), Arturo Uslar Pietri (1906–2001), and José Tomás Jiménez Arráiz (1904–1981).

Many of these young people, some of whom would later become presidents [most notably Betancourt], celebrated writers, political activists, and above all gravediggers of the autonomous workers movement, had access in one way or another to anarchist ideas, be it through written text or conversations. One example is the marxist writer Miguel Otero Silva, who in his stories refers to anarchism. One example of this is the discussion between the characters Victorino Perdomo and his father in his notable work *Cuando quiero llorar, no lloro* (When I Want to Cry, I Don't):

> The graveness of the matter is that we believed anarchism was dead, buried by Marx, Engels, Plekhanov, Lenin, Stalin, by its own madness, and suddenly in the midst of the twentieth century it rises from its mausoleum and you're speaking like an anarchist, Victorino, which is something like being treated for appendicitis by a witch doctor.[88]

Otero Silva always referred to anarchism and anarchists in a disrespectful tone, almost comparing them with troglodytes. Otero Silva considered anarchist like pebbles in one's shoes.

He eventually became the managing editor of one of Venezuela's largest-circulation periodicals, *El Nacional*, which would consistently tie anarchism to violence, chaos, and slovenliness.

As regards the small but certain influence anarchism had on Generation '28, the historian Jesús Sanoja Hernández states in the prologue to the book *Del Garibaldismo Estudiantil a la Izquierda Criolla* ("From Student Garibaldiism to the Creole Left"): "The '28 Generation while in jail partook of the books of" authors including Dostoevsky, Barbusse, Sorel, and Lenin. " Betancourt had well-thumbed copies of Rosa Luxemburg and Marx's *Capital*, and even used them in courses."[89]

For his part, Rómulo Betancourt (cited by Manuel Caballero), recalled things differently:

> The tyranny was not only concerned with punishing the insurrectionists [students], but wanted to provoke society to reject a specter that had haunted [the

world] for almost a century. They accused the students, in the words of government minister Pedro Manuel Arcayá, of being communists, of being part of a communist insurrection. This, of course, had no basis in reality. The majority of the young people involved in the revolt had hardly heard of communism, mostly as a synonym for anarchy, and the most learned had barely heard of what had happened in Russia in October 1917.[90]

What's little known is the role that Pío Tamayo played in the diffusion of radical left ideas among the '28 Generation. He carried out this work in great measure during his long imprisonment in the Puerto Cabello castle. Prominent figures such as Miguel Acosta Saignes, Rodolfo Quintero, and Jóvito Villalba remembered the teachings of the poet of El Tocuyo.

Regarding the ideas that were circulating in prison, Miguel Acosta wrote:

It was only in the Puerto Cabello castle that one could read things which were prohibited in Venezuela, such as . . . Kropotkin, George Sorel. These authors were read freely in the jail, and people would ask, "How and why were prisoners allowed to read this?" It was because in the time of Gómez prisoners were considered the living dead.[91]

Concerning the anarchist literature that passed from cell to cell in Castillo Libertador, Juan Bautista Fuenmayor said:

There was an anarcho-syndicalist book by the Frenchman George Sorel, which I believe was titled *The Future of the Revolutionary Unions*, which had a lot of impact on us. This resulted in confusion, because we took anarcho-syndicalist concepts as if they were leninist concepts, when in reality they weren't. There was a book by the famous French geographer [and anarchist] Elisee Reclus who had written a monumental work on geography. In [the book we had] he spoke of historic materialism, and explained through a series of events what was happening in Europe. And we had others whose names escape me, but they comprised the arsenal we had at our disposal: formative reading matter."[92]

In this regard, Venezuelan writer Isaac J. Pardo comments:

Juan Batista Fuenmayor, with the desire to initiate discussions in a form that would be well remembered, from his pulpit/hammock, would begin by saying, "In the name of Marx, Engels and Bakunin." [For non-Catholic readers, that mocks the traditional Catholic benediction, "In the name of the father, the son, and the holy ghost."] That is to say, this was a combination simply inadmissible from an ideological viewpoint, given that Marx and Engles were not only op-

posed to but would fight to the death the ideology of Bakunin, and vice versa.
. . . Thus came our confusion about this, given that a person of clear talent, as
he had demonstrated through his life and written work, could come up with
such a mishmash. This is to say, that we did not have clear ideas about these
matters. Did Fuenmayor start to become acquainted with these things from
Tamayo?[93]

Regarding Tamayo's influence, the historian Raúl Agudo Freites wrote:

These discussions of Pio Tamayo enthused the leading prisoners from the Student Federation. They organized another series of talks, given this time by the
students themselves. Beyond cultural ends, they did this to put their interminable idle time to good use.[94]

Another Venezuelan writer, José Antonio Jiménez Arráiz adds:

Pio Tamayo wasn't released when the students were released from jail. . . . He
remained there only being released two or three months before he died. Now
those who were prisoners with Pio in the castle say that undoubtedly he was the
initiator of political consciousness in the country.[95]

It's certain that marxism was the principle fount from which the '28 Generation drank. Nonetheless, Rodolfo Quintero says, "I have to state that my
first contacts with organized workers back in 1928 were mainly with anarcho-
syndicalists, men with an anarchist mentality who were mostly industrial
workers who had come from the Old World.[96]

To deny the influence of anarchism upon the university students, as some
liberal bourgeois and marxist Venezuelan writers have done, represents an
omission from the collective historical memory.

The Hidden Work of the Cultural Centers

Simultaneous with the development of the workers organizations, workers cultural centers—creole versions of the celebrated [in Europe] proletarian
atheneums and libraries—arose and anarchists were their principal instiga-
tors. More specifically, the workers who arrived in the petroleum fields from
Margarita Island [which comprises Nueva Esparta, one of Venezuela's 23
states] were the ones who spread the concept.

Facundo López recalled how he met in January 1932 with about a doz-
en other workers, including Juan D. Velásquez and Francisco Monteverde

Adrián, in the old electric plant in Juan Griego to discuss matters related to holding events, the repressive measures of the dictatorship, and the attitudes of the '28 Generation. Then there were the meetings of the Comité Cachete [roughly, the Cheeky Committee], which according to Nicolás Bor oriented itself to the cultural struggle for social good, and which led to the founding on February 12, 1932 of the Sociedad Benefactora de Juan Griego (Beneficent Society of Juan Gregorio), which in turn led to the creation of the Biblioteca Dr. Agustín R Hernández (Dr. Agustín R Hernández Library), which included a school and also a shelter for the disabled. This example spread through the island, leading to the creation of the Federación de Centros Culturales del Estado Nueva Esparta.

Later in Zulia State, several similar cultural centers appeared: Centro Cultural Tubores, Centro Cultural Antonio Díaz, Sociedad Pro Nueva Esparta, Sociedad Pro Arismendi, Sociedad Pro La Guardia, La Rosa Roja, etc. These featured music recitals, discussions of the problems of the barrios, literacy classes, and libraries including the works of such authors as Victor Hugo and Emile Zola. The schools also served as sites for clandestine political activities against the Gómez dictatorship. [Shortly after some of these centers appeared], Antonio Granado proposed the creation of a cultural center federation, with the purpose of political resistance.

Many of these centers were sponsored by petroleum workers, among them anarchists. These centers grew in popularity. They provided schools where hundreds of people attended who couldn't afford private education or who didn't want to subject themselves to the lessons given in [scanty] public education.

These centers, these atheneums, became meeting places and hangouts for local people, and they were focal points of diffusion of libertarian ideas through their newsletters, publishing of books and pamphlets, trips to the country, theater performances, classes in Esperanto, discussions of sexuality, conferences, debates, and free libraries. They promoted a style of life and thought in accord with the libertarian ideas they advocated, which in turn sprang from the anarchist educational movement, especially that of the workers movement in Spain.

One means used by the syndicalists to hide their incendiary teachings was to use the names of Christian saints and deities as the names of their unions and cultural centers. This was purely for show.

Rodolfo Quintero comments:

The streetcar workers, for example . . . had a very strong and combative organization. According to them, they had a patron saint: the Virgin of Carmen, and it was truly interesting and even eccentric to see them in the places with streetcars prostrating themselves before the virgin, praying, and concentrating on that for several minutes. Later these same workers . . . were the most combative, the most aggressive and those who were involved in the largest union battles in the country.[97]

Many of these centers continued to exist until the end of the 1930s, while others were gradually absorbed by the country's first marxist and socialist parties. Nonetheless, these learning and meeting centers continued to play an important part in the development of class consciousness and the country's first unions.

The Sunset of Gomezism

Both internally and in exile, the anarchists continued to be enemies of the Gómez dictatorship. One example of this in print form was the periodical *Culmine* (Culmination), which was published in Buenos Aires by the militant anarchist Severino Di Giovanni (1901–1931).

As well, in great measure the products of the events of the Week of the Student, there were the revolt of the guards at the Miraflores prison and the attack on the San Carlos barracks on April 7, 1928. The Miraflores revolt was coordinated by Lieutenant Agustín Fernández, Leonardo Leefman, Rafael Antonion Barrios, and Captain Rafael Alvarado, with the support of students tied to the Week of the Student. The uprising failed, and those responsible were tried and imprisoned or managed to flee into exile. One of its leaders, Lieutenant Leonardo Leefman, stated that one of the revolt's inspirations was Pío Tamayo.

These and other such events provoked a fierce repression against groups on the left, which the Gómez regime considered "communist."

Taking advantage of the repressive atmosphere, police prefect and Gomecista Elías Sayazo directed three series of raids against communist cells in Caracas in 1931, 1932, and 1934. In the 1932 raid, according to police statements, a bomb was supposedly found along with mimeo machines, stamps, and literature about the Paris Commune. The police also made accusations about supposed conspiracies and phantom uprisings. Their seizures and statements about those seizures served as justification for the infamous Lara Law, which we'll deal with later.

It's necessary to emphasize that the criminalization of dissent during that time is notorious. People were arrested, accused, and tried in an inquisitorial manner, with no recourse, and were convicted on fabricated evidence. Examples include Manuel Bogan, accused of conducting "revolutionary" correspondence from New York, and Elio Montiel, Ramón Bolívar, Angel Senior, Domingo Mijares, and Manuel González Pedrique, who were jailed for distributing "anti-government propaganda." This repressive atmosphere limited in great measure, and for a considerable time, anarchist political work.

In this atmosphere, and after suffering from tuberculosis, José Pío Tamayo died in Barquisimeto on October 5, 1935 after being released shortly before his death because of his poor health. He was a man of both words and action, and ahead of his time. He's considered by many historians as one of the first and principal advocates of advanced social ideas in the region during the 20th century, and he contributed greatly to the diffusion of anarchist ideas. Before his death, one of Tamayo's comrades in the literary group Diogenes' Cave asked Tamayo what he'd say of the proletariat. He replied that they were the "future of the world."[98]

Two months after Tamayo's death, the dictator Gómez died in Caracas. He was one of the most despotic and tyrannical rulers Venezuela ever had. Following his death, the congress named as president of the republic his Minister of War and Navy, General Eleazar López Contreras. During Gomez's almost thirty years in power, he tortured and persecuted political and social dissidents of all stripes, and turned Venezuela into a secure and energetic font of riches for foreign powers. During this period of its history, Venezuela became a raw-materials exporting country with ties to foreign capital, especially that of the United States, and remained under that country's political and cultural influence.

While all this was going on, the petroleum boom continued to attract rural people to the city. Thousands upon thousands of campesinos moved their households to urban petroleum-producing areas, giving rise to the formation of belts of misery surrounding the urban centers. At the same time, the commercial business class, a legacy of Gómez, began to consolidate its power, displacing the traditional latifundistas as the dominant class.

Gómez had taken advantage of the growth in petroleum revenues not only to maintain himself in power, but also to modernize Venezuela in the context of international business. During his reign, the dictator had canceled the foreign debt, increased the wealth of the banks, revalued the bolivar [national currency], gave oil concessions to U.S. oil companies, and provided support to German imperialism. Of course, all of this weakened the agricultural and livestock industries which had formerly been the economic backbone of the country.

Culturally, the iron curtain which had held back progressive ideas also condemned the people to the political status quo. The political and social ideas brewing in other countries were unknown to most people in Venezuela.

The universities only churned out lawyers, doctors, dentists, engineers, and and pharmacists. They didn't train philosophers, economists, agriculturists, geologists, etc. And a high proportion of the populace was illiterate. The percentage of the budget devoted to education was very low, only 9.3 million bolivars in 1935.

A determining factor in the Gómez period was the creation in 1910 of the Academia Militar de Venezuela, which gave way to the Fuerzas Armadas Nacionales, with which the state assumed a monopoly on violence, and institutionalized it along the lines of the Prussian military. In juridical matters, the gendarmerie of Gómez was as reactionary and conservative as its predecessors, but despite this labor organizations and their actions helped lead to improvements in labor conditions, one example being the Mining Law of 1915, which established safeguards regarding [work-related] accidents and illnesses, the [length of the] workday, and overtime, and which prohibited the "truck system" of paying miners with company scrip. This law took effect in a very restrictive environment, and the gains it granted were small and of course nonrevolutionary, being in nature more populist than progressive.

As regards other laws, one arbitrarily repressive measure, the Ley de Tareas (Law of Tasks), passed by the Congress in 1916, mandated that both political and common criminals be forced to labor without pay on public works [much as prisoners in the U.S. are enslaved]. Likewise, campesinos who wanted to be exempted from military service had to work [without pay] for the government two days per month for two years.

In 1917, the Congress passed the Ley de talleres y establecimientos públicos (Law of Workshops and Public Establishments), which truly was a first step in general labor law in Venezuela, but whose reach was limited by the police codes mentioned in the previous chapter.

To close the book on the labor laws enacted under Gómez, the legislators in the service of the caudillo passed the Ley del Trabajo (Work Law) in 1928, which was as coercive and nonprogressive as the other Gómez-era labor legislation. The laws of this period were the tools with which the Gómez regime tried to suppress growing labor discontent, and it dictated them in moments of boiling class struggle, such as the strike against the Bolivar Railway Company Limited in Aroa.

As one might expect, anarcho-syndicalist militants played a leading role in the labor struggles in the country [during the Gómez era]. They helped in organizing workers, provoking labor conflicts, and spreading anti-capitalist propaganda among the petroleum and urban workers. But by the beginning of the 1930s they were severely weakened by the constant police raids; nonetheless the most outstanding labor militants, who after Gómez would figure in the public arena, received their first lessons in class struggle from the anarchists.

Rodolfo Quintero stated that, in the same year Gómez died, "sections of workers organized themselves into unions, impressing upon their leaders ideas learned in courses [in the atheneums] and in the semi-clandestine meetings in which Spanish anarcho-syndicalists participated."[99]

Víctor Alba, in his book, *Historia del Movimiento Obrero en América Latina, adds:*

> The dictatorship of Juan Vicente Gómez wasn't favorable ground for the development of unions of any type, and even less so for unions led by anarchists. There's reason to believe that the anarcho-syndicalists contributed, even though they had to hide their ideas, to the organization of the unions that began in 1923 with the Unión Obrera Venezolana (Venezuelan Workers Union). Many of them later worked effectively in the union movement.[100]

After the death of Gómez, [the social-democratic] Acción Democrática (AD), in its embryonic stage [as the PDN, Partido Democrático Nacional, founded in 1936], and the Communist Party of Venezuela (PCV), absorbed that movement almost entirely.

The Free Unions

Regarding the influence that anarchist ideas had within the Venezuelan unions, and how the AD had to deal with those ideas, Manuel Caballero says:

> The political party [PDN/AD] had to share the terrain with other organizations such as unions that were founded or dominated in their beginnings by anarchists who not only opposed the existence of the state, but also the very idea of politics: they abhorred political activity, proclaimed their abstention [from politics], and completely rejected political parties.[101]

A pertinent example of this was provided by the syndicalists Salom Mesa and Francisco Olivo, considered by many to be anarchists, and who throughout their lives were militant members within the Acción Democrática party.

Salom Mesa mentions in his book *La Vida me lo dijo, elogio a la Anarquía* (Life told me this, Elegy to Anarchy) a bit about Francisco Olivo's libertarian adventures:

> I joined the National Democratic Party (PDN) and within it I heard a lot of admiring comments about a carpenter named Francisco Olivo, who was known on the street as Blanco, and was tall and strong, and would walk down [the street] with planks across his shoulders. . . . He was the son of a physically powerful man, but had grown up in economic misery. . . . For me, he was a wise man who I enjoyed listening to. From 1936 to 1940, the time in which we met each other, he was reading fervently . . . In his rebellious words, spoken without any egotism whatsoever, he explained to me what he had discovered. How greatly his teachings have benefited me! He advocated anarchism even after the founding of the AD. For a worker who felt in his bones the exploitation, the inequality of the system, and who wanted to live freely, what other ideas could fill his heart?

> One day in 1942, when we were walking down the Avenida Sucre . . . I said, "Let's break with Acción Democrática and espouse anarchism." He looked me in the eye and replied, "let's meet tomorrow at [my] house." . . . He had thought about it and reached these conclusions: a) the people were too backwards to be receptive to libertarian ideas [at least labeled as such]; b) as a result of that, it would be very risky to adopt my proposal; and c) through political action it would be possible to arrive at the triumph of libertarian communism.

> I accepted his reasoning. It was easy enough for him to convince a nearly illiterate youth, such as I, who had hardly begun to experience humanity, and who was full of fears and insecurity, and who had hardly begun to speak of [political] ideas.[102]

The historian Libertad Olivo, daughter of Francisco Olivo, says of her father, "His pole star was his great passion for justice and liberty, and I'm certain that papa died as a libertarian communist, with his rectitude, personal honesty, and manliness, with his not playing at politics."[103]

The journalist Rafael Poleo would write of Olivo:

> He was an archetype of the exceptional human being with his seriousness and rectitude. From the unionists he demanded austere personal conduct. He warned against the [politicking and infighting] into which social democracy [i.e., the AD] was descending, without the smallest possibility of success.[104]

In his memoirs, Salom Mesa, whom we can consider one of Olivo's disciples, says:

He was among those who strongly opposed the integration of labor leaders into Acción Democrática at the founding of the party [in 1941]. In the end, though, he decided it would be wise to join them. The public statements of Acción Democrática [despite being from a political party] continued to be openly anarcho-syndicalist and many times openly anarchist or libertarian communist.[105]

Regarding Olivo's anarchist influence within the PDN, Mesa, in his posthumous work *Cartas para Carlos* (Letters for Carlos), says:

The PDN cell I joined consisted of laborers and shop workers, and the carpenter Francisco Olivo had great influence within it; everybody admired him. He felt, thought, and acted as a libertarian communist, as an anarchist, and would say to everyone, everywhere that we'd arrived at a politics that would serve as a medium for social revolution, "A world without the exploited, without the humiliated, without the privileged. A world without governors who drive people as if they were beasts. A world in which all men and all women govern themselves for themselves guided by the norms of solidarity and justice that they will freely determine. A world worthy of human greatness. . . . "

All of us who formed that [PDN] cell of ten persons felt complete identification with the philosophic and moral thought of Olivo, because not only did he proclaim wonderful ideas about social action by the dispossessed, but also because his personal conduct was of exemplary sobriety and rectitude."[106]

These were difficult times for the Venezuelan working class, and many others probably felt as Mesa and Olivo did, [but many joined the AD]. Perhaps the most perceptive analysis of the reasons for this came from professor Domingo Alberto Rangel:

How was it possible that in the period of the greatest labor struggles, from 1936 to 1945, that Acción Democrática had in its ranks men such as Salom Mesa and Francisco Olivo, who held anarchist or anarcho-syndicalist ideas, or in any event were libertarian socialists? . . . AD in those days had many reactionaries . . . and not a few social climbers and thieves, but it also included in its ranks the most radical men in Venezuela. And the anarchists of all types had no other political alternative. In the Communist Party (PCV), in which Olivo participated for a time, stalinist dogmatism arrived at its apotheosis . . . which was dissuasive. To remain in the PCV it was necessary not only to adopt the Marxist credo as interpreted by the [stalinist] Third International, but more importantly to follow the strange positions on all fronts held by comrade Stalin. It was in those times that militant communists had to recite and memorize a tedious catechism . . . in which they were treated like kids in primary school. It's easy enough to see that there was no room for anarchists, even though they were closer to the stalinists' theoretical [economic] analysis than they were to the populist AD. But at least in the AD they were free to express their opinions.[107]

So is shouldn't seem strange that within the AD there were anarchists in this epoch. It should be remembered that AD was a populist party embracing many parts of the political spectrum, and its leaders were only interested in increasing their influence, swelling their ranks, and giving the party the appearance of being powerful; so it accepted members of all tendencies on the ideological spectrum. Rómulo Betancourt, with characteristic cynicism, said to Francisco Olivo at a meeting convened by the PDN member Alejandro Oropeza Castillo, prior to Olivo's joining the PDN, "Yes man, it doesn't matter that you're an anarchist. Here everyone fits in."[108] Betancourt and other leaders of the party guaranteed Olivo that he would have absolute liberty to formulate whatever approaches he wanted, and this was precisely because Olivo was a well known labor organizer.

For the nascent electoral machine into which the embryonic AD would transform itself, Olivo was a necessary figure in penetration of workers organizations. It was precisely the liberty that he had within the AD/PDN to express his anarchist views,that sealed the deal for Olivo. It was why he joined them and not another political group, such as the clandestine PCV, which he had become acquainted with thanks to Miguel Acosta Saignes (1908–1989), but which he rejected because of its stalinist and dogmatic character.

* * *

Here it's necessary to state that Rómulo Betancourt never was attracted to anarchism, and that he came to explicitly reject it, even though he had been exposed to anarchist ideas while a member of the Costa Rican Communist Party.

The journalist and investigator Sanin confirms this:

> Rómulo the anarchist! He never was, not even in the days in which he was most tormented by ideological doubts. Betancourt always rejected anarchism . . . because of its rejection of state authority and because of its promotion of absolute and spontaneous liberty. [This badly misrepresents the anarchist concept of liberty. —tr.] . . . He had read Proudhon and Bakunin. From when he was very young he had reacted negatively to the[ir] ideas which rejected the state . . . [I]n Costa Rica he had always shown his love of a strong state and authoritarian govern-

ment as a means of realizing social change. . . . At the same time, he rejected terrorism, nihilist violence, preferring instead the methodical organization of the workers as a base of political action. Likewise, he disagreed with the anarchists' reflexive anti-militarism, seeing in the army a means of changing the structure of the state. . . . For him, anarchism was only an item to be studied.[109]

Up Against the Minister of War

Eleazar López Contreras, in contrast to his predecessor, was a sophisticated man who'd had a good education, and using it he initiated a new epoch in Venezuela. But this didn't mean an improvement for Venezuela's anarchists and other leftist tendencies, despite the new president's old friendship with Biófilo Panclasta, which had little effect on his policies, as the following will show.

On February 14, 1936 there was a large demonstration at the Plaza Bolivar in Caracas; the demonstrators were protesting the suspension of constitutional guarantees on January 5 of that year. The historian Manuel Beroes states that the demonstrators were peaceful and that some bore placards bearing slogans such as "We want a free press," We're not communists," and "We want [constitutional] protections." Around nine in the morning the demonstrators approved a proposal to form a Patriotic Council, whose members would be Jorge Luciani, who had denounced the censorship board the previous day, Miguel Acosta Saignes, Rolando Anzola, Manuel Felipe Rugeles, Ernesto Silva Tellería, Hernani Portocarrero, and Raúl Osuna. Several of them addressed the protesters promising to keep up the struggle for democracy and exhorting them to organize themselves for civic action.

Then they were suddenly attacked by soldiers from the federal government building, and five people were killed and over 100 wounded. But despite this deadly attack by the government, the demonstrators stood their ground. In the midst of all this some protesters painted slogans on the walls of the government and other buildings using the blood of the wounded, using phrases such as "Death to Galavis!" [governor of the Federal District] and "Down with the murderers of the people." Meanwhile others, who were enraged [by the brutal attack], sacked the residences of persons tied to Juan Vicente Gómez.

Concerning these events, the journalist Eleazar Díaz Rangel wrote:

> It was around ten or eleven when the desperate Lieutenant Contreras yelled "Where are you going?" to a group that approached [the federal building]. The reply was "Down with Galavis!" Frightened, he fired his .38 revolver. His men

took it as a signal and opened fire, shooting some of the protesters down. The others threw themselves down to the ground or ran to protect themselves. Up to a hundred wounded were taken to the Red Cross Hospital and about forty to the Hospital Vargas. . . . On the wall of the Casa Amarilla [Venezuelan Ministry of Foreign Relations] someone wrote "Murderer!" in blood, which served as the spark that ignited the sacking of the homes of Gómez supporters.[110]

The historian Manuel Caballero states that this event affected different people in different ways: The politician Jóvito Villalba saw it as an expression of anarchism, as Caballero relates:

The uprising of an entire people demanding their rights would remain forever in his thoughts and in his writings. He saw it as democracy revealing itself on one great day . . . Betancourt had a very different take. For him, the demonstration was an instrument of political and social structure, but not the only one and not even the most important. He had years of leninist experience, and because of this it's not unreasonable to say that his first reaction to the events of February 14 was distrust due to its primary character: spontaneity. . . . Lenin was the great enemy of spontaneity . . . For Betancourt . . . the only way to channel the tumultuous impulses and to take power was to construct a centralized project, a political party. And a party couldn't be built in a day.[111]

In the view of Manuel Caballero there were three key dates in Venezuelan history: February 14, 1936; January 23, 1958 [overthrow of the dictator Marcos Pérez Jíménez]; and February 27, 1989 [the start of the Caracazo"uprising]. He considered two of these [1936 and 1989] to be the two greatest expression of anarchism in the country.

Regarding February 14, 1936, he wrote:

In effect, the events of February 14 can be considered the first real act of anarchy [in Venezuela]. Because of the demonstration on that afternoon, and almost without prior organizing, nearly spontaneously, almost the entire adult population of Caracas took to the streets. . . . Despite the demonization in the conservative press, overall and with but a few excesses from uncontrollable elements, the events of February 14 were peaceful and orderly.[112]

During the mournful events of February 14, the vengeful sentiments of the repressed flourished. On the 22nd of that month, the Program of February was signed, under which the chief executive, under the banner of "Calm and Sanity," promised to respect the rule of law.

On that same day, Biófilo Panclasta decided to write an open letter to his old friends and political compañeros, Elbano Mibelli and Eleazar López Contreras. It was published in *El Diario Nacional* in Colombia. In the letter, he subtly tried to make his old comrades in arms understand the necessity of introducing new revolutionary changes within Venezuela, setting the country on the path to more liberty and social equality.

In May of the same year, Biófilo sent two letters to the Colombian president, Alfonso López Puma Rejo (1886–1959), asking him to expedite issuance of a passport allowing him to travel to Venezuela, confident of protection provided by his old compañero López Contreras, but López Puma ignored the letters. Six years later, still in exile and exhausted, Biófilo died in an old folks home in Pamplona, Colombia, passing over to being a popular and anarchist legend.

In the year 1936, there was also a rise in working class activity. In the words of Nelson Prato Barbosa, there existed in the heart of the government "a struggle against the 'state of anarchy' on one hand and on the other 'a struggle for the establishment of political and social liberties' that was unleashed immediately after the death of Gómez."[113]

An example of this struggle was the creation of the Frente Obrero (Workers Front), organized by Leonidas Monasterio, Augusto Malavé Villalba, Luís Hernández Solís, Francisco Olivo, Ramón Quijada and others at the first great workers conference in the country, held at the metropolitan cinema in Caracas. The Federación Sindical del Distrito Federal (Union Federation of the Federal District) also appeared, and on December 12, 1936 the Congreso Obrero de Trabajadores (Working Congress of Laborers) self-organized and elected Francisco Olivo as its treasurer.

In parallel with these sprouts of liberty, Carlos Brandt returned to Venezuela after a long and public exile in Argentina in which he had published his most anarchist work, *El problema económico-social*. In it he said that "the human ideal, socially speaking, is the suppression of capital and all [other] coercive forces." In the book he maintained his lifelong pacifist posture, saying that this ideal state "cannot be arrived at except with time and through the means of pacifist propaganda."[114]

While the PCV and PDN/AD were peddling the illusions of the Bolshevik revolution, Brandt in this book alerted readers to the fiasco of attempting to change social-political reality through the taking of political power:

> We know very well that the so-called dictatorship of the proletariat is a farce that flatters the vanity of the workers so that they'll defend their new boss. . . . There are no workers' states just as there are no watchmakers', tailors', shoemakers', or astronomers' states. . . . No matter how laudable many find the socio-economic efforts of the Soviets, the facts are that anarchists are persecuted

in Russia neither more nor less than in the time of the tsars. . . . What is certain is that such a revolution [based on violence and coercion] will never achieve [revolutionary ends].[115]

Thus Brandt fits into the anarcho-pacifist camp, derivative of Tolstoy, arguing that only an elevated morality, near to primitive Christianity, will serve to eradicate the inequalities within society via nonviolent direct action. Until his death, Brandt continued to contribute to the periodicals *El Nacional*, *Ultimas Noticias*, and *El Universal*.

Positivism Reigns in Anarchism

In great measure the product of growing social agitation, the constitution [that took effect on] July 13, 1936 was a reformed version of the 1931 constitution. However, Article VI of this magna carta declared:

> It is considered contrary to the independence, to the political form and social peace of the nation, communist and anarchist doctrines, and those who proclaim, propagate, or practice those doctrines will be considered traitors to the country and punished in accord with the laws.

> At all times, the federal executive, whether or not constitutional guarantees are suspended, will impede the entrance to the territory of the republic [of such persons] or will expel them for a period of six months to a year if they are citizens, or for an indefinite time if they are foreigners, individuals affiliated with the forementioned doctrines, if their entrance to the republic or their presence here would be dangerous or prejudicial to the public order or social tranquility.

In the same epoch, the National Congress, at the petition of the Minister of Interior Relations, Alejandro Lara Núñez , passed the Law of Public Order, better known as the Lara Law, that not only set and limited the rules of social conflict, but also restricted anarchist propaganda. This legal instrument was approved with the ends in mind of regulating political demonstrations by opposition [parties and movements] and repressing them if necessary. In general terms, the Lara Law consisted of five chapters.

The first chapter was "On the organization and surveillance of public and private meetings," which among other things required organizers to apply in writing for permission 24 hours in advance of any demonstration, allowed the government to deny permission, and held organizers responsible for any unlawful acts.

The second was "On associations," and it regulated all aspects of their formation.

The third chapter, "On strikes in relation to public order," prohibited politically motivated strikes, general strikes or work stoppages, and strikes by public employees, with penalties ranging from one to six years imprisonment.

In the fourth chapter, "On illegal political propaganda," articles 33 and 37 stand out. The first of these stated, "those who create propaganda about communist, anarchist, nihilist, or terrorist doctrines or methods . . . shall be penalized with one to three years imprisonment." The second article specified fines of one to five thousand bolivars for publishers or radio stations that distributed such propaganda, with fines doubling on the second offense.

This law closed off any opening whatsoever for anarchists in public life. It forced them back into clandestinity, weighed down by the possibility of fines, imprisonment, or exile. The Lara Law was a tool to persecute and criminalize any political activity considered leftist.

The writer Arturo Sosa comments:

A good part of the political debate during these years was carried out on this thorny terrain not only in discussion of diverse theoretical political positions, but also in the throwing back and forth of labels with the intention of delegitimizing one or the other social group and also to provoke repressive measures on the part of the government [against groups labeled] "anarchist or communist," whose activities were constitutionally prohibited.[116]

Rodolfo Quintero notes:

The constitution which sought to hide the class problem, and the persecutory Lara Law, were seen up close by striking workers and their comrades in other unions. They saw an apparatus that upheld the dominant class and that sought to destroy the labor movement. The police, the army, the lawyers and courts, the bought-off press, the governors, the laws—all of these were put in the service of destroying any movement that sprang from the "lower" class.

The workers understood that only they themselves, through their organization and combativity could produce the improvements, the well-being to which they had a right.[117]

The legal prohibitions, along with the very poor conditions of the petroleum workers, produced in December 1936 a strike in the states of Zulia and Falcón. In its class-struggle and revolutionary formation, it was the workers' vanguard in the struggle against the successor to the Gómez regime. This movement was molded by agitators such as Isidro Valles, Dilio Morin, Juan

Bautista Fuenmayor, José A. Mayobre, and Felipe Hernández, who managed to mobilize public opinion in favor of the workers.

The income of the petroleum workers was the highest in the country, but their conditions of life were very bad, the majority of them living in unhealthy galvanized-metal shacks, without medical help, which allowed the spread of malaria.

Even though the strike had a strong leftist character, the list of demands kept strictly to labor issues (equal wages for foreign and native workers, recognition of the union, a minimum wage of 10 bolivars per day, etc.). More for ideological than economic reasons the corporations refused to meet the demands, and so provoked the strike.

The government of López Contreras through its Minister of Labor attempted to mediate the conflict, but in vain, due to the instructions from the directors of the oil companies to their representatives to refuse to negotiate with the workers. From this impasse, mutual aid and support committees sprang up, but in the face of this the government sided with the foreign petroleum companies and broke the strike in March 1937.

It also invoked Chapter 6 Article 32 of the constitution and expelled from the country 48 strike leaders accused of being anarchists and communists. Among them were future high government officials including, most prominently, future-president Rómulo Betancourt as well as Gonzalo Barrios, Juan Salvador de la Plaza, Raúl Leoni, Gustavo Machado, Guillermo Mújica, Miguel Otero Silva, Rodolfo Quintero, Ramón Quijada, and Jóvito Villalba.

The failure of the strike combined with the forced clandestinity of leftist political currents debilitated the workers movement. In the words of Luís Enrique Villegas, this "demanded a reformulation of the struggle and its tactics."

In March 1937. in a protest in solidarity with the political activists and syndicalists expelled under Chapter 6, Ramón L. Meneses, Tito Hernández, and Francisco Olivo were arrested under the pretext of violating the Lara Law. Olivo was sentenced to three years imprisonment in the Cárcel del Obispo, and the others spent nine months in jail before being pardoned by López Contreras. During his imprisonment, Francisco's daughter Libertad Olivo wrote: "Papa passes the time reading, boxing, and doing his tasks as the leader and organizer of the prisoners union."[118]

One effect of the 1937 strike and the social ferment that accompanied it was the creation of two coercive social organizations: Cuerpo de Investigación Nacional (National Investigative Body)—later the Dirección de Seguridad Nacional (National Security Directorate)—and the Guardia Nacional which were armed agencies charged with controlling internal public order.

These two administrative bodies would become a determining factor in the struggle involving popular forces and revolutionary thought in the region.

The Short Summer of Anarchy in Spain

At the same time that the rebellion in Venezuela was hitting rough spots, changes were occurring in Europe. In Spain, the country in which anarchist ideas had resonated strongly since the 1860s when Giuseppe Fanelli (1827–1877), a disciple and friend of Bakunin, founded along with Spanish comrades the Federación Regional de Trabajadores de la Región Española (Regional Federation of Spanish Workers) which was the first International Workers Association (AIT) section in Spain.

Spain was fertile ground for libertarian ideas, and [what would become the world's largest and most important anarcho-syndicalist] union, the Confederación Nacional del Trabajo (CNT—National Workers Confederation) was founded in 1910. By 1936, it had two million members, and there were other important anarchist organizations such as the Federación Ibérica de Juventudes Libertarias (Federation of Spanish Libertarian Youths—FIJL), the Federación Anarquista Ibérica (FAI), and Mujeres Libres (Free Women)

On July 19, 1936, a military uprising led by future dictator Francisco Franco (1892–1975) took place with the intention of seizing power from the republican Popular Front government, which was comprised of nearly all of the leftist organizations (bar the anarchists) that existed in Spain at the time, and had been in power since 1931. The generals, in contrast, were supported by the Catholic Church, the Carlists (monarchists), the fascists, and the industrialists and other members of the bourgeoisie.

The military uprising failed in large parts of the country, including Madrid and Barcelona, the cradle of the libertarian movement in Spain since the beginning of the century. The CNT called for armed resistance to defend the republic against the coup, but also to initiate the process of social revolution.

As all this was taking place, Venezuela had a diplomatic legation in Madrid, led by Juan Tinoco, who decided to move the legation to Barcelona where it would do its job of protecting Venezuelan citizens in Spain. Besides this proper role, the Venezuelan consul also sent harmful dispatches to the Venezuelan authorities in which he told them about how anarchist developments in Spain could pose a threat to to the status quo in Venezuela.

These dispatches resonated in the Ministerio de Relaciones Exteriores and in the international policies of López Contreras, such as in the designation as Venezuelan consul of Ramiro Fernández Pintado and in the treatment of persons such as Martínez Pozueta, Rubio Villanueva, Manuel Pendas, Jesús Echeverría, Marcelino Sánchez, and Valeriano Quecedo, who were expelled from the country or placed under surveillance for being suspected purveyors of revolutionary ideas.

In Barcelona, one Venezuelan witness to the events in the summer of 1936 was Doctor Isaac J. Pardo, who was working in a regional hospital under the auspices of the Ministerio de Sanidad, Servicios Sociales e Igualdad (Ministry of Health, Social Services, and Equality). Among other things, Pardo witnessed the transformation of convents to hospitals.

The polarizing conflict in Spain found an echo in Venezuela, in the mobilizations of the PDN in favor of the republican forces and in the activities of the Unión Nacional de Estudiantes (UNE) in favor of the nationalists (Franco's fascists). On August 27, 1936 a group of 192 Venezuelans gathered in the Spanish consulate as "volunteers to fight in Spain . . . to defend the Popular Front in Spain," according to a letter signed by the Spanish vice-consul.

Following the military uprising and the counter-offensive by the productive people of Spain, there were almost three more years of bloody civil war where the anarchists were at the forefront in the trenches and at the barricades. During these years there were major self-management initiatives in Catalonia, Spain's most heavily industrialized region, where the factories were taken over and managed democratically by members of the CNT, and also in agricultural areas such as Aragon and parts of Andalusia. These showed the world that an anarchist, self-managed economic and political system worked, that it wasn't utopian daydreaming. [Despite the experiment being crushed by the Spanish fascists with the aid of Hitler's Germany and Mussolini's Italy, and the treachery of the PCE and Soviet Union], the Spanish Revolution provided a rich harvest of experience and examples for future sowers of libertarian ideas in other lands, among them Venezuela.

CHAPTER 4
Resistance and the Spanish Exiles

After the Spanish Civil War ended in March 1939, hundreds of thousands of men, women, and children fled to France, where they were put in refugee camps while the French authorities decided what to do with them. Several Latin American countries, including Argentina, Chile, Cuba, the Dominican Republic, Panamá, and above all México, allowed large numbers of Spanish exiles to emigrate to their countries. For its part, Venezuela remained silent and showed no type of solidarity with the refugees.

Upon the outbreak of the Second World War later in 1939, Venezuelan petroleum was put at the service of the Allies and their armed forces. This brought a huge influx of foreign currency to the country, and gave it strategic importance in the hemisphere, as it strengthened its military and economic alliance with the United States.

Venezuela did eventually allow some of the Spanish refugees into the country. The first ones came from the Dominican Republic, where they'd been unable to find work under the dictatorship of General Rafael Leónidas Trujillo (1891–1961), and where they'd also had to struggle against political repression aimed at "communists."

At this time there existed in Caracas the Centro Español, which provided social space under the name Casa España; it was located next to the Hotel Ávila. It was nonpartisan politically and all the Spanish immigrants who arrived in Caracas made use of it to help orient themselves and find work in their professions. Those who went to it included militants of the CNT, the FAI, and FIJL.

This was in the time of General Isaías Medina Angarita (1897–1953), who succeeded Eleazar López Contreras in 1941. The Medina government came to power after an election in which his opponent was the author Rómulo Gallegos (1884–1969). Despite being a military man and despite heavy accusations of being a "sympathizer of Mussolini and fascism," Medina Angarita became the most progressive president Venezuela ever had.

Upon his inauguration he instituted a series of democratic measures such as the release of political prisoners, legalization of the social-democratic Acción Democrática party in 1941 and the communist PCV party in 1945, eradication of the Gomecista elements in public administration, reform of the Constitution and the direct election of deputies to the congress, elimination of Chapter 6 Section 32 of the Constitution which had prohibited communist and anarchist propaganda, and he issued a decree that May 1 was to be celebrated as International Workers Day.

But it's important to understand that Medina Angarita wasn't a democrat, but rather an astute and agile politician. He intuited that he couldn't continue to govern as his predecessors had. The events of February 14, 1936, the petroleum strike, and the rapid spread of unions had shown him unequivocally that he had to propose a reconstruction of the nation's government and initiate a process of political opening.

This took concrete form in public policies such as institution of a minimum wage, obligatory participation in Social Security, the signing of the first union contract in the petroleum industry, an increase in the powers of the Workers Bank in construction of housing, and other reforms in the areas of the legislature, agriculture, petroleum production, and working conditions.

These actions, even though laudable, had a reformist character and were designed as a dike to hold back the wave of demands which had built up over more than a decade, coming from a social movement that had shown its claws during the events of 1936. Despite the reforms, Medina Angarita continued governing in league with the traditional sectors as a liberal but bourgeois politician.

Of course, presidential ambitions were also present in the sectors opposing him. Disputes broke out quickly in the recently created political parties, and especially between the workers nuclei within the AD and the government. On January 20, 1945, following a protest in front of the National Congress, the police arrested Francisco Olivo and Salom Mesa. Through the intervention of Gonzalo Barrios, they were released the same day. That was the first time that Mesa was arrested in what would be a long series of arrests and jailings.

While all this was occurring in Venezuela near the close of the Second World War, the country had needed a fluid immigration policy due to its need for workers in the petroleum industry. The economic abundance brought by oil exports made possible the arrival from all over Europe and South America of thousands of immigrants, among them anarchist militants who joined with the existing group at the Casa España.

As well, the friction between the militant elements of the AD and the government of Medina Angarita, resulted in AD militants finding nationalist allies in the nation's military academy, led by majors Julio César Vargas and Marcos Pérez Jiménez (1914–2001) and lieutenant colonel Horacio López Conde whose movement took the name of Unión Militar Patriótica (UMP), which was preparing the way for a civil-military uprising. For its part, the PCV, rather than remaining aloof from this inter-bourgeois military plotting closed ranks behind Medina Angarita.

The conspiracy formed in parallel with the negotiations between the AD and the government to elect to the presidency the diplomat Diógenes Escalante (1879–1964), who had promised to govern for only two years and to reform the Constitution, to the end of establishing universal, direct, and secret electoral voting. However, this initiative was frustrated by the sudden mental illness that befell Escalante. Betancourt refused to accept, under the same conditions, the replacement official candidate, Ángel Biaggini in September 1945. By that point the seditious military movement couldn't be stopped.

On October 17, 1945, Medina Angarita learned of the preparations for the uprising, which seemed to be confirmed by a meeting on that same day by the AD in the Nuevo Circo de Caracas, which essentially issued a call for a popular uprising. Medina Angarita's orders to restrict the military in Caracas and Maracay and to arrest three of the military leaders of the UMP plot (Marcos Pérez Jiménez, Julio César Vargas, and Horacio López Conde) set off the uprising. AD cells supplied logistic and armed support to the rebellion; one participant in these cells was Salom Mesa.

On the morning of October 18, 1945, the revolt broke out at the Escuela Militar de La Planicie (Military School of the Plains) in Caracas. By the afternoon it had extended in Caracas to the garrisons at the San Carlos, La Planta, and the Miraflores barracks, and also to the garrison in Maracay. At the San Carlos barracks a battle broke out between the insurgents and forces loyal to Medina Angarita, who prevailed and retook the barracks. Meanwhile there were skirmishes in the streets between AD militants and the forces of order. That night, upon analyzing the situation, Medina refused to attack the Escuela Militar for fear of causing the death of cadets, many of whom had been his students. This decision determined Medina's fate.

The successful civic-military uprising was hailed by the social-democratic militants and their organs as the second coming of the October Revolution in a clear echo of the Bolshevik sympathies of some within the AD. Hyperbole aside, the uprising led to what is known as the "Trienio Adeco" (the Three AD Years). In this period a Junta Revolucionaria de Gobierno, presidided over by Rómulo Betancourt and Carlos Delgado Chalbaud (1909–1950), held sway.

As regards anarchists, during these days a delegation from the CNT, formed by its Secretary General in Venezuela, José Serrano (who worked in the furniture industry and had come to Venezuela via France and the Dominican Republic) met with Rómulo Betancourt to ask him that the provisional revolutionary government in an act of "revolutionary solidarity" break diplomatic relations with the Franco dictatorship in Spain and with the Trujillo dictatorship in the Dominican Republic, in line with the pledge the new government had made upon assuming power, and Betancourt promised to do so.

There were also indications of cooperation between Spanish anarchists in the city of Mérida with the armed actions undertaken by Acción Democrática during the civic-military uprising. Regarding this Domingo Alberto Rangel wrote:

> The AD of Mérida was the most radical of all the regions in the country. To the students strongly influenced by Trotsky, you had to add the artisans and workers led almost always by Spanish anarchists of the CNT or FAI, who had arrived in the city after the defeat of Spanish republic.[119]

Nonetheless, even though some of the CNT and FAI anarchists were near to the new government, they continued to support their countrymen in the PCV who had backed the government of Medina. An example of this solidarity was the aid they supplied to the brothers Manuel and Antonio Trueba, exiled Catalonian communists who had taken part in the assault on the San Carlos Barracks where some communists had seized military equipment to use against forces of the coup.

Meanwhile the PCV "accepted the facts" and their peers in the Unidad Popular Venezolana adapted to "the new conditions that have arisen" and quickly became "defenders of the new public order," as the journalist Juan Bautista Fuenmayor put it. The anarchists, along with other noncommunist political groups in exile, decided to leave their quarrels to one side and to aid their "comrades in arms," the Trueba brothers, who were baselessly accused by the new government of being anarcho-syndicalists. Their efforts bore fruit when the brothers were expelled from the country and landed in Ecuador, where they spent the rest of their days.

At the same time, another political party appeared on December 10, 1945, the Unión Republicana Democrática (URD), a republican and electoral party. On January 13, 1946, the social-christian Comité Organizado Para Elecciones Independientes (COPEI) was formed, and which brought in a conservative Catholic element that sympathized with the Spanish fascists.

On July 18, 1946, to commemorate the tenth anniversary of the Spanish Revolution, the daily paper *El Nacional* dedicated an entire page to that Revolution, in which it hailed the actions of the Spanish anarchists. This piece was reproduced by clandestine publications such as *Verdad* (Truth), *CNT*, *El Socialista*, *Fragua Social* (Social Forge), *Mundo Obrero* (Workers World) and *Euzkodeia* (a Basque exile publication).

On December 17, 1946 Francisco Olivo was elected as an AD representative of the Capitol District (Caracas) to the National Constituent Assembly, which would approve on July 5, 1947 a new constitution replacing that of the one from 1936. His participation helped lead to a declaration of political rights for women, guaranteed education, social and workplace security (insurance), and making it easier for Spanish exiles to achieve Venezuelan citizenship.

The historian Ramón J. Velásquez, in his *Venezuela Moderna*, would write that, "One of the major voices in the Assembly would be that of Francisco Olivo who along with Augusto Malavé represented the growing importance that the union sector had in the new political order."[120]

In that same year, coming via Panama, José Peirats (1908–1989), CNT militant and author of the authoritative *Anarchists in the Spanish Revolution*, arrived in Venezuela. Despite being a learned man with an easygoing personality who was well suited to public speaking, he didn't manage to attract Venezuelan workers and intellectuals to anarchism. He only published some articles in the daily *El País* (The Nation) about anarchist historical figures such as Max Nettlau, Elisée Reclus, Peter Kropotkin, and a few others.

Also in the journalistic field, Miguel Campuzano García (1894–1964) worked for the daily papers *El País* and *Ultimas Noticias* (Latest News). He had been a member of the FAI and the director and a teacher at the rationalist school in Mataró (Spain), which was supported by the Glassworkers Union of the CNT. He remained in Venezuela for the rest of his life and died in 1964 working for the AD-oriented paper *La República*, whose library bears his name.

Regarding Campuzano, Iberian historian Miguel Iñiguez says:

In 1940 he made it to Santo Domingo (Dominican Republic) and three years later came to Caracas while suffering a life-threatening bout of malaria. He recovered and began a new stage in his life, becoming a professional journalist. He was the editor of *El País* (1943–1948) and *Últimas Noticias* (1948–1958), before participating in the founding of his final project, the paper *La República*."[121]

While in Venezuela, he didn't hide his libertarian convictions: iin 1946 he spoke favorably of the CNT in Venezuela; and he was held in high regard by the CNT subdelegation in the country. He also lent notable service to democracy in Venezuela, including during the dictatorial years, and he became highly regarded, winning the National Prize for journalism in 1963 and founding a library that bore his name.

Domingo Alberto Rangel, in his book, *Un socialismo para el siglo XXI* (Socialism for the 21st Century) wrote that for *El País* Campuzano read the foreign news and boiled it down for readers, expressing his views with mordant wit, for example calling Harry Truman "a son of a bitch, but because of his father"; and he recalled that when Campuzano read extracts from the sermons of Pius XII, he muttered a veritable "sonata of obscenities."

Rangel continues:

Miguel Campuzano worked with two packs of cigarettes and a thermos of coffee at hand. He was a walking encyclopedia of anarchism. Through him I came to know Proudhon, Elisee Reclus, and Bakunin, who he cited and commented upon daily, but also Spanish anarchists such as Anselmo Lorenzo [the CNT publishing house in Madrid is now titled Fundación Anselmo Lorenzo], Federica Montseny, and Angel Pestaña. He was intransigent to the point of being punctilious about workers struggles. One time one of the workers at *El País* was robbed and he went to the police. Campuzano almost grabbed him by the lapels asking how he could resort to bourgeois justice.[122]

Those near to Campuzano, Peirats, Serrano, and other CNT members, along with members of the AD, would join forces against future military totalitarianism.

The AD in Power

Following the Junta Revolucionaria de Gobierno, the first universal, direct, and secret presidential election was held on December 14, 1947, in which the writer Rómulo Gallegos, the AD candidate beat the COPEI candidate Caldera (1916–2009) and Gustavo Machado the PCV candidate.

On that same date, Francisco Olivo was elected city councilman in Caracas, where he worked in defense of workers' rights and for the well-being of the community. He also participated in organizing the II Congreso Sindical Nacional (the Second National Union Congress), where the delegates decided to revive the Confederación de Trabajadores de Venezuela; Olivo was named financial secretary by the congress.

On July 18, 1948, the two primary Spanish Civil War-era and pre-Civil War-era unions, the CNT and the Unión General del Trabajo (UGT—the Socialist Party union) held a public meeting in the Teatro Municipal in Caracas, which was also attended by several Venezuelans. It was presided over by Silvio Santiago; José Gregori spoke for the UGT and Domingo Torres for the CNT. This event, contributed more to discord than concord among the Spanish exiles. A group of CNT members opposed to the CNT faction of the speaker —there'd been a split in the CNT in 1945—provoked a disturbance. Those involved belonged to the Federación de Trabajadores del Distrito Federal y el Estado Miranda, the name of which showed that there was still a certain sympathy for the ideas of anarcho-syndicalism among the Venezuelan working class.

(Torres had an outstanding history in the CNT having been a militant at the port of Valencia, and had been designated mayor of the city at the outbreak of the Civil War. Following exile in France, he emigrated to Venezuela where he continued his political activities at the Casa España.)

However, despite the government instituting a series of reformist policies, within the "civil-military union" support in the barracks started to wain as the members of the armed forces began to see themselves as the junior partners in the political process that they themselves had helped to bring about. This situation worsened with accusations by the military chiefs that AD was organizing militias within its party and was trying to find followers in the military by having young party members enroll in the military academies.

The discontent this produced resulted in armed uprisings which the military commanders had to put down in order to maintain unity and discipline within the armed forces. Because of this, the heads of the military, Marcos Pérez Jiménez and Carlos Delgado Chalbaud, presented three demands to the government: 1) the expulsion from the country of Rómulo Betancourt; 2) the dissolution of the AD militias; and 3) the reorganization of the cabinet with independent persons not affiliated with the militant social-democratic policies of the AD.

Rómulo Gallegos and the political directors of the AD refused these demands, remaining firm against what they saw as blackmail by the military establishment. This refusal would soon bear a very high price for the social democrats and their anarchist allies.

The sabers are drawn again

On November 24, 1948, a new military coup put an end to the democratic government of Rómulo Gallegos. This new military uprising was perpetrated by a group of lieutenant colonels affiliated with the UMP, who had aided the AD in the events of October 18, 1945. Marcos Pérez Jiménez, Carlos Delgado Chalbaud, and Luís Felipe Llovera Páez (1913–1977) were the visible leaders of the coup, which led to formation of a Junta Militar de Gobierno presided over by Carlos Delgado Chalbaud.

There's speculation that in addition to the friction between the military establishment and the government of Gallegos, another reason for the uprising was the unhappiness of the foreign petroleum interests about the nationalist and social-democratic approach of Gallegos. He had signed the Reform of the Taxation Law on November 12, 1948, which imposed a 50% tax on the earnings of the petroleum companies on top of other taxes.

The junta dissolved the national congress, outlawed both the AD and the PCV, and expelled their leaders from the country. At the same time, the militants in both parties returned to clandestinity. The social democrats had to restructure their tactics and dedicate resources and efforts in preparation for an armed struggle against their former military colleagues. This had reverberations among the younger members of the AD, and Salom Mesa was no exception, rallying from the first call to organize resistance. He participated in coordination with the AD central committee in several armed actions, and became one of the key figures in the abortive plot to assassinate the military junta. For his part, Francisco Olivo was arrested and expelled to Chile on January 23, 1949.

While things were heating up following the coup, the Spanish anarcho-syndicalist Germinal Gracia arrived in Venezuela on December 24, 1949; with time, he became an enthusiastic promoter of anarchist ideas in the country, adopting the pseudonym Víctor García, which had formerly been used by Peirats, because he couldn't use his real name in the dispatches he sent to the CNT without being expelled from Venezuela.

The Spanish anarchists' love of liberty grew in exile to include embracing the right to rebel. The assault on the air base Boca del Rio and the attempted assassination of the Junta in Caracas were examples of this.

The assault on Boca del Rio

On May 5, 1950, during the middle of a petroleum strike called by elements opposed to the military junta, there was an attempt to seize arms from air base Boca del Río in Maracay. The operation involved a dozen military men of various ranks, and members of the AD and Spanish anarchists. With some firearms and machetes, they attempted to seize arms with which to radicalize the petroleum strike and hasten the downfall of the dictatorship. After briefly seizing the base, but out numbered and out maneuvered by the military, they surrendered unconditionally. They were detained, tortured, some were shot, and the rest held incommunicado in the Pabellón Militar N° 3 of the Cárcel Modelo in Caracas. The failure was the perfect excuse for the junta to argue for the complete elimination of the PCV and to brutally crack down on dissidents.

The writer José Agustín Catalán, in his *El libro negro* (Black Book), describes the assault:

With very few arms, 30-some men captured the base for an hour in the early morning from the Air Force. The government forces recaptured the base and [many—a subsequent news report said there were 18 survivors] of those who assaulted the base, despite their surrender, were machine gunned in cold blood. . . . The survivors of the assault, Francisco Peña Vázquez, Francisco Macara, Cruz Esqueda, Leopoldo Sequera, Claudio Mújica, Claudio Reran, Manuel Silva, Marcelino Cabrera, Ramón Carrasco, Cleofe Duran, Florentino Trumba, Pedro López, Juan Camacho, Froilán Blanco, Jacinto Balcázar were arrested and brutally treated. They were bayoneted, beaten with rifle butts, humiliated, and threatened with automatic arms. Later after being transferred to Caracas and the military police barracks, they were violently interrogated and mistreated, and again threatened with being shot. Later after being taken to the Carcel Modelo, they were thrown to the ground and left to rot as anonymous prisoners. . . . held incommunicado, sick, deprived of all contact with their families, sleeping in the dirt. They only got word out after ten months of incommunicado confinement in the form of a tattered, dirty sheet of paper passed from hand to hand in a chain from the prison to the street. . . . [In it the prisoners said,] "Some of us suffer from dysentery and see themselves on the brink of death without medical aid. Others suffer from strange [skin] eruptions and are in a constant state of physical desperation. We feed ourselves with crumbs of bread which the other prisoners give us. A majority of our sick can't raise themselves off the ground, where they remain for days on end."[123]

A majority of those detained from the assaulting force were workers and campesinos. Seven other civilians were subsequently arrested and jailed, as were at least eight members of the military. The possibility that militant Spanish anarchists participated in or helped facilitate the assault continues to be unresolved because of the clandestinity in which they had to operate and because talking about such actions would have been dangerous; any such participants likely carried their secrets to the grave.

An attempted assassination in Caracas

Parallel with the repression visited upon leftist militants, on November 13, 1950 an armed group, apparently without ideological orientation and under the control of Falcón state political boss Rafael Simón Urbina (1897–1950), who had participated in the PCV assault on the island of Curacao and the subsequent failed landing in the state of Falcón, kidnapped without much resistance the military junta's president, Carlos Delgado Chalbaud.

During the abduction and after a struggle between Delgado and his kidnappers, Pedro Antonio Díaz, Carlos Mijares, and Domingo Urbina, there was a bizarre series of events culminating in the killing of Delgado Chalbaud. Due to the magnitude of their acts, those involved decided to flee the capital and seek shelter among friends and fellow plotters. Urbina tried to take refuge in the Nicaraguan embassy seeking political asylum. Within hours, the mayor of Caracas, Carlos Morales, the chief of police, and the prefect Hernán Gabaldón presented themselves at the embassy and demanded that Urbina be turned over to them. He was, after the functionaries guaranteed he wouldn't be killed and that they'd bring him medical attention. Rather than take him to the hospital, they took him to a cell in the Cerro del Obispo jail. Urbina remained there from 8:00 to 11:00 pm, when state security showed up to transfer him to the Cárcel Modelo. However, what was supposed to be a simple transfer wasn't, and the Falcón boss ended up shot to death.

It's never been established exactly what the true intentions were of the kidnappers, or what motivated them. Some versions speculate that theirs was an act of vengeance against the junta due to its refusal to return funds to Urbina that he had embezzled; others say that it was a plan of Pérez Jiménez's to raise himself to the presidency; and still others speculate that foreign powers were behind it due to worries about Chalbaud continuing the petroleum policies of Gallegos.

Whatever the case, with the death of Delgado Chalbaud, a new president of the military junta was named: the attorney Germán Suárez Flamerich. Pérez Jiménez and Llovera Páez continued to hold high positions within the junta.

The "Nipples" and the "Special Apparatus"

On October 12, 1951, a group of AD activists and Spanish anarchists were arrested on charges of attempting to organize the assassination of members of the military junta; the anarchists were Pedro Beltrán Guells (or Wells) and Eusebio Larruy. Beltrán and Larruy and the AD militants were sent to the infamous concentration camp on Guasina Island in the Orinoco delta and held there until its closure on December 21, 1952, and were then transferred to the Prisión de Cárcel Nueva en Ciudad Bolívar and held there until 1956.

Little is known of Larruy other than that he arrived in Venezuela in 1948. After his imprisonment he became active again in CNT circles and participated along with Juan Verde in the Grupo Errico Malatesta, which published the periodical *Simiente Libertaria* (Libertarian Seed).

Miguel Iñiguez in his book, *Esbozo de una Enciclopedia histórica del anarquismo español* (Outline of a historical encyclopedia of Spanish anarchism), notes that Beltrán was among the reorganizers of the CNT Mercantile Union in Barcelona in 1931, that he fled to France and was interned in 1939, and later that year would reach Venezuela via Panama. He also "participated in the reorganization of the CNT and enthusiastically supported the Centro de Estudios Sociales."[124]

In regard to the attempted assassination, Moisés Moleiro, Secretary General of the Movimiento de Izquierda Revolucionaria (MIR—Movement of the Revolutionary Left) and a longtime militant in the AD, said:

> The AD was the first party in Venezuela that attempted, after the events of October 1945, to violently overthrow by force a government [the junta], resorting to direct action . . . The [AD] Special Apparatus was trained by Spanish anarchists and quickly learned to make bombs (the AD's very famous "nipples" bombs). Contacts with discontented military personnel were regularized and, cautiously, other types of actions and attacks were planned.[125]

Regarding the insurrectional activities Beltrán took part in, Salom Mesa relates that following the coup:

We started preparing for the uprising. We gathered any weapon that would kill. But we only obtained eight rifles and a few revolvers, of which none were new. . . . In consequence we proceeded to design bombs and incendiary devices . . . Pedro Beltrán Wells showed me the rudiments of making bombs. Other activists, whose names will remain unspoken, because they're still alive, also worked at making bombs. Many times I was present when these experiments turned out to be duds. I remember a test we did in El Junquito of an effective detonator that we adapted to the "nipple," but which required that it be used in very open spaces. We abandoned it because we needed devices that we could use easily and anywhere. Through a construction engineer we obtained some sticks of 40% dynamite. With Pedro Beltrán Wells and another anarchist . . . we did a test near Carmen de Cura, but the bomb didn't go off because the dynamite was too old. . . . For the incendiary devices we searched for a more effective formula than the Molotov, and we found one. It produced flames when thrown against an object and didn't need to be lit first. We called it the RAS in honor of doctor Federico Rodríguez, the anarchists, and Edmund Sánchez Verdú, who as a team had produced this effective device.[126]

Regarding the abortive assassination attempt on October 12, 1951, Jorge Dager, an active member of the resistance said:

It was 10:00 in the morning . . . In the house of Gustavo Leindenz we were listening to the live broadcast. They announced the coming arrival of the governing junta at the Columbus Plaza in Los Cabos, where we intended to unleash the actions that would do away with the dictatorship. The junta triumvirate arrived and the ceremony was concluding. We looked at each other quizzically because it was going on without interruption. The ceremony ended without what we had expected happening, the physical elimination of the junta. What had occurred? Had everything failed? At noon, Caracas had already been informed that a new "terrorist plot by the extinct party [AD]" had been uncovered.[127]

An article in the paper *La Esfera* (The Globe) under the headline "They threw a bomb in the way of the junta" summed up what had happened:

Yesterday morning . . . terrorist elements of the dissolved Acción Democrática . . . threw a bomb, intercepted by the military police escort, which failed to explode . . those responsible were arrested. Previous to this police authorities had seized a car near the route that the junta was going to take. . . . [The car] was occupied by four persons who had eight bombs, at the same time between the corners of Sordo and Guayabal [streets] the police found 100 bombs and proceeded to arrest eight members of the dissolved political organization previously mentioned, who were armed with rifles and pistols.[128]

The plot had been revealed to National Security by an informant named Chacín and by a blunder that took place the previous day, October 11. The blunder occurred in the home of AD militant Eloy Martínez Méndez in the Maripérez area in Caracas. The house served as the warehouse for the bombs that would be employed on the coming day. Due to human error, one of the bombs went off leaving Jesús Cherubini and Manuel Felipe Carías gravely wounded. This unfortunate event put the security apparatus on alert, and thanks to the treachery of Chacín the authorities knew a considerable number of names and address of those involved and of the armed action they intended to carry out the following day.

The plan of the social democrats and their libertarian allies had not only counted on the physical elimination of the principal figures of the military junta, via an action by commandos under the direction of Castor Nieves Ríos at the ceremony (commemorating Día de la Raza) at the Columbus Plaza, but a military uprising following the bombing and the taking of various military and police installations by the mutineers; these were to include the Cuartel General de la Policía de Caracas (General Police Barracks of Caracas) by a group directed by Rubén Charlita Muñoz, who had been involved with Salom Mesa; Mesa managed to escape the police roundup and continued fighting the dictatorship.

Carnevali's escape

This series of shocking events stimulated AD resistance as had the earlier armed rescue, led by Salom Mesa, of AD leader Alberto Carnevali from the Puesto de Socorro de Salas hospital on July 27, 1951. Here's a portion of an article from *La Esfera* describing the events: "Yesterday in the early morning four subjects dressed as doctors or male nurses entered the emergency room and threatened with pistols those on duty, thus covering the flight of Dr. Carnevali, who left the premises with the four gunmen."[129]

Salom Mesa himself described the series of armed actions when he was interrogated at the Seguridad Nacional headquarters on October 28 following the failed attempt on the junta.

The rescue of Carnevali was carried out as follows: 1) I knew that . . . Carnevali had been taken to Puesto de Socorro . . . . 2) I visited Puesto de Socorro and realized that it would be easy to snatch Carnevali, and I informed Ruiz Pineda of this saying that I would carry out the action if he was in accord and would provide a safehouse. Ruiz Pineda answered positively. 3) I returned to Puesto de Socorro again to better check out the situation in its exterior. 4) I spoke with Juan Regalado, Ruben Muñoz, "Negro" López, and they agreed to the act. 5) I talked with Carías (I don't know his real name) and asked him to lend me a car saying that I was going to a meeting. 6) In that car (a blue Nash) I and the others named arrived at the Puesto de Socorro in the early morning of the 26th/27th and entered by the left side door around 3:30 and captured two guards who we took along with Carnevali. . . . We took them to San Bernardino [and released them. We took Carnevali] to a unit in an apartment block situated on the Avenida Roosevelt that had previously been obtained by Ruiz Pineda.[130]

The rescue of Carnevali was a setback for the dictatorship and made a mockery of its repressive apparatus. So it undertook the use of extrajudicial execution to do away with the leadershipof the AD.

[Strangely enough, during this time, Spanish exiles continued to arrive in Venezuela.] The anarcho-syndicalist ex-minister of the Spanish republican government in exile, José E Leiva, arrived in Venezuela. He had been named to the post by the CNT (in hiding in Spain), and before that had been imprisoned for his clandestine activities there. He had also been actively involved in the Libreria Selecciones (Selections Bookstore) in Bolivia, and after being presented to the public in the pages of *Últimas Noticias* by Miguel Campuzano became the head of Agency France Press in Caracas. He would live in Venezuela until the end of his days.

* * *

After the death of Chalbaud, in an attempt to find a way to fictional institutional legitimacy, the military junta organized a presidential election. The only parties to take part were the [centrist] Unión Republicana Democrática (URD), COPEI, and the ironically named Frente Electoral Independiente (FEI), a party organized by the government.

On election day, November 30, 1952, it seemed certain that the winner would be the URD candidate, Jóvito Villalba, but the FEI stopped the count and rigged the results in its favor so that its candidate Marcos Pérez Jiménez was "elected" president, paving the way for a period filled with arrests and torture of dissident political activists, and sending Venezuela into a tailspin of chauvinism.

Repression and solidarity in the face of adversity

The failure of the armed actions by AD and the consolidation of the rule of the "gendarme de Michelena" (Pérez Jiménez) paved the way for a strong surveillance state watching over all sectors at cross currents with the hegemonic project. The Casa España, the epicenter of anarchist activities, was always under the vigilant gaze of the SN. Victor Sanz comments on this:

> Suspicion was general, as is demonstrated by the fact that on August 6, 1954 the Casa España had to send to the Dirección de Extranjería (Office of Immigration or Office of Alien Status) a report citing by name its members. But relationships [with the local people] weren't all negative, as can be seen . . . [in the fact that] not a few Spaniards participated in the struggle of the democratic Venezuelans against the dictatorship, and as a logical corollary, also in [being subjected to] the tortures, the jailings, and the concentration camps of the regime. But the most difficult days for all of the [immigrants'] institutions during this dark period were those during the preparations for the referendum called by the dictator to set himself permanently in power. The Portuguese Center and the Casa de Italia among others yielded to his demands [endorsing the referendum] in statements bearing many signatures [of their members]. A high official of the Seguridad Nacional visited [Casa España] calling for an immediate pronouncement . . . But in this trial by fire we were able to save our dignity: to the pressure and soft interrogations to which they were subjected in the SN headquarters, and the heavy surveillance that followed, [the Casa España comrades] never yielded, and the desired communique never appeared.[131]

Given all this, it's necessary to understand the reasons why some Spanish anarchists decided to join the AD resistance and not with that of other political parties. To begin with, the PCV was basically a Latin American office of the USSR, not to mention the confrontations the anarchists had had with the stalinists during the Spanish Civil War, differences which came down to armed confrontations in May 1937 in Barcelona.

For its part, the URD was a heterogeneous and illogical party, so contradictory that it bore the name "republican" in a country that had never had a local monarchy and in which there didn't exist strong partisans of monarchy.

As regards COPEI, it was a conservative, orthodox Christian party that at its beginnings had sympathized with the Spanish Falange (Franco's fascists).

With AD, the dynamics were different, not only for the welcome it gave to the CNT exiles, but because it had anarchists in its ranks, specifically Francisco Olivo and Salom Mesa Espinoza, who had given the name Faneli to one of his sons in honor of Giuseppe Fanelli, the Italian who had introduced libertarian socialist ideas to Spain in the late 1860s. Another reason was that the AD was a multi-class organization with an important agrarian sector, in contrast with the PCV which was a [single] class organization and urban. Also, some CNT militants such as José Serrano had managed to acquire small properties and had become employers. This clashed with the class thesis brandished by the PCV, and would also become one of the basic matters which would later factor into internal disputes within the CNT in Venezuela.

There were various reasons that individuals in the CNT collaborated actively with the AD's anti-Pérez resistance, reasons as much individual as ideological. Pérez Jiménez was an ally of the Franco regime, and among the first things the junta did after overthrowing Gallegos was to renew diplomatic relations with the Franco dictatorship. As well, the junta praised and sympathized with Dominican dictator Leonidas Trujillo. In sum, the junta was a true representation, a true prototype of the conservative, religious, pro-imperialist, capitalist, supporter of fascism. As such, the Spanish libertarians opposed it.

So, unsurprisingly, the corporate state that Pérez Jiménez was constructing scored propaganda points against the resistance when it managed to capture Salom Mesa on December 20, 1952. Regarding the arrest, the writer and editor José Agustín Cátala, in his book *Venezuela bajo el signo del terror* (Venezuela, under the sign of terror), relates:

> Salom Mesa Espinoza, a union leader, in irons and handcuffed, stretched out naked upon blocks of ice for ten days while he was tortured with electric shocks to the ears, his wrists twisted flayed from a torture device, being cut and beaten, suffered mental disturbances as a result of being tortured.[132]

The writer Guido Acuña, another victim like Salom Mesa of imprisonment and torture by the Seguridad Nacional, tells us in his book, *Pérez Jiménez, un gendarme innecesario*, of the agony of Mesa in the dungeons:

> I'm going to succinctly narrate my most acute prison experiences: Torture! I spent almost a month in the dungeons of Seguridad Nacional sited in Paraíso. The great majority of those who I saw there on October 22, 1951 were my friends and comrades: one widely admired figure was Salom Mesa. They brutalized him in bestial manner! . . . I had to witness the physical agony of this man; when he was taken prisoner his martyrdom had barely begun. Salom was "'handcuffed" with a device used in the countryside to flay the husks from seeds; they used this device to "persuade" prisoners. . . . After this they laid him

out, face up, with the "handcuffs" still on, on a block of ice. The ice tormented him greatly and bit into his body [shredding his skin]. Then they left him [tied down on the ice]. The first moments were bearable, but with every movement the "handcuffs" bit deeper into his flesh, the flesh being slowly stripped away. . . . The torturers watched in silence and every now and then forced him to move. They took turns watching, smoking, waiting. . . . The tortured man felt an infinity of time between real and the unreal.[133]

So legendary was the torture and beating of Mesa by the SN that the novelist Miguel Otero Silva was inspired to use it in his novel *La muerte de Honorio* (roughly, Death of an Honorable Man), which was set in a prison in which political prisoners clung to a fragile brotherhood. Like Mesa, Otero Silva's protagonist had attempted to assassinate a dictator but had been apprehended immediately before the attempt.

In the same era of terror and military tyranny, another Spanish anarchist, Pablo Benaige, arrived in Venezuela. He had been a well known antiauthoritarian fighter, and had been the secretary of the bus drivers union in the CNT during the Social Revolution. He'd been arrested by the Nazis in France but managed to escape and pass into clandestinity. At the end of the Second World War he took part in the libertarian union in Burdeos (France) and helped Jose Peirats write his celebrated book, *Historia de la CNT*. After arriving in Caracas, he was arrested by the SN and accused of being a communist, but after a short time in jail was released.

Another CNT member who'd arrived in Venezuela, was Antonio Escobar (1913–1996), a survivor of the Nazi concentration camp Mauthausen-Gusen who had fought in the anarchist Transport Workers Battalion during the Spanish Civil War. He was expelled by Pérez Jiménez in 1951 [but later returned] and was active in the group around Casa España, the CNT in Venezuela, and the Colectivo Autogestionario Libertario (Libertarian Self-management Collective); he also also worked on the Venezuelan anarchist magazine *El Libertario*.

[Others were caught up in the wave of repression during the dictatorship.] The archives of Seguridad Nacional contain a record of the arrest and imprisonment of the Argentine anarchist Carlos Kristof Fiala:

Argentinian. Plumber. Communist. Arrested March 22, 1954. Given the task by the Communist International of establishing contact with various unions in several South American countries under the orders of the Federación Obrera Regional Argentina (FORA), with the object of setting up an assembly meeting to reconstitute the Asociación Continental Americana de Trabajadores

[ACAT]. Said foreigner was the one who wrote a defamatory article about the Venezuelan government titled Despotismo en Venezuela, which he sent to the daily paper "CNT" in France, for publication. Transferred to the Cárcel Modelo sentenced to six months imprisonment prior to expulsion. Expelled to the destination Buenos Aires on June 8, 1955.[134]

[This record demonstrates the political ignorance of the SN.] The FORA is the anarcho-syndicalist central in Argentina, and it advocates anarcho-communism a la Kropotkin—hence the mistaken identification of Kristof as a communist. And the ACAT was the Latin American affiliate of the AIT. (In 1997, the AIT attempted to revive ACAT, but without success.)

The Argentine writer Carlos Penelas in his book *Ácratas y crotos* (Anarchists and Bums), provides a sketch of this libertarian agitator:

Carlos Kristof from his youth participated in the great social struggles. . . . He was secretary general of the plumbers guild, fought the sellouts and climbers within the workers movement, and created a [presumably plumbers] union free of the tutelage of the government and political parties. His combativity earned him misery, sorrow, persecution, and imprisonment. He led through his actions and example. He wrote for magazines, bulletins, also wrote manifestos and memoirs, and also wrote for the FORA. He was also a typesetter and hod carrier, and was familiar with many [Argentine jails]. He was an exceptional figure within the Argentine union movement . . . an exceptional orator, a militant filled with idealism, integrity, and understanding. . . . He died before his 55th birthday on May 17, 1976.[135]

* * *

While the generalized climate of repression persisted in Venezuela, AD militants in exile organized, along with other armed Latin American groups, the Frente Internacional Antidictatorial. This coordinating group was formed in Mexico and encompassed Juventudes de AD (AD Youth), the Alianza Popular Revolucionaria Americana (a continental social-democratic party based in Peru), M26J (Movimiento 26 de Julio, a wide front self-defined as democratic, anti-imperialist, and nationalist, led by Fidel Castro), Movimiento 14 de Junio in the Dominican Republic, Juventud Democrática Nicaragüense (JDN, which would later be known as Juventud Revolucionara Nicaragüense—it contributed to the formation of the Frente Sandinista de Liberación Nacional), Directorio Revolucionario (social-democratic Cuban group that grew out of the Federación de Estudiantes de Cuba), and Juventudes Antifranquistas (Anti-Franco Youth, whose representative was Octavio

Alberola). This front had a platform to which the various groups promised to contribute once the dictatorships in their countries had been overthrown. Venezuela, during this period, appeared to have two separate realities. On the one hand, a vertiginous development expressed as the Doctrine of National Well-being with the slogan "New National Ideal," and on the other the persecuted and tortured who resisted the government's nationalistic ambitions. The price of petroleum was going up thanks to foreign military conflicts, and took off during the Korean War. With this increase in revenue, ambitious plans to construct infrastructure could be carried out to perfection. There were also important gains in such areas as hydro-electric generation, mining, steel making, and construction. All of these raised the level of prosperity.

Other policies promoted immigration of both capital and individuals, primarily from European nations such as Spain, Italy, Portugal, and Hungary. This gave impulse to a vast, ambitious program of infrastructure building using reinforced concrete in the construction of buildings, large and modern highways that linked the states and cities, bridges, and other major works that modernized the country.

However, even though Venezuela appeared to be living in a period of splendor and consumerism it had never before seen, the desire in society to experiment with electoral democracy began to produce cracks in the foundation of the regime. The political opposition of the Marcos Pérez Jiménez period commenced with the AD and PCV, which were followed by the URD and COPEI. Besides the four parties there were growing independent sectors such as guilds and other association, the church, dissident military elements, and militant Spanish anarchists from the CNT.

On June 14, 1957, the Junta Patriótica formed with a nucleus of AD, CO-PEI, URD and PCV, with the goal of organizing a popular insurrection against Pérez Jiménez's plan to organize a plebiscite and elect a new president, but to remain the hidden power. On November 17 students at the Universidad Católica Andrés Bello and also a bunch of high school students called a strike and organized a demonstration for the 21st of the month in Caracas. This was strongly suppressed by the SN.

The crowning event occurred on December 15, when the plebiscite was held and Pérez Jiménez won with 2,374,790 votes in favor and only 364,182 against. This, along with the political persecution, intimidation, and torture with which the country lived, set the scene for the convulsive events which would soon shake Venezuela.

Despite the Pérez Jiménez regime's policy of providing incentives and perquisites to the military elite, there was discontent within the military. A group of mid-rank officers sensed the popular clamor for democracy, and weren't impressed with the squandering of government money on their higher-ranking colleagues.

On January 1, 1958, in the early morning hours, Air Force planes flew over the city of Caracas and strafed the presidential palace and the Seguridad Nacional headquarters. This coincided with an armed uprising of officers and troops in the garrison stationed at Maracay and the taking of a radio station in that city. At the same time in Caracas, two tank units under the command of colonel Hugo Trejo (1922–1988) appeared on the streets from the Urdaneta de Catia barracks and made for Maracay, rather than the presidential palace which was a few kilometers away.

Lack of coordination of the mutineers, inadequate preparation, and a betrayal to the government caused the uprising to take place five days before it was planned, and led to its failure. Nonetheless, this surprising revolt helped to create more fissures within the regime, which began to gradually crumble.

Beginning on January 10, acts of protest began to increase: the inflamed masses could no longer be repressed by Seguridad Nacional. On the 16th, student protests continued and Andrés Bello [high school attached to the university] was shut down. And on the 21st, the press guild complied with the strike called by the Junta Patriótica. During these critical events, some anarchists took part in street actions. As an example, CNT member Octavio Bardetas was wounded in the street skirmishes in Caracas while attempting to assault the SN headquarters.

On January 22, a military junta headed by Wolfgang Larrazábal (1911–1970) and dissident sectors in the Navy demanded the resignation of Pérez Jiménez. On the 23rd, Pérez Jiménez, his family, and his closest collaborators fled to the Dominican Republic.

Rebirth of anti-Franco Hope

The events of January 23, 1958 served as an inspiration for the Spanish exiles [and their allies] struggling for the liberation of the Iberian Peninsula. As one example of this, a few years later the Scottish anarchist Stuart Christie, arrested on August 11, 1964 while transporting explosives for an assassination attempt against Franco, said, "Our expectations of what was possible we saw reflected in the struggle against the Pérez Jiménez tyranny in Venezuela in 1958."[136]

In Latin America, as an example of that inspiration, the JDN held an international conference on January 12, 1960 to denounce the dictatorships of

Fulgencio Batista (1901–1973) in Cuba and Trujillo. [Batista had just been overthrown on December 31, 1959; the conference had been planned well in advance of that date.]

But perhaps the group that had benefited most from the social-democrats' overthrow of Pérez Jiménez was M26J. According to anarchist Spanish historian Octavio Alberola, in an e-mail on January 13, 2009, "After the fall of the dictatorship in Venezuela the AD Youth pressured their party to comply with its contracted obligations, and finally [then-president] Betancourt gave a million dollars to Fidel Castro's M26J."

Another example of actions inspired by the Pérez Jiménez overthrow was the invasion on June 14, 1959 by the Movimiento de Liberación Dominicano in the areas of Constanza, Maimón, and Estero Hondo in the Dominican Republic. The invasion failed, even though it had logistical support originating in both Cuba and Venezuela; in the failed invasion, 80 Venezuelans died in firefights. But despite its lack of success, it sowed the seeds of actions to come against the Trujillo regime.

Also, following the fall of the Pérez Jiménez, the CNT renewed its struggle against the Franco regime, and some anarchists came to be advisers to the Confederación de Trabajadores de Venezuela including José González Navarro as its secretary general. Other CNT activists in Venezuela at the time included Avelino Gonzáles Entriago, who had been a member of the CNT National Committee in Madrid and Valencia, and who had fled to Latin America after the civil war, and Luis Montoliu, who had participated in the clandestine struggle in Spain after the war, and was active in the organization of the CTV. Another Spanish anarchist, Jesús Maella, became secretary of the Venezuelan radio and television workers union.

* * *

The collaboration of some sectors of the CNT with Acción Democrática had strengthened the AD's efforts to end the Pérez Jiménez dictatorship, and after the overthrow many libertarians decided to join the files of Acción Democrática. Regarding this, Antonio Serrano says that even though many joined, "they all continued to collaborate one way or another with the CNT and the anti-Franco resistance."[137]

In the same year, 1958, those who had taken part in the uprising in Boca del Rio in 1951 were put at liberty.

On April 13, 1958, an event took place in the Sports Palace of Caracas in which activists of the UGT, the PSOE, and the CNT took part. Public personages who took part included Rómulo Betancourt, Rómulo Gallegos, Jóvito Villalba, Gustavo Machado, and Fabricio Ojeda (1929–1969). The speakers for the CNT and the Movimiento Libertario Español were José Leiva and José Consuegra, who both denounced the Franco regime and praised the democratic process unfolding in Venezuela.

Nevertheless the closeness of some of its sectors with the AD was generating strife within the CNT. To combat what they saw as reformist tendencies within the organization, a collective formed called the Grupo Libertario Errico Malatesta, and commenced publishing a periodical called *Simiente Libertaria* (Libertarian Seed). Members of the group included Juan Verde, Pablo Benaige, Vicente Sierra, Eusebio Larruy, French anarchist Francisco Portela, who joined the CNT after emigrating to Venezuela, and José Cazorla, who had been wounded while taking part in anti-Franco attacks during the clandestine period in the 1940s. Cazorla, even though a member of the Grupo Malatesta, also worked as secretary of the local CNT. *Simiente Libertaria* was published monthly for over a year, with 16 issues appearing. It attacked those the Malatesta group considered "collaborators" with the new Venezuelan governors.

Another anti-collaborationist group called El Grupo Buenaventura Durruti, composed of Mateo Rodríguez, Mariano Tejero, and José Mateu appeared in the city of Maracay. This group represented the most conscious edge of the CNT in Venezuela. It maintained that some CNT members used pretexts such as the AD government being widely supported, a defender of labor rights, and anti-communist, as well as reasons of personal survival (freedom to express anarchist ideas, work, etc.), as excuses to support the "revolutionary" government without reserve, leaving to the side the conflicts inherent in class struggle and the power relations in any state, even one in populist garb.

These differences within the CNT would have serious future repercussions internally, and would have a negative effect on growth of the anarchist movement within Venezuela.

Another group that arose from the Casa España was the Venezuelan section of Solidaridad Internacional Antifascista (SIA) that was a global network of anti-fascist groups created during the Spanish Revolution to supply aid to persons and groups suffering under fascism in other countries. The Venezuelan section, to which Juan Verde and Vicente Sierra belonged, issued a monthly bulletin published under the name of the network until July 1965, publishing 30 issues in all.

The Punto Fijo pact and the advent of representative democracy

On October 31, 1958 at the residence of the leader of COPEI, Rafael Caldera, there was a celebration of the Pact of Punto Fijo [named after the city
of Caldera's residence]. This accord established a commitment to defend the
constitution, to govern in accord with electoral results, to govern for national
unity, to put an end to single-party hegemony, and to put forth a common
basic program. The parties to the pact recognized the supposed latent threats
against the democratic government and solidified the basis of a unified government, which was unprecedented in the era. Those subscribing to the pact
included Rómulo Betancourt, Raúl Leoni, and Gonzalo Barrios for AD; Jóvito
Villalba, Ignacio Luís Arcaya, and Manuel López Rivas for URD; and Rafael
Caldera, Pedro del Corral, and Lorenzo Fernández for COPEI.

But the organizers excluded the PCV from the pact, one of the parties that
had taken part in the struggle against the dictatorship. This omission would
create great problems in the near future.

On December 7, 1958, a presidential election took place in Venezuela,
from which the vaunted leader of the AD, Rómulo Betancourt, emerged victorious with 1,284,092 votes, 49,18% of the total, beating Rafael Caldera of
COPEI and Wolfgang Larrazabal who was supported by the URD and PCV.
Betancourt would rule Venezuela from 1959 to 1964.

In a climate of great social conflict, the Betancourt government took office and faced a series of strikes in the civil sector (campesinos, workers, students). Nonetheless, the AD government retained the support it had gained
in the previous decades from the union and agrarian movements, as well as
from intellectuals.

Betancourt initiated a process of constitutional change to guarantee the
legal basis of representative democracy. But his unstable government reproduced and widened the repressive governmental practices that had previously
characterized the country, being from the start marginal in the area of human
rights. Betancourt used new expressions and political arguments intended to
pull the wool over the eyes of citizens. But this was not a simple problem of
semantics. What it did was open the way for a model of representative democracy in which economic and political interests would come together to
create a society in which exploitation, domination, and blind consumerism
were the expressions of a model of production and development: extractive,
dependent capitalism.

The fiction of "a government of all," put forth in all of the epochs of our national history, was finally given the lie. The government of Betancourt became an administration that responded to the dictates of the international business sector, avid for primary materials; the native financial and industrial bourgeoisie; the latifundistas; and speculators on the importation of food. Representative government limited itself to guaranteeing citizens the right to vote every five years. Conceptually, it meant that during those five years the elected would speak and act in the name of the people. The people lacked a mechanism to directly and continuously participate, because they had transferred their power to their so-called representatives. For a society under the sway of the caudillismo of the elite and the military, this was perceived as a great advance.

During these years, the logic of representative government included its ability to buy off dissidents and to repress adversaries. From the first moment it was evident that there was a dichotomy between what the political parties said [regarding popular well-being] and the growing possibilities of their enjoying the benefits of the state through the exercise of power. This process unfolded slowly, discretely, and it encountered resistance on the part of ethical functionaries and parts of the leadership of the different parties. Nonetheless, the process became ever more apparent and common as the years went on.

Even before this [corrupt] process was unfolding, months before the election of Rómulo Betancourt, a group of Spanish anarchists began work on the magazine *El Libertario*. They were based at the Instituto Albert Einstein in Chacao, and Juan Campá was managing director. Its editorial group included, José L. Herrero, Emilio Sánchez, Aurelio Lorente, who had been secretary of the CNT manufacturing and clothing union in Barcelona before and during the Spanish Revolution/Civil War, and CNT and FAI member Antonio Ortiz who had been politico-military commander of the Sur-Ebro Column during the Civil War, and who had fought with the Allies during World War II. The magazine defined itself as the Vocero del Movimiento Libertario Español (Voice of the Spanish Libertarian Movement) and had a small office in Conde de Caracas. During this first stage, three issues of the magazine appeared.

At the same time some young libertarians coexisted with the group of [older] anarchists at the Casa España and began publishing the magazines *Crisol Juvenil* and *Juventud Libre* (Youth Crucible and Free Youth). And the CNT managed to arrange three expositions, one of Spanish painters, another of documents from the Spanish Civil War, and the third of photographs of the Social Revolution of 1936.

All of these activities unfolded after July 18, 1958, a few months after the overthrow of Pérez Jiménez, and all shared the goal of developing and spreading anarchist ideas.

Among other things, the Casa España relocated to the La Florida housing project, and the publication *Crisol Juvenil*, using the masthead Portavoz de la Federación Ibérica de Juventudes Libertarias (Megaphone of the FIJL), began appearing in 1959 and at least eight issues were published. It was distributed via the Casa España and among Spanish families living in Venezuela. Even though it was a "youth" publication, a lot of older writers appeared in its pages, including José Consuegra, Acracio Bartolomé, and Luís Montoliu.

During these years the CNT managed to rent a shop front in which members gave talks, held meetings, had a library, showed films on Saturdays, and which was frequented by Francisco Olivo and other leading workers who belonged to the CTV. It was called the Centro Cultural y de Estudios Sociales (Cultural and Social Studies Center) and was located at Avenida Alameda, nº 8 in the San Bernardino area of Caracas. The principle responsible people were Juan Verde, Víctor García, and Pedro Beltrán.

An article by Francisco Escamilla Vera, "Pablo Vila and the Spanish Exile," mentions that in addition to the other activities the Centro also served to organize trips around the country for up to 120 people at a time, had a theater group, and financed publication of and promoted books ranging from Erich Fromm to a tome on turtles of the Orinoco. Vera notes that "almost all of the activities were free and were financed by the Spanish exile families that funded the Center."[138]

On November 14, 1959, the Third Congress of Venezuelan Workers took place. It encompassed both leftist and centrist labor tendencies, from socialists, to anarchists, to communists, and from the Christian democrats to the AIT. The AIT representative was Spanish anarcho-syndicalist José "Germinal" Esglea (1903-1981), who had been an advisor to the Departamento Económico de la Generalitat de Cataluña during the Civil War, had been rescued from a concentration camp by anti-fascist French guerrillas, had served as both secretary general of the CNT in exile and also had served from 1958 to 1963 as secretary general of the AIT; he was also the compañero of Federica Montseny, who had served as the anarcho-syndicalist Minister of Health in the Popular Front government during the Spanish Civil War.

Regarding Esglea's visit to the Third Congress, Salom Mesa said that Esglea told him and Francisco Olivo, the two of whom financed Esglea's trip: "If I speak I won't make concessions of principle, and this could lead to an element of discord in your assembly, and I think I wouldn't be doing you any favors by doing so." Mesa goes on to say:

Nonetheless, the curiosity of many delegates led them to seek out conversations with Germinal. Very quickly—during a plenary session—I observed delegates leaving their seats and going down to the ground floor. There was Germinal, surrounded by a great number of workers who were listening to him attentively. He spoke smoothly but with great persuasive power. I asked him to dissolve this unscheduled assembly, which he had not instigated, so that the delegates could get back to the regular assembly [and he apparently did call an end to it].[139]

During the Congress, the CTV suffered its first major schism. Sectors near to the PCV decided to separate themselves and form their own labor confederation, the Central Unitaria de Trabajadores de Venezuela. The Spanish anarchists who were collaborating in the reconstruction and strengthening of the CTV didn't join them.

In August 1960 at a CNT congress in Limoges (France), the disputing parties reunited in the struggle against the Franco dictatorship, with the entire anarchist movement uniting under the name Movimiento Libertario-Confederación Nacional del Trabajo (ML-CNT).

Venezuela during this time had acquired the reputation of being a rich country, and for that reason a delegation from that CNT congress had visited Venezuela to gather funds for the anti-Franco struggle and also to reunify the disputing sectors of the Spanish exiles that had become estranged, including those that had been at odds since a split in 1945.

Among the members of this trip in June, prior to the official reunification in August, were Juan García Oliver (1901–1980) who came from Mexico. He was arguably the most famous leader of the anarchist movement and a man with had a unique capability as an orator. He was a member of both the CNT and FAI, had taken part in the celebrated armed group Nosotros, and had been the anarcho-syndicalist Minister of Justice in the Popular Front government during the Civil War. Taking advantage of his days in Caracas, the Spanish anarchists there organized an event in the Asociación Venezolana de Periodistas (Venezuelan Association of Journalists) hall, which would later be converted to a movie theater. Despite scant publicity, the hall was filled to overflowing. Antonio Serrano tells us that "the more than three thousands persons who attended the event weren't all [anarchists].

. There were people from all of the Spanish political factions, though the majority were from the ML-CNT."[140]

The young Spanish anarchist Octavio Alberola, a militant in the Juventudes Libertarias in México, was also a member of the delegation. He would later go on to participate in and organize armed actions against the Franco regime under the names Defensa Interior (DI) and Grupo Primero de May, which later became Movimiento de Solidaridad Revolucionaria Internacional (MSRI).

Regarding the delegation's visit, Alberola would say:

[One of the reasons for it] was the meeting scheduled between the secretary of coordination, Juan Pintado, of the SI (Secretariado Intercontinental de la CNT in exile in Toulouse) and the secretary general of the CTV, one Navarro. The Venezuelan compañeros had arranged this meeting because Navarro had assured them that the CTV would aid the CNT in its struggle against the Franco regime. It appears that some CNT comrades had been imprisoned with Navarro during the Pérez Jiménez dictatorship. In addition to the meeting with Navarro Pintado had to talk with García Oliver about an assassination attempt against Franco that the SI wanted to organize and in which Floreal "Florico" Ocaña and I had promised to participate. . . . When I arrived, the meeting with Navarro had already taken place at the CTV headquarters. ([Oliver] had no contact with the AD.) Navarro had made vague promises of armed aid and had also promised to set up a radio transmitter in Venezuela to broadcast propaganda to Spain. Later a radio station would be built, but it wasn't on the air for a long time. Due to the nature of my visit, I didn't have [large] meetings with the CNT compañeros, and only individual, private meetings with a few individuals with whom I'd had contact from Mexico.[141]

On July 18, 1960, sectors of the ML-CNT, taking advantage of the visit of García Oliver and the others in the CNT delegation, decried the Franco tyranny and convoked a demonstration by CNT members and sympathizers in Cagua, Aragua State to support [and publicize] the peaceful general strike that had taken place in Spain in June of that year.

In Caracas, there was a peaceful demonstration [a vigil] on July 19 in front of the Spanish embassy, and in the early morning hours some youths with anarchist sympathies threw Molotov cocktails against the building. Considering it an act of provocation, the demonstrators captured those responsible and turned them over to the police, accusing them of being Falangist provocateurs, with Rafael de Monteys, one of the organizers of the vigil, presenting himself to the authorities to confirm the accusations.

But it was difficult to believe that the group—among whom was the niece of the anarcho-syndicalist ex-minister in the Popular Front government, Juan Peiró, who the Falangists had shot precisely because he refused to collaborate—were provocateurs in the service of Franco. In the end, all three of the accused were put at liberty.

One product of all this political activity and the reorganization of the CNT in Venezuela was that the largely unknown organization, the Directorio Revolucionario Ibérico de Liberación (DRIL) decided to launch an armed propaganda action from Venezuela.

DRIL was an odd group formed in 1959 by exiled Galician separatists, anarchists, and communists, with the support of Portuguese rebels [against the dictatorship of general António de Oliveira Salazar]. It was led by Humberto Delgado and Xosé Velo Mosquera. It was born from the confluence of the Federación de Mocedades [Youth] Galeguistas and the Unión de Combatientes Antifranquistas Nacionalistas Gallegos based in Venezuela.

On January 22, 1961, DRIL, operating from Venezuelan soil, undertook what it dubbed "Operación Dulcinea," which consisted of commandos hijacking the ship Santa Maria that plied the transatlantic Caracas-Vigo (Spain) route. The commando group consisted of 24 militants who had embarked from Guaira, and it was commanded by captains Henrique Galvão, José Velo Mosquera, Humberto Delgado, and Jorge Sotomayor, a Spanish communist widely admired by the leninist Bandera Roja party in Venezuela.

The operation would be studied over time as the first act of political hijacking on the high seas. Even though DRIL was an ideologically mixed group, the assaulting force had only a few anarchists, one of whom, Francisco Rico, would in 1969 write the book El asalto del Santa María, which was published by the FIJL in Caracas.

To assume that Santa Maria operation was a quixotic anarchist affair would be wrong given the very few anarchists who took part. To illustrate this, Rico only mentions one single other hijacker with some interest in anarchism: "Basilio was a little more conscious [than the other hijackers] and had some knowledge about the political-social struggles in Spain in the time of the republic, and his father had taken part in the Socialist Party and would later join the CNT."[142] As well, Octavio Alberola, in an interview conducted for this book, said that the most active members of the CNT were unaware of the operation, and that the DRIL had asked some anarchists in Mexico for aid, but nothing came of it, and [the CNT] was surprised by the affair.

The Santa Maria, which the hijackers renamed Santa Liberdade, ended up surrounded by U.S. warships, and after several days the hijackers disembarked on February 2 in Brasil thanks to that country's offering them political asylum.

Even though it was a [nonanarchist] anti-fascist action, many exiled Spanish anarchists lent aid to the hijackers [after the event]. A while later, one of the hijackers, Federico Fernández would return to Venezuela and be arrested at the Maiquetía airport. He was freed through the intervention of Minister González Navarro, which once again demonstrated the tolerance of the AD government for Spanish anti-fascists.

Passions unleashed in the CNT-Venezuela

On August 9, 1961, about 500 CNT militants from all over the country held a meeting in a CTV hall in an attempt to reunify those elements on the margins with the bulk of the CNT-Venezolana, as had happened with the CNT overall at the reunification meeting in Limonges. Over six hours, they discussed possible reunification and also expressed solidarity with the Venezuelan dockworkers in La Guaira, who for several weeks had been refusing to unload the cargo of the Spanish ship Churruca. A piece in the publication *Crisol Juvenil* described the dockworkers actions as being motivated not only by anti-fascist economic solidarity, but by refusal to allow the ship to take Falangist mercenaries to Santo Domingo (Dominican Republic) to support the Trujillo dictatorship. The piece went on to add:

> The Churruca returned to the [Iberian] peninsula not only its cargo, but also a message from Venezuelan workers to their Spanish brothers who fight for liberty and against the Franco tyranny. This magnificent gesture by the Venezuelan port workers should be imitated in other countries so that their governments become aware of the power of proletarian solidarity and so that they'll decide to break relations with the bloody Spanish despot.[143]

But in regard to its main task, there wasn't complete unity at the conference, and it split into two blocs. One of them was the collaborationist [with the AD government] Fuerza Nueva, led by Juan Campá, Jesús Maella, Joaquín Ascaso Valeriano Gordo Pulido, Martín Andrés Terrer, and Antonio Ortiz Ramírez. Of these, Joaquín Ascaso had been involved in the armed group Los Indomables (The Uncontrollables), at the outbreak of the civil war had been named president of the Regional Defense Council of Aragon, and had fought in the Durruti Column. Gordo Pulido had participated in the pre-civil war anarchist armed groups in Barcelona and had fought in the Ortiz Column in

Aragon during the civil war. Tercer was a lifelong anarchist and had fought and been wounded in the civil war.

The more purist group was led by Juan Verde and Juan Cazorla among others. From there on out the CNT in Venezuela would be divided.

Perhaps no one is better placed that Victor García to comment on the disputes within the CNT in Venezuela, disputes which ended up leading to the end of an important libertarian organzation in the country. At the time of the split, García was the secretary general of the organization. He stated, in a letter written to Carlos Díaz: "At the end [of the conference] we declared unity, and I settled into the job of being secretary. I thought the opposition would be heavy (astonishingly!) to ourselves. That same month we launched *Fragua Social* (Social Forge) as our organ."[144]

That paper was presented as the official organ of the CNT; Manuel Rico, brother of Francisco Rico, functioned as principle organizer. Many well known writers appeared in its pages, including José Peirats, Antonio Serrano, Víctor García, José Leiva, José Consuegra, and Benjamín Cano Ruiz. Its first issue appeared in January 1961, and it contained a letter wishing it well from González Navarro, who at the time was president of the CTV. The magazine had a short run, and its final issue appeared in April, done in by the infighting within the CNT.

As one might have expected, the celebration of the declaration of unity between the two opposed CNT blocs didn't last long. In another letter written by García to Díaz, dated February 3, 1961, García comments:

> The unity continued without everything being resolved. There are always a multitude of blockheads who throw obstacles in the way of all types of good intentions. This was always a problem with the presence of the ex-compañeros who had become business people. In Chile, Mexico, Brazil, and other Latin American countries the compañeros had been able to avoid and ignore this. If an ex-compañero wanted to come [back] to the movement to help, to put his shoulder to the wheel, he was welcomed with no problem. In the end, it's not economic goals but rather the anti-Franco struggle and the desire to return to Spain that are most important to the CNT in exile. This is the present situation, and if we're not going to be more Catholic than the pope, we shouldn't reject the help of a compañero who, often without even realizing it, has passed from one class to another. In the end, from the point of view of speculative ideology, a boss can never be an anarchist. But the ideas are not what's in play now. . . .
> In my view, there is no more fertile ground for the development of anarchist ideas than Spain, and the ivory towers of the ultra-purists are useless unless they help in the return to Spain with at the minimum the necessary freedom to spread our ideas. Venezuela can't be anything other in the struggle against

Franco than a source of economic aid. The position of the ultras leads in the opposite direction. The really odd things is that the majority of the ultras come from bourgeois backgrounds.[145]

The quarrels stemming from this continued until the death of the CNT as an organization in the mid 1970s. The "business people" ("patronos") García refers to were the Fuerza Nueva, who had come to own businesses employing workers or who had gone to work for the AD government in some capacity. On the other side, the "ultras" were orthodox but were better positioned ideologically in that they refused ascent to the employing class [or working for the state in any capacity]. They regrouped as Federación Local de Caracas-CNT.

As regards the literary ambit of the CNT in Venezuela, in 1961, the same year *Fragua Social* briefly appeared, the CNT published the book *La militancia pide la palabra* (Militancy Asks for the Word), by Víctor García in which he expressed appreciation for both sides in the dispute and issued a final call for unity.

[The book did little good.] The quarreling within the CNT had become so heated that because of it one of the issues of *Fragua Social* that had already been printed never reached the streets: the issue was pulped.

Armed Struggle and "National Liberation"

The triumph of Fidel Castro in 1959 and the initiation of a process of national liberation on the island revived the adventurous spirit within young people in Venezuela and the rest of Latin American. The youths who launched the "storming of heaven" in 1961 and 1962 were convinced that a revolutionary utopia was possible. Fidel Castro had demonstrated it. There was an attempt to do the same thing in Venezuela by the Juventud Comunista and leftist youths in the AD, who left the party and founded a group known as the Movimiento de Izquierda Revolucionario (MIR—Movement of the Revolutionary Left).

The fuse was lit within a year [of Castro's taking power] at the Third Congress of the PCV, and the MIR set March 2, 1962 as the date for an insurrection against "the government of AD-COPEI." They created the Fuerzas Armadas de Liberación Nacional (FALN) as their military initiative and the Frente de Liberación Nacional as their political initiative, and they initiated guerrilla warfare via sabotage, armed attacks, expropriations, and plane and ship hijackings.

There's been a lot of groundless speculation about anarchist participation in the the actions undertaken by the FALN and other groups raised by the MIR, all without evidence. I contacted the ex-guerrilla, Pablo Hernández Parra, a militant in the Célula Van Troi of the MIR and political-military commander of the Bandera Roja-Marxista Leninista, about the presence of anarchists in the armed groups. He said:

> Whoever tells you that is talking crap. In the MIR there were only left social democrats, petit bourgeois radicals, and very few of us dedicated ourselves to studying and applying historical materials as a method of analyzing reality.[146]

In the face of this new uprising, Salom Mesa decided to close ranks with the constituted authorities. Functioning as an AD deputy in the National Congress, he expressly repudiated armed struggle, putting himself at odds with his own former revolutionary militancy. Taking the part of Rómulo Betancourt, he execrated [armed] dissidence. (Later we'll see several other examples of this contradictory attitude.)

For their part, the Spanish anarchists who still held to principle greatly distrusted the Castro regime which they considered far from truly revolutionary, and that unfortunately was repeating all the same evils and atrocities that had been done in the USSR in the name of social transformation. In addition, Castro and his followers had untertaken a ferocious persecution of the anarchists who had organized as the Asociación Libertaria Cubana (ALC). Many Cuban anarchists were killed or imprisoned for very long times in the jails of the Castro regime. Others managed to flee to the United States where they regrouped as the Movimiento Libertario Cubano en el Exilio (MLCE).

The historian Frank Fernández, in his book *El Anarquismo en Cuba* [slightly expanded edition published in the U.S. as *Cuban Anarchism: The History of a Movement*], comments on the aid that Venezuelan anarchist circles gave to the Cubans: "[I]n Venezuela, the Grupo Malatesta . . . in the course of a campaign for the liberation of Luís M. Linsuaín [condemned to death for an attempt on Raúl Castro] . . . . had to be careful to 'clarify' and to explain exactly what the anarchists wanted . . . and to demonstrate that they weren't reactionaries."[147] That campaign probably had some effect given that that Linsuaín's sentence was reduced from death to thirty years imprisonment. It's well worth noting that this libertarian had been a militant in Castro's M26J and had fought in the Sierra Maestra.

As well, the MLCE in collaboration with the CNT managed to publish a booklet that went through three printings that denounced the deviations of the Cuban revolutionary process. [Also, from 1979 through 1992 the MLCE published 52 consecutive issues of its well written anti-Castro magazine *Guángara Libertaria* {Libertarian Jest}.]

On September 1, 1961 in Caracas, Manuel Monreal and, from the ML-CNT, Manuel Rojas gave a press conference to announce the formation of a provisional council of war to direct the struggle against Franco from Venezuelan soil. On the same date, arriving from Cuba and fleeing the Castro dictatorship, ALC anarchist Santiago Cobo arrived in Venezuela. He had occupied positions of responsibility within the secretariat of the Federación Nacional del Transporte, one of the largest and most important unions on the island. His visit to Venezuela helped to consolidate the ties of friendship and solidarity between the ML-CNT in Venezuela and the Cubans in the MLCE.

In March 1962, in the Casa del Periodista (House of the Journalist), there was an announcement of the creation of the Council of Anti-Franco Resistance, with Antonio Soler being the representative of the Frente de Resistencia Interior and Juan Campá being the CNT representative. The object of this council was the gathering of funds for the anti-Franco resistance in Spain.

In October of that year, a new anarchist magazine appeared in Caracas, *España*, edited by Leoncio Pérez. It was short lived, running to only eight issues. Among other things it published pieces by José María Llopis on Francisco Ferrer, the founder of the Modern School—a libertarian, secular, rationalist school in Barcelona that Ferrer founded in 1901—and Ferrer's persecution and murder by the Spanish authorities. And on December 21, the Casa España began a series of conferences on anarchist ideals in which Víctor García, José Consuegra, Pedro Bagalló, and José E. Leiva participated.

Also of note, in that same year Víctor García was the driving force behind the creation of the Federación Ibérica de Juventudes Libertarias (FIJL) of Caracas, which created the bimonthly publication *Ruta* (Route or Road) as its organ. Among the FIJL's activities were excursions to the countryside that always featured discussion and debate. Besides Victor García those involved included the siblings Andrés, Ana María and Vicente Sierra, Alberto Espiés Sanz, Leonardo De Francesco, and Aurelio Lorente. The FIJL of Caracas also published three books, *España hoy* and *Juicio a Franco* (Spain Today and Judgment on Franco), both written by Víctor García, and *Portugal Hoy* (Portugal Today), edited by Edgar Rodrigues.

Taking advantage of May Day celebrations, on May 1, 1963 the UGT and CNT issued a communique to Venezuelan workers asking them to show solidarity with the under-the-yoke Iberian workers suffering under Franco. And on July 19 of that year [the anniversary of the Social Revolution in Spain in

1936], the CNT had a fundraising dinner at Casa España to collect funds for the political prisoners in Franco's prisons, counting on the aid of the UGT and Socialist Party to do so. Regarding such fundraising dinners, Antonio Serrano commented, "Since 1951, every May Day and 19th of July, dinners and parties were held not only to commemorate the days, but also to collect funds to send to Spain."[148] In that same year, the AD organized a series of conferences in the city of Maracay. Taking advantage of this, professor Demetrio Boersner, used one of these meetings dedicated to the discussion of contemporary political ideas to hold a talk on anarchism.

The FALN was also active. On August 24, a group of FALN commandos directed by Paúl del Río ("Máximo Canales") kidnapped the Argentine soccer player Alfredo Di Stéfano in Caracas. They held him for two days, and the reason for the kidnapping was to call world attention to the armed struggle in Venezuela and to denounce the Franco dictatorship. The participation in the crime of Paúl del Río, son of Spanish anarchist Jesús del Río, led to the persecution of the entire family and its later relocation to Mexico, which was facilitated by the SIA and in large measure by AD leader Gonzalo Barrios.

As Betancourt's mandate came to a close, Venezuelan democracy found itself under the shadows of violence, that of the FALN, several armed uprisings within the military, including four in 1962, at Castro León, La Guiara, Cárupano, Puerto Cabello, and one the previous year at Anzoátegui in which at least 50 people died. All of these had PCV and MIR involvement.

As regards energy policy, there was a marked strengthening of nationalist energy policies during Betancourt's reign with the creation of Corporación Venezolana de Petróleo (CVP) and the Corporación Venezolana de Guayana, as well as the creation of OPEC in 1960, in which Venezuela took part.

In contrast to these nationalist moves, in a conciliatory gesture toward the U.S., Betancourt agreed that Venezuela take part in John F. Kennedy's Alliance for Progress, an investment program designed to counter the influence of the Cuban revolution in Latin America. And the U.S. did in fact invest a large amount of money in Venezuela, including financing the construction of over 3,000 grade schools and 200 high schools. The number of graduating students increased from 847,000 in 1958 to 1,600,000 in 1963. At the end of Betancourt's administration, more than 90% of school-aged children were attending school, and the graduation rate had doubled. This was the beginning of mass education in Venezuela and would assure the future triumph of the social democrats.

On December 1, 1963 there were new elections in which Raúl Leoni of the AD was elected with 32.81% of the votes, the highest amount among the seven candidates: Rafael Caldera of COPEI, Jóvito Villalba of the URD, Arturo Uslar Pietri of the newly formed rightist Frente Nacional Democrático (FND), Wolfgang Larrazábal of the newly formed leftist Fuerza Democrática Popular, Raúl Ramos Jiménez of the leftist AD-Oposición, and Germán Borregales of the ultra-right Movimiento de Acción Nacional.

The triumph of Raúl Leoni assured the continuation of the policies implemented by the AD, though his government had the challenge of overcoming the obstacles posed by the armed actions impelled by the MIR and PCV. Like his predecessor, Leoni created a coalition among opposition forces to support his administration, his "government with a wide base"; this "wide base" included both the URD and the FND.

* * *

Shortly after the 1963 election, on February 27, 1964, the writer Carlos Brandt died in Caracas of a stroke at the age of 89. Brandt, a unique man and product of this land, summed up his thoughts as follows: "The practical anarchists are those who adopt naturism, proclaim their sobriety, which is what will put an end to the tyranny of capital and the state."[149]

In an article regarding Brandt, Antonio Serrano said:

> I saw him a few days before his death . . . upright as he'd always been throughout his life, a practicing vegetarian and naturist. Jailed by general Gómez, he went into exile and came to live in Spain, in Barcelona coming into contact with the naturist group Generación Consciente, which was encouraged by anarchist groups, for whose journal he wrote while writing books and traveling throughout Europe, leaving behind friends with whom he maintained copious correspondence, including George Bernard Shaw [and] Leo Tolstoy, Elmer Lee, Benedit Lust, and the writer Evalenko who translated [Brandt] into Russian. Angel Cappeletti in his masterful book *Anarchism in Latin America* [notes that] he worked on *Estudios, Tiempos Nuevos* and other organs of the Spanish libertarian press."[150]

Brandt represented for his countrymen a luminous break, in both writing and practice, with belligerent, war-like symbols in a country attached to such symbols. The beneficiary of a privileged education, he lived his life in accord with his ideals, practicing naturism and vegetarianism until the last moments of his life. He was a pacifist of total conviction and an anti-militarist, modest and self-abnegating like the disciples of Tolstoy. He was a defender of pantheism and a promoter of anarchism as a way of life. His existence has been little studied and his theoretical contributions relegated to the closet of proscribed texts. An [obituary] note in *El Universal* remembered him as "living in sacrifice, humility, and poverty."

Later in the year Brandt died, to celebrate May Day, the CNT in Venezuela put out the magazine *Volveremos* (We Will Return). In this special edition there were pieces by M. Lara, José Consuegra, Juan C. Claverol, Víctor Alba, Juan Campá, Domingo Torres, Antonio Ortiz, and Diego Abad de Santillan. That group held a large dinner on the tenth of May at the Casa España to raise funds for the CNT.

That same year the FIJL in Caracas published the book *La Internacional Obrera* (The Workers International), by Víctor García, in which the author rescued from oblivion material on antiauthoritarian activity within the First International.

Other actions weren't so pacific. In that era the guerrilla struggle continued both in the countryside and in the city, with the Unidades Tácticas de Combate (Tactical Combat Units) acting as urban guerrilla cells with a strong presence in the Universidad Central de Venezuela. They committed kidnappings, armed assaults, and hostage-taking.

Because of all this, on November 11, 1964 Salom Mesa, then an AD deputy in the National Congress representing the state of Barinas, took to the floor of the chamber to praise a speech by Carlos Andrés Pérez as politically "lofty," and to attack fellow deputy José Herrera Oropeza of the Vanguardia Popular Nacionalista, which was near to the FALN, calling the FALN "a great monster."

In another speech, transcribed under the title la "Universidad esta siendo utilizada como Centro de Conspiración Extremista" (The University is being used as a Center of Extremist Conspiracy), Salom Mesa attacked Herrera Oropeza again, calling him a "murder weapon" and "chicken[shit] politician."[151] He also presented documents that detailed the activities of the PCV and MIR in the UCV, and worse, denounced to the authorities the guerrillas by their full names.

During these years, the press had a field day displaying its ignorance of the meaning of the word "anarchy." [Translator's note: Such gaudy ignorance is still regularly displayed in the American corporate press and in the online writings of authoritarian leftists, liberals, and conservatives.] Here are the titles of a few of the articles that appeared at the time in Venezuelan papers: "el anarco-putschimo del PCV" (Carlos A. D'Ascoli, *La República* 22-6-1962); "la anarquía del Congo" (Juan Liscano. Balance, *El Nacional* 31-12-1960); "Fidel, con Raúl y el 'Ché,' son incapaces de gobernar a Cuba. Para salvarla de la anarquía y la ruina a que la llevaron, la han entregado a la Unión Soviética

(Luís de Zulueta." *El Universal* 3-1-1961). But the grossest of all these pieces appeared in the daily paper *El Nacional*, which was notorious for its pejorative use of the word "anarchy." The Spanish anarchists denounced this in the pages of *Ruta*, with Víctor García calling the paper the "one-word press."

After several informal meetings, on April 19, 1964 a meeting of primarily Spanish- and Argentine-exile anarchists from around the country formalized the Grupo de Amigos de la AIT, which would later become the Federación Obrera Regional Venezolana, which would publish the bulletin *AIT*, which would appear quarterly until February 1978. The editors included Juan Verde, E. Duran, Vicente Sierra, T. Uzqueda, and Aurelio Lorente. At the start they printed a thousand eight-page copies, but in 1970 they began publishing two thousand 12-page copies. It was a free publication supported by its readers and sympathizers, was distributed to unions in Venezuela by the Casa Sindical de Paraíso (Caracas), and was intended as an outreach tool for the rest of Latin America. It never tried to achieve general circulation in Venezuela nor to be sold on newsstands. [In the '70s it faded away], with at the end Juan Verde being the only member of the editorial staff.

In 1966, Víctor García moved to France with his family, leaving behind the editorship of *Ruta*. By the time of his departure, *Ruta* had published 46 issues in a totally independent manner. It would continue to appear under different editorship until October 1967.

Also in 1966, the FIJL, published in Caracas the previously mentioned book *El Asalto al Santa Maria*, by Francisco Rico and *A la polémica Determinismo y Voluntarismo* (On the Polemic between Determinism and Free Will), written by Benjamin Cano Ruiz and José Peirats, and with a prologue by Víctor García.

In October of that year the anarchist Luís Andrés Ede, a member of the CNT in Exile, and five other members of the group Primero de Mayo were arrested in Spain while planning armed actions. The FIJL agitated in their favor at the Estadio Universitario (University Stadium) in Caracas. At about the same time the [arts and] culture magazine *Bohemia* published an article titled "Los Anarquistas de 1910, una estela de sangre y muerte" (The Anarchists of 1910, a trail of blood and death), in which it equated the actions of all anarchists with those of the Bonnot terrorist gang in France. The FIJL refuted this all-too-familiar calumny in the pages of *Ruta*.

The following year, on November 12, 1967, the Grupo Primero de Mayo, this time under the name Movimiento de Solidaridad Revolucionaria Internacional, claimed responsibility for setting off a bomb at the Venezuelan embassy in Rome, part of a series of such actions in different countries against "yankee imperialism." The MSRI said the bombing was in solidarity with the guerrilla groups operating inside Venezuela.

In parallel with these quixotic actions taking place in Europe, there was a parting of ways between the AD and the MIR, and the creation of a new party, the Movimiento Electoral del Pueblo (MEP). The reasons for said separation were internal disputes over power and disagreements between the president of the AD, Luís Beltrán Prieto Figueroa, and the presidential candidate, Gonzalo Barrios.

The new party, the MEP, defined itself as revolutionary, nationalist, and a proponent of democratic socialism. Salom Mesa left the AD to join the MEP, and became the secretary general of the sectional executive committee of Caracas. Regarding Mesa's participation in the MEP, UCV professor and ex-MEP member Nelson Méndez said:

> I was a member of that party for several years, and even though there was a curious tolerance toward libertarian ideas in that ambient, there was never a recognizable anarchist group despite Mesa's youthful sympathies being well known and there being a young [MEP] leader from La Vega (Paco Plata) who considered himself an anarchist.[152]

Attorney Humberto Decarli comments:

> Salom Mesa Espinoza, who was a great fighter against the Pérez-Jiménez dictatorship, Paco Murillo Font, who became the national youth secretary, and Luis Potellá, all called themselves anarchists in this political organization. That was strange, above all for an electoral movement and whose leader, Luis Beltrán Prieto Figueroa, bragged about being anti-communist.[153]

The split in the AD ended the presidency of Raúl Leoni and his "wide base" government. During his administration, the process of the [economic] extraction model deepened, which produced great benefits over the short term, as the Leoni government encouraged both foreign and domestic investment. The production of petroleum in the country reach 3.6 million barrels per day at a price that never passed $1.35 (US—just over $10 today) per barrel. The growth of the petroleum sector in this period was 2.2% annually, and the growth in the nonpetroleum sector averaged 6.5%.

During Leoni's time in office the National Congress approved a new Ley de Impuesto Sobre la Renta (income tax) that increased the monies received by the Venezuelan state to 70% of the income of petroleum companies, and also demanded from these companies the repayment of taxes they had evaded in the years from 1951 to 1965.

As well, the privately owned steel company, the first steel company in the nation, Corporación Venezolana de Guayana Siderúrgica del Orinoco appeared, as did the state-owned CVG Aluminio del Caroní, S.A, the first aluminum company in the country. Iron production also increased, which became Venezuela's second most important export.

Parallel with this, during Leoni's administration Venezuela and its neighbors created a tariff union on exports, sticking together in the Comunidad Andina de Naciones and the Alianza Latinoamericana de Libre Comercio, which began an [economic] integration process in the region.

The government of Leoni also opened the way for the "Gran Venezuela" (Great Venezuela) boom, which began to buzz in the ears of of the foreign investors in a society that had begun to live out the spectacle of conspicuous consumption.

University Reform and Turmoil in "Gran Venezuela"

In 1968, there were new presidential elections in which Rafael Caldera emerged victorious with 29% of the vote, beating Gonzalo Barrios of the AD, Miguel Ángel Burelli Rivas of the URD, and Luís Beltrán Prieto Figueroa of the MEP. During Caldera's term the process of "pacification" began in the country. Many guerrillas were tired and had become convinced that armed struggle wasn't right way to achieve their objectives, and had decided to come down from the mountains and out of clandestinity to enter into political life under the rules of participation imposed by their adversaries.

The military defeat experienced by the insurgents was the product of political errors, betrayals, and false promises made by their leaders, but above all was because of the unpardonable error of placing the military struggle as the leading edge of the people the guerrillas said they represented. It was primarily a movement of students, with weak support among workers and campesinos. The guerrillas' defeat marked the end of a path to liberation that fit neither the sentiments nor actions of the great majority of Venezuelans.

As well, the invasion of Soviet troops into Czechoslovakia [to oust the reformist Dubcek regime] was the straw that broke the ideological camel's back. It led to several schisms within the PCV, giving rise to the Movimiento al Socialismo (MAS—ideologically similar to the pragmatic socialism of Salvador Allende in Chile) and the self-defined "movement of movements" Causa Radical (Causa R). Even before these splits, a grouping of militants headed by Douglas Bravo formed the marxist-leninist Partido de la Revolución Venezolana-Ruptura(PRV).

For its part the MIR shed factions that would later become the Bandera Roja party—which in turn would split again into the BR-Marxista Leninista and the maoist BR-Frente Américo Silva—and the marxist-leninist-maoist Organización de Revolucionarios (OR).

The defeat of the guerrilla insurgency [and the splits in the marxist parties]—even though the PRV, OR, and Bandera Roja continued with insurgent activities until the end of the '70s, and still other splinter groups into the 1980s—strengthened both the AD and COPEI parties.

With the failure of the armed struggle, two of the principal MIR figures, Domingo Alberto Rangel and Simón Sáez Mérida, began a process of teaching and radicalization within the cloistered atmosphere of the universities; the first of these promoted [electoral] abstentionism as a mechanism of social disobedience, and the second through the written word, via the pages of the magazine *Al Margen* (To the Margin or To the Edge) which he edited in the city of Caracas.

Even though in Venezuela in 1968 the concept of social transformation had taken a backward step, the ideas were being rejuvenated in the streets of Paris where the nonrevolutionary statist and dogmatic concepts that had ruled the continent since World War II were being rejected. The awakening of radical youths attuned to the counterculture, spontaneity, direct action, federation, sexual liberation, and above all affinity with anti-colonialist Third-World politics all unfolded in the events of May 1968 in Paris.

This outburst had echoes all over the world, in the United States, West Germany, Mexico DF, Italy, and Czechoslovakia. There was a skeptical attitude toward Soviet "socialism," the "free market," and the ruling social democracies. This represented a generational change, a rejuvenation, and a rebirth of anarchism, which had kept a low profile since the Second World War.

In this atmosphere, questioning began within the faculty of the UCV about what role university students should play, in the context of Venezuela [as a whole] and their lives after receiving their degrees.

For professor Nelson Méndez, the situation had three overlapping outcomes: 1) The objective situation (the boom in graduates, of instructors, and administrators); 2) A process of internal "modernization," the slow bureaucratization of the political parties (PCV, COPEI, AD) within the universities; and 3) The failure of the armed experiment of the marxist groups.

[Analysis was soon followed by action.] The University Renovation Movement reached its high point between March and October 1969, with occupations of facilities, demonstrations, and street clashes with police forces. All of this was tied to criticism of the political parties, the curricular structure, and testing; all this with massive participation of students, professors, and university employees. COPEI categorized this unrest as an "anarchist conspiracy" and the PCV called it "a Bakuninist ideological deviation that is so attached to the juvenile radicalism of the petit bourgeoisie."[154]

In accord with the rebellious and anti-institutional flavor of the process, groups flourished linked to direct action and bottom-up organization, such as the Comité Coordinador de la Renovación in Engineering, the Comité Renovador de Acción Estudiantil in Sociology, and their equivalents in other disciplines; they were formed by independent leftists and autonomous militants radicalized by the schisms in the traditional political parties (MEP, AD, PCV, COPEI) who formed groups such as Poder Joven (Youth Power) which some participants, such as Alonso Moleiro and Ivan Feo, considered "anarchist."

Regarding the presence of anarchist militants in the Renovación Universitaria, leftist activist Alexis Miguel Romero Salazar says that there was only one "organization, if you could call it that, formed by the compañeros, called itself 'Grupo Anárquico,' which was . . . very small."[155]

Years later, the anarchist writer and sociologist Rafael Uzcátegui would recognize the influence of Poder Joven in the counterculture in Barquisimeto:

> The first countercultural publications I noticed for our incipient history were mimeographed pamphlets under the name Poder Joven, a movement centered in Caracas at the end of the '70s influenced by the hippie movement in San Francisco. The "Turn on!" with which they ended their manifestos signified, perhaps, the first response to the system from a revolutionary perspective that wasn't manipulated by the political parties nor by traditional leftist groups.[156]

In reference to how Poder Joven functioned, the economist Rafael de la Cruz, in his book, *Venezuela en busca de un nuevo pacto social* (Venezuela in search of a new social pact) says this:

> Poder Joven is the most inaccessible but perhaps the most interesting student movement. Despite there being some groups that tried to coordinate common actions, and so achieve a character as an organization with regional and national reach, the spirit of spontaneity that presides in Poder Joven works against the success of any reifying organizational attempts. The ideas that inspired May 1968 [in Paris] along with the very Latin American ideal of the "new man" preached by Che Guevara were its bases of action until about 1973. Whoever within the Poder Joven "wave" wanted to write something on the wall and sign it with the initials of the movement became the mouthpiece of the same. And this is what makes Poder Joven a point of condensation of the new

responses to the cultural vacuum. With no central leadership declaring policies, this movement managed to coherently express the refusal of that which exists."[157]

The process of Renovación Universitaria extended to other universities in the interior of the country, but the insubordination had an abrupt end when Rafael Caldera executed "Operation Kangaroo" in which the army entered and shut down the UCV on October 25, 1969. The writer Eduardo Casanova-said that "it's evident that this was done to put the brakes on the uncontrollable and libertarian student movement."[158]

This expression of rebellion [at UCV] had a fatal flaw as a focus of social transformation: its urban, downtown location. [After the army takeover] it remained closed for almost two years. Its facilities and residence halls taken over by the army, and its green spaces trod by authoritarian boots. Operation Kangaroo achieved its objective of stopping youthful dissidence and dispersing youthful movements that challenged [the status quo].

At the same time all this was happening at the UCV, exiled Spanish anarchists in Venezuela continued to support the Cuban anarchists who had been forced into exile. In *Cuban Anarchism: The History of a Movement*, Frank Fernández mentions several such Spanish exiles who lent support, including Agustín Souchy, Gaston Leval, Juan Campá, Ricardo Mestre, and Fidel Miró.

As regards informational activities, in 1969 Vicente Sierra opened a small publishing house in Caracas called Tierra y Libertad, which published several pamphlets on anarchism as well as the massive three-volume tome *Enciclopedia Anarquista*.

For his part Solom Mesa had been elected as an MEP deputy to the National Congress representing the Distrito Federal (Caracas), and had turned to writing, with Imprenta Nueva in Caracas publishing his book *El gallo de Machillanda* (The rooster of Machillanda), which even though fiction contained innumerable references to anarchists including Élisée Reclus ("The man is nature made conscious of itself"), August Spies ("The price of the truth is death. Dry your tears those who suffer! Take heart, slave! Rise up!"), and several others. One of the characters in the book even makes a speech about anarchism.

In 1970, Monte Ávila, the largest publishing house in Venezuela, located in Caracas, published *Anarquismo Ayer y Hoy* (Anarchism Yesterday and Today), by the Chilean-French sociologist Louis Mercier Vega. And in the same year Libreria ABC (ABC Bookstore) opened its doors in Caracas. Its backers were in large measure members of the CNT, and its manager was the militant anarchist and Spanish Civil War veteran Antonio Serrano. Even though it was a general-interest bookstore, it served as a meeting place for anarchists and it distributed antiauthoritarian literature. It remained open until 1978 when fire destroyed the premises.

In May 1970, using his own money, Víctor García, in Caracas, started publishing *Ruta* again. This time, rather than identifying itself as the organ of the FIJL, it billed itself as anarchist. The issues were bound in book form, averaged 30 pages, and had multi-color covers. It had both cultural and informative value, and 40 issues appeared, the last in March 1980, when financial problems, especially the cost of printing, drove it under. The Spanish writer Carlos Díaz says that rising costs forced García and his family to devote an ever-increasing portion of their income to the magazine, despite all of the labor necessary to producing *Ruta* being voluntary. [In a scene familiar to anyone who's worked on a low-budget anarchist magazine, he describes part of the production process]: "Compañeros walked for kilometers around a huge table collating the magazine" [gathering up the sheets in order from piles of individual pages, placing the collated pages in a stack, and then repeating the process over and over].

Ruta was a milestone in its time for being a high quality publication, but it's necessary to understand that the magazine wasn't written for the Venezuelan public; it didn't deal with local matters and focused on anarchist efforts against Franco [and fascism]. Antonio Serrano said that it dealt not only with the anti-Franco struggle, but also with "the internal technical problems of what anarchists within the movement should do." He also notes that, "In its second epoch (1970–1980), the magazine turned into a monograph, with every issue dedicated to a single matter, with the entire issue written by a single writer."[159]

[In a curious echo of the Mexican anarchist Ricardo Flores Magón's Partido Liberal Mexicano], during that period Oswaldo Alcalá decided to found the Partido Ácrata de Venezuela (Venezuelan Anarchist Party) in an attempt to bring together all of the anarchist tendencies in the country. He even registered the party with the National Election Council. But as one might expect, his initiative never bore fruit due to the anti-bureaucratic nature of anarchism.

Another relevant event occurred during the first third of the decade of the 1970s: the arrival in the country of the French anarchist anthropologist Pierre Clastres (1934–1977), who along with French anthropologist Jacques Lizot lived for a brief time in a Yanomami village. Clastres achieved worldwide notoriety shortly thereafter for his book *La Sociedad contra el Estado* (Society Against the State) which was based on his time with the Yanomami and the Anché people in Paraguay. He set forth an evolutionary critique of Western society, rejecting the notion that the state was the foundation of human society, setting as a contrary example primitive societies that rejected a power structure separate from the core of society, societies "without the state, without [religious] faith, without law, without a king," in which power was shared among the people living together in harmony and without hierarchicalization and institutionalization of human dynamics, in which people were always struggling against the prestige of their leaders being converted into power over the people.

* * *

The government of Caldera ended up facing a radical left that was uncoordinated, ineffective, and boxed in by the [petroleum] economic bonanza. Among other things, the government raised taxes on the energy companies, began construction of the El Tablazo petrochemical complex, and built the Poliedro sports arena, Universidad Simón Bolívar, and the Hospital del Seguro Social Miguel Pérez Carreño in Caracas.

In 1973, there was another presidential election, which Carlos Andrés Pérez of the AD won with 48.70% of the vote, besting Lorenzo Fernández of the COPEI and Jesús Paz Galárraga of the MEP. During his time in office Andrés Pérez managed to nationalize part of the petroleum industry and deliver to the country for a short time a handful of benefits that created rising expectations among the people. This "petroleum bonanza" occurred within the framework of a world energy crisis, which created skyrocketing oil prices, and brought to the country enormous amounts of money; it was used to prop up the client system endemic to representative democracies, which unfolded in the most corrupt bureaucracy the country had ever known up to that time.

But Andrés Pérez did not have universal backing within the AD. Fancisco Olivo was among those opposing him. Salom Mesa outlines the reasons for the opposition:

> Inside the AD, Olivo opposed the candidacy of Andrés Pérez and history shows why. . . Olivo proved that Carlos Andrés Pérez—already the AD candidate— had accepted large amounts of money for his campaign from labor leaders within the AD that had come from shameful sources.
>
> More, he announced that he would ask for an investigation of the origin of the income of some party members who were also members of the CTV; these in

turn threatened to ask the AD for an exhaustive report on what it had done with the money received from the United States for the election campaign."[160]

Olivo himself wrote that "Carlos Andrés Pérez in his thirst for power was capable of anything."[161]

* * *

This period of the petroleum bonanza known as La Gran Venezuela was the time when Argentine anarchist militants fleeing the military dictatorship in that country began arriving in Venezuela. Among them were professors Ángel Cappelletti (1927–1995) and Alfredo Vallota.

Cappelletti was an outstanding anarchist thinker and theoretician. He held a PhD from the Universidad Nacional de Buenos Aires and gave classes in history, philosophy, logic, sociology, Latin, Greek, and the history of political ideas. He held posts at the universities in Cuyo and Litoral in Argentina, the Universidad de Montevideo in Uruguay, and Universidad Simón Bolívar and Universidad de Los Andes en Venezuela. He published more than 70 books, many of them relating to anarchism.

He arrived in Venezuela in 1968, but didn't begin giving classes until1972 when he began teaching at the Universidad Simón Bolívar.

The artist José Planas says that Cappelletti was "a corpulent, solid man like a quarry worker, with a dark face, eyes half-open, incisive and intelligent looking, topped by a strong head that hid a powerfully intellectual brain, in sum a head worthy of being chiseled by Rodin."[162]

* * *

By this time the activities of the CNT in Venezuela were in serious decline. The local organization remained in the hands of the "collaborationists" and bit by bit they were ceasing to do anything. They arrived at such a state of inactivity that no one even answered the mail sent from the CNT headquarters in Toulouse to the Venezuela section. With the passing of the years and the deaths of many of its members, the Venezuelan CNT vanished.

On December 21, 1974, near to the Plaza Venezuela, Francisco Olivo was felled by a heart attack. His sudden death left the CTV without its chief executive.

Regarding his death, his daughter Libertad Olivo wrote:

All that was left was to prepare the physical goodbye to our father, and we didn't have to wait long for the calls to start coming; they wanted to know where [his body] would be taken first: the Congress, the [AD] party, or the CTV. We had to explain that his desire all his life for when died was to be buried as quickly as possible, in the most simple manner and without being taken anywhere that wasn't a cemetery. He didn't want either flowers or priests, and with the first he'd always wanted to enjoy them in life, and with the second the presence of clerics would have been in contradiction to his beliefs.[163]

Olivo's death took Salom Mesa by surprise; he commented:

He died disgusted by the turn his party had taken in recent years, and for the most part was disillusioned with his fellow labor leaders. These, through their miserable morals, had accelerated the end of his precious life.[164]

Olivo was a unique man both in his ideas and in the context in which he worked. Even though a leading member of Acción Democrática, he never abandoned his interest in anarchist ideas and did what he could to propagate them.

His daughter Libertad Olivo said this of him:

While we were growing up, it wasn't difficult to understand the pride papa had in being working class. . . . perhaps this is the reason he had such courage. His struggles to obtain the betterment of the conditions of life for the masses of workers was a constant throughout his life, and also the acceptance of the necessity of a political movement to attain the objectives of social and economic transformation of society. He had to choose between solitary struggle or participating in a political party that appeared to have sufficient principles for the struggle to improve the conditions of work and life for Venezuelan workers.[165]

The Kidnapping of a "CIA Agent"

On February 27, 1976, William Frank Niehous, vice-president of the American bottling company Owens-Illinois, was kidnapped and accused of being a CIA agent by the self-styled Grupos de Comando Revolucionarios (GCR), a marxist-leninist group with little experience in armed struggle that had split from the PCV.

There was a massive repressive turn in the country after the kidnapping. Liga Socialista (Socialist League) leader Jorge Rodríguez was tortured and murdered by agents of the intelligence agency DISIP, and League members Aquino Carpio, and Wilfredo Silva were also killed. The government unleashed ferocious repression against revolutionary factions, jailing among others Carlos Lanz Rodríguez, David Nieves, Fortunato Herrera, and Salom Mesa Espinoza, using the kidnapping as an excuse to strip parliamentary immunity from Herrera and Mesa who were deputies in the National Congress.

The new misadventures of Salom Mesa commenced on July 28, 1976 when he gave a speech in the National Congress on the death of Liga Socialist leader Jorge Rodríguez. The national executive censured the speech and prohibited its distribution. On the 3rd of August, Mesa was seized and held for 23 days in the Cuartel San Carlos by order of the Tribunal Tercero Militar de Caracas, in violation of the Constitution.

In August 25, the Politico-Administrative Division of the Supreme Court, by a 3–2 vote asked that Mesa be stripped of his parliamentary immunity. On the 26th, he was released to house arrest for a single day, but the Delegate Commission of the National Congress by a vote of 12-11 stripped him of his immunity and he was jailed again on the following day.

On December 15, charges were read against him before the Permanent Council of War, accusing him of cooperating with the kidnappers by acting as mediator between them and the government; the military attorney asked for a sentence of 35 years. From that day until February 22, 1979, he was jailed at the Cuartel San Carlos.

Pablo Hernández Parra, second in the political-military command of the group Bandera-Roja at the time, later speculated that Salom Mesa had an "interest in some lands in Guaribe and wanted to negotiate with Owens to produce glass. I believe that he had an economic interest."[166]

The kidnapping of the American executive was one part of a series of kidnappings. Not only was the GCR responsible, but also the Liga Socialista and its armed wing, the OR, to which Salom Mesa's two children belonged, and other groups such as Bandera Roja and its schismatic offspring, BR-Frente Américo Silva and BR-Marxista Leninista.

Regarding Salom Mesa's two offspring, and Salom Mesa's giving them help, Hernández Parra said: "I don't know if his son was involved [in the kidnapping] . . . but Norelkys, his daughter, was the wife of Orlando "cabezón" [big head] Yajure, the leader of the OR."[167]

Salom Mesa was finally released on February 22, 1979 when the military court bowed to the decision of the people of the Federal District. His release was the product of an extensive campaign of solidarity and of the elections at the end of 1978, when the people of Caracas voted in favor of his release.

During his stay in prison, Salom Mesa wrote two books, the autobiographical *Por un caballo y una mujer* (For a horse and a woman) and *Tres vidas*. The first was a quite good literary journey through the life of a self-contradictory and passionate man of action. The second was a scant, rather unimaginative work of fiction.

Regarding the detention of Salom Mesa, there have been various hypotheses and suppositions, none of them proven. [In contrast to the conjectures of Hernández Parra,] Humberto Decarli, a part of [Salom Mesa's] legal team who represented leftist activists in the epoch, said:

> The kidnapping of Niehous was surrounded by a series of mysteries that have never been resolved. Salom Mesa was imprisoned because of an old quarrel with Carlos Andrés Pérez who never forgave him for pointing a revolver at his chest during a meeting of the MEP celebrating a triumph in union elections which had been disrupted by DIGEPOL (Direccion General de Polcía). Carlos Andrés had to shamefully back down, and he never forgave Mesa for it. Mesa's only involvement in the matter was trying to intervene in good faith as a negotiator; meanwhile (fellow deputy) Fortunato Herrera intervened in the case in order to make some money.

Nelson Méndez said, "Almost everyone concluded that it was payback by Carlos Andrés Pérez."

Salom Mesa himself said, facing the Council of Permanent War: "I am a prisoner through the will of the president Carlos Andrés Pérez. I'm a victim of his immense cowardice."

The kidnapping of Niehous came to an end on June 29, 1979 with his rescue at a cattle ranch in Guyana, the rescue supposedly financed by an American millionaire.

While all this was going on, the Spanish and South American anarchists in Venezuela devoted themselves to the elaboration and spreading of ideas. In 1976, Editorial Editexto de Caracas published the book *A la memoria de Paulino Díez, un anarcosindicalista de acción*, with a prologue by Víctor García. Meanwhile, Angel Cappelletti issued a series of books about anarchism, among which were *Francisco Ferrer y la Pedagogía Libertaria*, *La Teoría de la Propiedad en Proudhon y otros momentos del pensamiento Anarquista*, and *Etapas del Pensamiento Socialista* (Stages of Socialist Thought). The first two of these were published by Editores Mexicanos Unidos in Mexico City, and the third by Ediciones la Piqueta in Spain.

The economic bonanza begins to break down

The legacy of the Niehous kidnapping, combined with the success of the "Democracy and Energy" policy of Andrés Pérez, produced a negative outcome for the local insurgents and for all radical leftist currents in the region.

The term of Carlos Andrés Pérez would be known in the country's history as the "Venezuela saudita" (Venezuelan Saudi Period) due to the surpluses brought about by nationalization of the petroleum and mining industries. Pérez undertook an interventionist politico-economic policy with the small and medium-sized companies that benefited the huge economic conglomerates such as Grupo Cisneros and big businessmen such as Siro Febres Cordero, Edgard Espejo, Pedro Tinoco, Diego Arria, Carmelo Lauría, Gumersindo Rodríguez, and others who would become Venezuela's economic elite.

The elevated petroleum income allowed Andrés Pérez to pursue populist economic policies such as a law of Full Employment and a law prohibiting unjustified firings, as well as scholarship programs. He also reestablished diplomatic relations with countries in the socialist camp such as Cuba, Romania, China, and the USSR, and provided aid to the Frente Sandinista de Liberación Nacional in Nicaragua, which was fighting the Somoza dictatorship. All of this earned him sympathy among many Venezuelan leftists.

Nonetheless, the drunken spending spree produced by petroleum nationalization generated cases of corruption such as the "Caso Sierra Nevada" and the squandering of money such as that of presenting a ship to the [landlocked] Republic of Bolivia; all this contributed to the slow degeneration of Venezuelan social democracy.

* * *

The 1970s were of vital importance in the theoretical development of Iberian anarchism in exile. From Caracas and through the FIJL press, to José Leiva and Víctor García, anarchists undertook the task of writing antiauthoritarian books and texts. In 1970 Leiva and García co-authored the book *El Anarcosindicalismo en España, Comunistas y anarquistas frente a frente* and in 1972 *Para una monografía de escritores anarquistas*. And in 1974 they co-edited *Anselmo Lorenzo. Prolegómenos de la CNT* (Anselmo Lorenzo: Prologue to the CNT).

Meanwhile Víctor García wrote *El protoanarquismo* and *Las Utopías de la Arcadia a 1984*, both in 1971; *El anarcosindicalismo, su origen, su estrategia*

(1972); *Las Utopías, inmersión en el pesimismo y Bakunin, hoy* (The Utopias, immersion in pessimism and Bakunin today) (1973); *Kropotkin, su impacto en el anarquismo* and *Kropotkin, la sociedad fue primero* (1974); *Kotogu, Osugi y Yamaga, tres anarquistas japoneses* (1975); *Centenario de Barret* (co-authored with Ángel Cappelletti) (1976); and finally *Godwin y Proudhon* (1977).

These theoretical undertakings by the CNT veterans didn't have great impact on the Venezuelan people who had achieved middle class status, living a vertiginous life filled with consumerism, waste, and frivolity. The class-based teachings of the Spanish anarchists were seen by the rest of the population as naive paleontological undertakings by old rebels who refused to accept the inevitable course of history..

The anarchists would continue to enjoy for a time the benevolence of the AD, exempting them from persecution for their ideology, but the new generation in the AD would be less favorably inclined [in part because of not sharing the hardships and oppression with the anarchists during the struggle against the Pérez Jiménez dictatorship].

Until this time the Spanish exiles kept the flame of anarchism alive in the region. Besides those already mentioned, it's necessary to pay tribute to all of the antiauthoritarians who gave life to libertarian thought in these lands. Many of the most notable are listed in the footnote below.*

We also can't forget that it was the Spanish anarchists who blazed the path for a new generation of young people sowing the seeds of antiauthoritarianism in the lands of the Caribbean.

But soon the modernist impulse reflected in Venezuela as a country in the vanguard of the region would have an abrupt and ominous ending which the citizenry would be unable to forget.

---

* Emilio Tesoro, Lucia Albanell Codina, Ricardo Albero, Candido Armesto, Fabián Barros Cela, Amalio Canella, Salvador Canovas Cervantes, German Carod Pastor, Gabriel Crespo Albacete, Jesús Maella, Marcelo Cros Camarillo, Lorenzo Campuzano, Jose Silvestre Granell, Diego García Almagro, Flora García Armesto, Carmen Hernández, Pedro Bargallo Cerveró, Roberto Gonzáles, Gloria Gonzáles de Herrera, Helena Guijarro, Sirio del Solar, Antonio Barea, José Luís Herrero, Fermín Lacarra Pastor, José Lara Sánchez, Ramón López, Ricardo Lozano Camara, Ángel Martínez Jerez, Vicente Leiva, Antonio Parra, José Pérez Martínez El Negus, Ángel Jesús Rodríguez Diez, José Ovidio Rodríguez González, Anastasio Segundo Calzacorta, Sirio del Solar Romero, Pablo Vila Dinares, José María Villegas Izquierdo, and Francisco Verdiell.

CHAPTER 5

The Seditious Resurgence of Anarchism

The 1980s were a propitious time for a renewal of anarchist activity in Venezuela. The marxist-leninist parties and factions were in crisis for a number of reasons: the failure of the guerrilla strategy in the previous decade, splits, fights for position among the leadership, opportunism, lack of power in the political system, etc. With the fall of the USSR and the Eastern bloc, the crisis of the M-L parties would deepen further.

This led to the re-examination of anarchism by activists seeking a different path: anarchist books and periodicals found new readers. As well, by different routes, anarchist-inspired initiatives were being discussed and put into action in unions, neighborhood and student organizations, and in the environmental and feminist movements. In general terms, the discrediting and exhaustion of the political parties' formulas and the corrupt nature of the bourgeois democracy of the era made the anarchist concepts of self-management and direct action more and more attractive to growing numbers of people.

On May 16, 1981, in the Extraordinary National Assembly of the MEP, Salom Mesa Espinoza was elected as its presidential nominee, representing the MEP in the open primary elections. Over the next year, from July 23, 1981 to August 21, 1982, he recorded 327 short programs that were transmitted over Radio Rumbos in the primary campaign. The great majority of these messages, in contradiction to their political-party origin, dealt with anarchist principles such as self-management.

Also in 1982, within the national army, a small group arose calling itself the Ejército Bolivariano Revolucionario (EBR-200—Bolivarian Revolutionary Army, later MBR-200, Movimiento Bolivariano Revolucionario), which set the year 2000 as the date it would take power. The "200" made reference to the 200th anniversary of Simón Bolivar's birth, which would take place on July 24, 1983. EBR-200 was a classic embryonic conspiracy aiming at the seizure of power.

Among its founders were Hugo Chávez Frías, Francisco Arias Cárdenas, Felipe Acosta Carlés, and Jesús Urdaneta Hernández. In another sector of the army, William Izarra was organizing the group Revolución 83, which would later change its name to Asociación Revolucionaria de Militares Activos (AR-MA—"weapon" in Spanish) and had ties with dissident political groups such as the PRV (Adán Chávez, brother of Hugo, was an active member), La Causa R, the MEP, and Bandera Roja, in preparation for a civic-military uprising that, at least in theory, would put an end to the "partyocracy of AD-COPEI").

On January 23, 1982 there was a celebration commemorating the 24th anniversary of the overthrow of the Pérez Jiménez dictatorship and that paid homage to the Venezuelan left. Salom Mesa gave a speech, including the following:

> We've proved that in politics there are as many merchants as there are in commerce. . . . [P]ublic prestige is a tool with the public's faith being held by those who probably don't don't deserve it. One after another's [supposed] values come crashing down before us . . . What clown[s] disguised as social activists! And here we touch on the sad truth. What has cost us blood to construct is now at the service of our enemies, the enemies of the workers. . . . [T]o be or not to be. To choose between the advantages of power, that so fascinate the traffickers in it, or to send that to the devil for not [working] for the people. . . . Into the breech! . . . Down with unfounded symbols and beliefs, on with the struggle as men, toward the order of justice and peace that we embraced as youths.[168]

This [speech] clearly broke with the old order, and with it perhaps commenced Mesa Espinoza's most anarchist stage. From there forward, he would break definitively with conventional politics to blaze paths encompassing antiauthoritarian ideas, solidifying his affinity with the ideas he had embraced during his youth, and helping with the coordination of new antiauthoritarian groups bursting upon the public stage.

At this time, as always, anarchism continued to be misrepresented in the corporate press. On July 18, 1982, the Venezuelan writer Pedro Berroeta, in his column "Vuelta de hoja" (Turn of the page) in the daily paper *El Nacional*, accused anarchism of being both at fault and the genesis of the reigning disorder and chaos in Caracas. Antonio Serrano wrote a reply titled "Anarchy is another thing, Señor Berroeta" that was [surprisingly] published in the same paper.

In the same year, in the Cantaura region in Anzoátegui state, there was a clash between the Frente Américo Silva and a military force composed of Air Force, Army, Marine, and DISIP forces. The guerrillas were taken by surprise and the one-sided firefight left 23 of them dead, many shot dead after they were already wounded. This action effectively finished off the few remnants of the guerrilla struggle in the country. It also caused the nation's revolutionary young people to reconsider "armed struggle" as a means of political action.

One example of renewed interest in anarchism was the appearance in the city of Maracaibo in 1983 of the magazine *Papeles Anárquicos* (Anarchic Papers). It was, however, more of a literary and freethinking magazine than an anarchist one. Its editorial group consisted of Bernardo Martín, Alvaro Nistal, Carlo Maglione, and Francesc Xavi. Alvaro Nistal would say in an interview, "The only anarchic thing about it was the way in which, and with the love, it was produced."[169]

As well, Cappelletti wrote the pamphlet *Fundamentos filosóficos del pensamiento de Malatesta* (Philosophic Fundamental's of Malatesta's Thought), published by the Spanish publisher Estudios Valladolid and also wrote the book *Prehistoria del Anarquismo* issued by another Spanish publisher, Queimada.

During the term in office of COPEI's Luís Herrera Campins (1979–1984) there was a crack in the AD-COPEI model of political domination. On February 18, the bolivar was devalued against the dollar, an event dubbed "Black Friday." This caused a rise in price of almost everything [in import-dependent Venezuela] and also caused the end of the local currency being one in which speculators would invest.

For Venezuela, Black Friday was a milestone in the country's economic history. It marked the end of the officially maintained stability of and confidence in the bolivar which had reigned since the century's second decade, with a final fixed exchange rate, before the devaluation, of 4.3 bolivars per dollar. After the devaluation, the steady decline in the value of the bolivar, added to the complications in paying the country's foreign debt, plus the implementation of an exchange-rate control called the Régimen de Cambio Diferencial (RECADI) put an end to the consumerism of the previous years.

The reason for Black Friday was a fall in petroleum prices, which reduced petroleum income from $19.3 billion in 1981 to only $13.5 billion in 1983, a fall of 30%. That produced a flight of capital of almost $8 billion and a corresponding drop in the country's reserves.

Regarding the impact of the devaluation of the bolivar, the writer Margarita López Maya says:

> Since 1979 there has been in Venezuela an inexorable decline in the development model based on petroleum income, expressed in the first place in the

stagnation of economic activity. In 1983, the combination of this stagnation with the setbacks of Herrera Campins' government in refinancing the foreign debt . . . resulted in the government's decision to devalue the bolivar and go to a system of preferential exchange. . . . A headline from that time sums up the feelings of the people: "The party is over.'"

With the devaluation of the bolivar against the dollar, a stage in the history of Venezuelan anarchism closed. With the fall of the bolivar as a reliable currency, the hopes embedded in social democracy began to fade away, and a new generation of activists took to the streets.

During this era, a group of libertarian organizations organized a series of talks and workshops in the UCV School of Philosophy to discuss anarchist ideas and anarchist history and fundamental beliefs. These conference were held on Saturday mornings, and Angel Cappelletti, Germinal Gracia, Pablo Benaige, and Ruperto Arocha, among others, participated.

An organization grew out of these workshops, the Colectivo de Autogestión Libertaria (CAL—Libertarian Self-management Collective), composed mostly of immigrants from Spain, Argentina, Uruguay, and Chile. Among them, we should mention Angel Cappelletti, Antonio Serrano, Alfredo Vallota, Nelson Méndez, José Luís Soldini, Nicolás and Mauricio Torres, Juan Rodríguez, Paoli, Armando García Miragalla, and autodidact and Spanish Civil War veteran Emilio Tesoro. According to Nelson Méndez, meetings typically had about 40 people in attendance.

This group began publishing a tabloid with a 2-color cover called *El Libertario*, which disappeared after only nine issues. CAL did its best to reach Venezuelan workers with this publication, distributing it for free at the exits of factories in Caracas. CAL also held forums and meetings regarding anarchism and anarcho-syndicalism within unions such as the Confederación General del Trabajo (CGT).

Out of all this grew the Primeras Jornadas de Reflexión sobre la movilización popular (First Reflective Conference on Popular Mobilization) in September 1986. This and many other CAL meetings were held in the CGT meeting hall. CAL also participated in the same year in the Encuentro Nacional de Trabajadores (National Workers Meeting) that was held on the premises of the textile union MANTEX in the city of Valencia, and which was intended to join together a wide movement of class-conscious unions.

CAL also maintained collaborative relations with the Movimiento Nacional Campesino Autogestionario (MONCA—National Movement of Campesino Self-management). With time and because of internal disputes and individual quarrels, CAL put distance between itself and MONCA.

Here it's necessary to mention that the CGT [which was important to CAL] originated on April 24, 1974 as a result of a schism in the social-christian union CODESA. The CGT's principles were based in autonomy, rejection of union ties to political parties, humanism, communitarianism, and class consciousness. Even though it held certain libertarian positions, such as defending self-management (or workers' autonomy), it would be erroneous to classify the CGT as an anarcho-syndicalist union.

The Breech Widens

In 1984, the AD candidate Jaime Lusinchi won the presidential election with a large majority. His government used the slogan "Austerity with Sensibility," and it had the strategy of constructing a new social pact along with reforming the state. To that end, on December 26, 1984 it called the Comisión Presidencial para la Reforma del Estado, whose goals included the democratization of regional governments (universal participation in direct and secret elections, and the creation of the post of mayor [in towns and cities]).

But despite this initial push, the critical economic situation at the beginning of Lusinchi's administration was worsening due to the devaluation policy of his predecessor. The growing disparity between the bolivar and the dollar grew to match the rate of inflation, deepening the dependent, mono-industry [extraction] nature of Venezuela's economy. In the face of this situation, the government decided to refocus its policies, increase wages, control both prices and [the exchange rate] of foreign currencies, all of this to create the illusion of economic stability.

This period was also characterized by both moral scandals and scandals regarding the abuse of power. As one example, the extramarital relations of the president with his private secretary, Blanca Ibáñez, was denounced in the communications media due to her notable influence on presidential decisions.

As regards anarchist media, in this epoch Cappelletti published in Caracas one of his most well known works, *La Ideología Anarquista*, which summed up the most important points in, and arguments about, libertarian classics. A year after this he published *Bakunin y el socialismo libertario*.

In 1985, in an interview with the paper *El Nacional*, the president of the Instituto Autónomo Biblioteca Nacional (National Autonomous Library Institute) said that anarchism is a genetic defect. She said, "Anarchism and authoritarianism, our defects, make themselves present when least expected."[170]

Once again, Antonio Serrano replied, defending libertarianism in the pages of that daily.

* * *

On May 8, 1987, the Masacre de Yumare occurred in a rural zone of Yaracuy where DISIP ambushed a group of young leftist activists called Corriente Histórica-Social (Historical-Social Current) and murdered nine of them. They exhibited their bodies to the press as guerrillas and presented the operation as "a triumph of the anti-guerrilla struggle." However, three survivors of the massacre came forward to give lie to DISIP's account.

This massacre along with the two previous ones, Cantaura and Tazon, helped to create the general perception that the government favored the attacks and that impunity was the order of the day. In response, leftist activists and students began to think about self-defense, to responding to violent government attacks with violence.

Shortly before the Yumare Massacre, on March 13, 1987, Luis Carballo, a student at the Universidad de los Andes, was shot several times by AD lawyer Bernardino Navas Vera, who had ties with the Mérida government and was vicepresident of the Mérida Cattlemen's Association. He'd become upset that, during a graduation celebration, Carballo had urinated in the entry to his garage. The students suspected that because Navas Vera was an influential man, he wouldn't be charged with the murder, and they attacked and burned his house, with the lawyer and his family being rescued by a DISIP squad.

Generalized rioting then broke out throughout the city for five days. The AD headquarters was burned, military storehouses plundered, and the government declared martial law. In the end, more than 20 people were injured and over 500 arrested, classes were suspended, and damage was estimated at 10 million bolivars. Writer Margarita López Maya in her book, *Del Viernes Negro al Referendo Revocatorio* (From Black Friday to the Revocative Referencum) said that "The disturbances in Mérida involved the students just as much as the common people, who had good reason to suspect that justice wouldn't be done, because in this type of crime [the murder] those with powerful influence tended to have impunity."[171]

At the time, students possessed a strong self-identity and the murders and brutality by the government provoked a reaction of students in other areas. The street protests of the students in Mérida were followed by similar protests in Caracas at the Instituto Universitario Pedagógico of the UCV, with car burnings and a raid by the National Guard on the Centros de Enseñanza

(Teaching Centers), with similar events happening at the Universidad de Oriente, and in Maracay, Barquisimeto, and Maracaibo, in which students began using hoods to cover their faces so as to avoid being identified by DISIP and the PTJ (Cuerpo Técnico de Policia Judicial—Technical Body of the Judicial Police, Venezuela's largest police agency), and this became a constant in the continuing demonstrations.

In the same year, 1987, an agrarian conflict broke out between campesinos of Cañizos-Palo Quemao, in Yaracuy state, and the landowners and hacendados of the region regarding the occupation and ownership of lands—a renewal of a conflict dating back centuries. Thugs employed by the landlords destroyed the village of Los Cañizos-Palo Quemao, and as a result the campesinos went to the Agrarian Court and asked for its aid. It restored the legal status of the village and recognized the campesinos' right to remain on the lands [controlled] by the Instituto Agrario Nacional.

However, that Institute didn't give the campesinos the land, but on the contrary persecuted them, jailed them, and destroyed their crops. This conflict was echoed in other parts of the country, and resonated on the campuses where leftist students began to support the campesinos in their struggles.

In the midst of these turbulent times, university professors Nelson Méndez, Alfredo Vallota, and José Luís Soldini regrouped in a new collective that they dubbed Círculo A, and began publishing the magazine Correo A (Anarchist Mail), with its eventual 28 issues having an average printing of 5,000 copies. Its design was simple, with all of the illustrations and layout done by hand by the editorial group. Its contributors included Ángel Cappelletti, Julio Rojas Ávila, and Leonardo Sánchez It was widely distributed in places including Caracas, Valles del Tuy, Maracay, Valencia, Barquisimeto, Mérida, Yaracuy, San Cristóbal, and Barcelona-Puerto la Cruz.

In addition to putting out Correo A, they also published anarchist pamphlets, both classic and contemporary, organized forums and conferences, showed films, took part in many social struggles, established permanent contact with the international anarchist movement, and sent their overseas comrades news of the anarchist undertakings in Venezuela.

The second act of violence in the epoch that shook the country was the killing of fishermen from Amparo, in which the Comando Especial de Contrainsurgencia José Antonio Páez (CEJAP) was responsible. CEJAP killed 14 fishermen and then accused them of being members of the Ejército de Liberación Nacional (National Liberation Army) from Colombia. But, just as in the Yumare Massacre, there were survivors who brought to light what had actually occurred.

The Masacre de El Amparo, as it became known, would shake up both civil and religious sectors during the final days of the Lusinchi government, producing large demonstrations that ended in riots and lootings, similar to what had happened in Mérida after the Yumare Massacre, indicating that the Pact of Punto Fijo was in its final days.

In the midst of this tumult, on July 23, 1988, Salom Mesa issued a manifesto titled "Hacia la revolución social libertaria de los anarquistas venezolanos al pueblo" (Toward the social revolution of the Venezuelan anarchists to the people) and from August 3rd until January 18, 1989, he wrote a column for the daily *Últimas Noticias* titled "El Camino, espacio de reflexión y difusión anarquista" (The Way, a space for anarchist reflection and dissemination).

After he stopped writing this column, he returned to book writing, with his book *La vida me lo dijo, elogio a la anarquía* (Life told me this, elegy to anarchy), published by Editorial Hermanos Vadell, in which he made a call for the construction of an antiauthoritarian society.

An important occurrence at this time was the appearance of the political group Desobediencia Popular, which was formed by Denis Boulton, Vanessa Davies, Damelis Guerra, Ricardo Dorado, and Carlos Lanz among others. Even though it was near to marxism and guevaraism, it embraced some libertarian methods, such as direct action; it employed a strategy of focused disturbances and street protests that contributed to the youth rebellion already being promoted by Bandera Roja via the Unión de Jóvenes Revolucionarios (UJR—Union of Revolutionary Youth) in many educational centers.

On the night of October 26, 1988 an event foreshadowed what was to soon come: on that night two columns from the Juan Pablo Ayala battalion of the Fourth Brigade of the army's armored strategic commandos, commanded by Major José Domingo Soler Zambrano, and Captain José Manuel Echeverría Márquez moved out from Fuerte Tiuna with the objective of taking the presidential residence, La Viñeta, and the Ministry of the Interior. They arrived at the sites without opposition, and without even being reported to the authorities.

According to declarations from Major Soler, the mobilization of the units was a response to an alert about a supposed coup against the minister of the interior and secretary to the president Simón Alberto Consalvi. Nevertheless, the action was fishy given that the Ministry of Defense had no knowledge of it and the military high command denied issuing the order to move.

There were two hypotheses about this affair, the first of which was that it was a frustrated coup, which failed because the plotters didn't manage to seize or kill Consalvi. The second was that it was a probe inspired by MBR-200 to see how the military establishment would react. In either case, "the night of the armored cars" prefigured the rupture that was nearing.

The term in office of Jaime Lusinchi was marked by administrative scandals produced by the mismanagement of the RECADI system of exchange; these included the purchase of 65 autos by the state for use in the AD's electoral campaign, the invention of thousands of state companies that never existed with the purpose of siphoning off state funds, and misuse of monies marked to pay down the external debt, which stood at $50 billion (US) in 1988, up from $27 billion in 1984, most of which was supposed to be paid down in short order. There was also the matter of the Banco Central de Venezuela reserves, which in December 1985 were $10.251 billion (US) and by 1988 were down to $3.092 billion. [As a result of all the mismanagement and theft] debt payments were suspended on January 2, 1989

Despite all this, during Lusinchi's time in office the government constructed the Paseo Vargas in Caracas (a huge downtown park), the Complejo Habitacional Juan Pablo II (housing project), the extension of the Metro de Caracas Zoológico/Las Adjuntas-La Paz line, the Represa del Río Turimiquire dam (in Monagas state, the first stages of construction of the Autopista de Oriente (Turnpike of the West), and 331,615 low income housing units.

[Near the end of Lusinchi's time in office] the Colectivo Ezequiel Zamora, whose staff included the brothers Nicolás and Mauricio Torres, relaunched *El Libertario*, but only managed to publish one issue. Meanwhile Víctor García published in Caracas what would be has last book in Venezuela, *Antología del anarcosindicalismo*.

* * *

On December 4, 1988, new presidential elections were held in which the AD candidate Carlos Andrés Pérez was elected to the presidency for the second time, with a total of 3,868,843 votes, besting his COPEI rival, Eduardo Fernández, owing at least in part to the promises of AD to return to the "Gran Venezuela" of Andrés Peréz's first term in office. This election saw the greatest turnout ever, a record that would last until 2006, though that record was due in part to growing population, and there was an 18% abstention rate.

Once in office, Carlos Andrés Pérez's government sought to change the country's economic course through a series of economic "reforms" promoted by the International Monetary Fund (IMF) dubbed "the economic package," and which were designed to produce long-term economic changes. Some of these "reforms" were applied immediately and others gradually, though over short periods. The "package" comprised measures regarding political change, foreign debt, foreign trade, the financial services, taxes, public services, and social policies. The lifting of price controls and the fixed exchange rate would be a shock for low-income people, and this would open the floodgates for the torrent that would be unleashed a few weeks later.

27 February: An anarchist rebellion?

On February 27, 1989, the Ministry of Energy and Mines [in line with the IMF "reforms"] announced a rise in the price of gasoline and a 30% increase in the price of public transit. This was the straw that broke the camel's back: it unleashed popular fury. The popular reaction began in the Caracas suburb Guarenas with protests by students and workers over the price increase of public transit. For several hours on the morning of February 27, people came down from the hills of Caracas and from its low income zones (Catia, El Valle, Coche, and Antímano) and filled the streets. At first the television stations showed scenes of looting carried out in a peaceful manner, with the police looking on. But the looting soon turned extremely violent, turned into riots.

The protest, the "Caracazo," grew massive, catalyzed by the communications media that transmitted events live. This spurred similar outbreaks of looting and attacks on the forces of public order in other Venezuelan cities including La Guaira, Maracay, Valencia, Barquisimeto, Mérida, and Ciudad Guayana.

On the 28th of the month, Andrés Pérez suspended constitutional guarantees and issued an unprecedented order for young people to remain at home. The people were demonstrating that the "economic readjustment" couldn't take place unless social problems were addressed. In response, the security agencies began a brutal round of repression.

In Caracas, they activated the "Plan Ávila," which gave the army control of the city, and authorized the use of firearms to control the demonstrations. Some demonstrators used guns to defend themselves or to attack the military, but the number of deaths among the police and military was very small in comparison with the number of civilians they killed. The official estimate was that between 73 and 100 people were killed; thousands were also wounded, and material losses were enormous. Independent sources estimated that the number killed was at least 400, with the repression being especially severe in the poorest parts of the capital.

For several days, the city was submerged in chaos, restrictions [of movement], food scarcity, raids, political persecution, and the killing of innocent people. It's estimated that 900 corner groceries were looted along with 130 grocery stores, 95 hardware stores, 72 office supply stores, and 850 stores of other types. There were also an estimated 154 arson attacks, including some against AD offices. The number of people arrested during the raids by the security forces was 91, almost all of them leftist university students.

When the waters began to recede on March 1, the government delivered the final blow when it lifted price controls on goods and services.

The bloody repression the government unleashed against the people led the youth of the time to decide to put an end to AD/COPEI duopoly. The Caracazo was a key event in the growing distaste for representative democracy in the country. The Caracazo was definitely the match that lit the fuse in the anarchist reawakening in Venezuela. A first sign was the special edition about the Caracazo published by *Correo A*.

To help better understand how valuable the explosion on February 27th was, here's the editorial on the matter from *Correo A*. After explaining that anarchy is not synonymous with chaos, *Correo A* goes on to explain why the uprising was anarchist in nature:

> It was anarchist because it was spontaneous, without chiefs or an "illustrious vanguard" that would guide it, without theoreticians who would evaluate the participants. It was born from the depths of the people . . . It grew in the solidarity of lifelong friends in the barrio, of brothers. It rejected political power, and a block from the Miraflores [presidential] palace there was a people's barbecue with meat taken from an adjacent market. It was anarchist because while we've heard for years that everyone is guilty of the ills of the country, this time, yes, we were responsible, but not to blame; on February 27 other values ruled. There was no theft, because property is theft . . . There were only the self-imposed obligations of solidarity, without the threat of penalties, and the laws made for the benefit of the exploiters were forgotten.
>
> We were free and equal, together taking back what had been stolen from us. . . . It ended when the protagonists returned to their homes, to their barrios, exhausted by a previously unknown liberty. Later came the repression reaping its quota of death, more in vengeance than in justice, with all the force never used against speculators, narcotics traffickers, and whoever else loots the country. It came with guns, tanks, and grenades, as from a beast hungry for blood . . .
>
> On February 27, we joined Paris [in 1870 and 1968], Spain [in 1936], and the soviets [in 1917/1918] in showing the world that everyone, even when they don't express it, identifies property and authority as their oppressors. The question that remains and that each one of us needs to answer is, Will we be capable of making this freedom and equality permanent in an anarchist society, and do we want to do it?[172]

The spontaneous events of February 27 and 28, 1989, the Caracazo, would be debated in the social sciences as to whether this popular explosion against the neoliberal "reforms" was an expression of "anarchism" due to its anti-capitalist, anti-statist nature and the expressions of solidarity and mutual aid among the looters.

As a product of all the commotion, there was a series of anarchist talks and discussions within the UCV. Ángel Cappelletti, Nelson Méndez, José Luis Soldini, and others participated in these gatherings.

The visual artist Eduardo de la Mano says of these meetings:

> There were a lot of things with an anarchist perspective going on in the UCV; at the start there was a series of coversations called "the garden of Epicurus" in which hippies, punks, sociologists, delincuents, UJR, M80 participated; many of them would later carry out anarchist initiatives with which we're familiar. This went on for five years."[173]

This allowed for a slow rearticulation of anarchist ideas in the most important university in the country. A symbolic event occurred when brothers Erick and Héctor Gutiérrez interrupted the visit to the UCV of the USSR ambassador to Venezuela bearing a banner commemorating the anarchist uprising at the Kronstadt naval base against the Lenin dictatorship in 1921. This brush up ended in shoves and shouts, and helped to show that youths were escaping from the traditional leftist canons.

The Caracazo opened a period of tension and conflict in which leadership and influences didn't come from the leftist political parties, but rather from emergent social movements such as those of students, neighborhoods, ecologists, indigenous people, and human rights. The youth of the epoch would create new channels in which to express their discontent.

The Descendants of Radical Rock

Parallel with this social agitation, there were signs all across the country, most notably in Caracas and Barquisimeto, of youthful unrest inspired by the counterculture and the punk movement. Inside the counterculture, 'zines were a means of propagating both libertarian and marxist ideas among the youthful nonconformists; some of the 'zines worth mentioning were *El Caleidoskopio, Caput Juves, El Provo, Panfleto Radical, ¿Qué hay de nuevo viejo?, Vía Subterránea, S.O.S., Mentes Abiertas, Anoche-ska, La Cuarta Hoja del Trebol* and *No Sumisión*, all from Barquisimeto, and from Caracas Carakas *resiste y ataka, Anacreonte en horas muertas, Anti-Sumisión, Corrupción CAP, Kronica Klandestina, Antitodo, Acción de Masacre, Reporte Latino,* and *La Gazeta.*

Young people began to form bands inspired by punk and hardcore, based philosophically in anarchism or marxism. Among these were 27F, CHIKRAK-CHIK, En Contra, Odio que?, Discordia, Ejercito Rojo, Venezuela Hard-core, Des-k-rriados, Claustrofobia, Desarme Nuclear, Primero Venezuela, Alternativa Radical Hard-core, Solo por Diversión, Devastación, Grito de Odio, Total Miseria, Acción Directa, Combate Nacional, Holocausto, Pérez serás tu, Allanamiento Moral, Victimas de la Democracia and Autogestión.

Among these, we should mention that Autogestión is considered the first anarcho-punk band formed in Venezuela. Even though the [punk] anarchist current was already old news and had been around [in Venezuela] since the early '80s, it wasn't until after the Caracazo that a band properly identified appeared. In their lyrics they talked about anarchism, and leading their social involvement toward liberty their bandleader was Leonardo "Vampiro" Sánchez. The band later changed its name to Grupo-A and after that Oktavo Pasajero, a name which they'd keep [until their presumed breakup] in 1994. Besides Leonardo, their group consisted of Wolfang Lara on guitar, Neil Ochoa on drums, and Juan Carlos Amado on bass. Allanamiento Moral (Moral Raid), was another notable anarcho-punk band of the era, and it managed to put out a demo tape. Its members were Julio Rojas Ávila on bass, Darwin Abreu on guitar, Julio Moros on vocals, and Zoúm Domínguez on drums.

Regarding the band Allanamiento Moral, formed in 1989 in Caracas, its bassist, Julio Rojas Ávila, said in an interview conducted for this book:

> The band's style was principally that of Punk Rock, Ska, and Hardcore via such bands as the Sex Pistols, La Polla Records, Kortatu, The Specials, and Los Intocables, among other. The band name was an expression of our questioning of the political and cultural domination imposed by force by the groups in power
>
> The emergence of the band corresponded to the political discontent of its four members who were influenced by the emergence of the punk movement in the country in 1980s and 1990s. We decided to organize to denounce, among other things, the abuses of President Carlos Andrés Pérez, who during his second term imposed harsh neoliberal economic policies delivered to him by the IMF, and who plunged the people and their organizations into one of the worst periods of repression, economic crisis, murder, and violation of human rights in the history of the country, showing its worst face during the social outburst of the Caracazo.
>
> The lyrics of Allanamient Moral dealt with themes such as the American and other foreign [interference in Venezuela], the contradictions of the capitalist

system, repudiation of police abuse, the struggle for human rights, equal access to opportunities and to the economic, cultural, and historical riches of the nation, as well as the right to self-determination of peoples, cultural resistance, solidarity and popular organization.

Allanamiento Moral has been frequently cited as a . . . propelling force in the musical and political history of the Venezuelan underground [and] leftist militancy (starting from socialism and arriving at anarchism), and the foundation and consolidation of the self-managed music scene in the country.[175]

Many of these musical projects and some of the 'zines had a radius of action in what was known as the Colectivo Rajatabla (To the Letter Collective), which was based in the cultural center known as Bellas Artes. It wasn't properly speaking an anarchist collective, but within it discontented young people of various stripes, anarchists, communists, and punks, met. Some modified the symbol of the Liga Socialista, incorporating a raised fist into it, which made it look like a youth with a Mohican.

In reference to the Rajatabla collective, the historian Claudia Heredia says:

I don't really know where or how it started. What I can say is that I started visiting Rajatabla in 1986 if memory serves. . . . In truth there existed diverse interests or groups within the collective . . . (music, 'zines, theater) and as a collective we supported each other in attending concerts, in our works, sharing 'zines, etc. . . . We also attended anti-government marches, with our banner bearing the slogan, "This is only the start, the struggle continues" . . . of course it had a circle A and a punk with a raised fist.(178)

Félix Tarazona, a member of the band Víctimas de la Democracia, said the following regarding the collective:

Rajatabla was visited by youths, punks of that epoch. The first time I went was in 1987 . . . when I was 15 years old. . . . [Politics] weren't my priority then, but with time the ideology grew within me, analyzing various things about society, religion, and politics [and accepting the results of that analysis] was for me very difficult . . . In Rajatabla many types of people met, and as Rajatabla was a cultural center there was a certain tolerance for different ideological points of view, which made for many interesting points of encounter. There were people there involved in art, theater, music, and later the publishing of 'zines. I think it reached its high point at the beginning of the 1990s. Music was the thing that attracted many, and many bands came out of it. At this time our ideology was clear enough that it formed a basis for our actions.[176]

Regarding the band Victimas de la Democracia, sociologist Rafael Uzcátegui says:

During the first years of the 1990s there was a flourishing of punk bands and hardcore bands in Venezuela, among which Victimas de la Democracia stand out . . . In the first place, they stood above the other local bands in their songwriting, with various types of songs which were catchy and with good hooks. In the second place, despite the lyrics' pamphlet-like radical nature, many of the lyrics contained intelligent metaphors and poetic touches from their vocalist Elías Yanez. And in the third place, for their use of guerrilla visuals and the punk aesthetic in the streets of Caracas, from their scruffy logo to the quantity of posters with which they plastered the streets. The band was certainly influenced by The Dead Kennedys, but also by the omnipresent sound of Iberian punk . . .[177]

With time, the youths attracted to marxist-leninist currents remained in Colectivo Rajatabla, while the anarchists moved to another site in Caracas known as the Plaza Altamira, and would become known as Los Anarkos. As for the motives and ideology of those who participated in Rajatabla and Los Anarkos, in an interview for the magazine *Plátano Verde* (Green Banana) Elías Yanez, vocalist for Víctimas de la Democracia, said:

We were looking for a way out. We were desperate, searching in socialism in anarchy. We believed in something and wanted to fight for it, and because we wanted solutions for the problems. The way was socialism, but it felt hopeless at the time, seeing all of the problems it had: repression, misery . . . In the present situation, the essence continues to be anarchy: no god, no masters, no owners. . . . We were against any and all forms of control.[178]

One common point of reference among the youths who were radicalized by the politico-economic circumstances in which they lived, was the bookstore Lectura del Centro Comercial Chacaito that was run by Antonio Serrano. Regarding this, Julio Rojas would say in an interview:

The search for texts that would deepen my adolescent understanding, at 15 or 16 years of age, of what I understood to be anarchism from the punk movement, would after a time lead me to several bookstores in Caracas with the idea of finding a bibliography about the matter. I clearly remember arriving at the bookstore Lectura, located in the Centro Comercial Chacaíto asking about books on anarchism. The man who waited on me, a person with European appearance and about 50 years old, commented that it was interesting that someone as young as I would be interested such matters, and I shortly found myself talking with a 70-year-old Spaniard with grey hair and on the fat side, who was shorter than most of the people working in the store. The Spaniard, upon being informed of my interest, asked me what had called my attention to anarchism. I replied that I didn't want to remain with a superficial concept of it and added that I was part of the dissident groups in Caracas that had touched on the theme through the punk movement. The Spaniard suggested a book on anarchism (frankly I remember neither the title nor the author), and I bought the book with the emotion of having encountered something extraordinary. I had hardly paid for it, when the Spaniard told me that if I wanted to learn more, on certain days of the week there were anarchist meetings at the UCV. So, I attended my first anarchist meeting at the Universidad Central de Venezuela, invited by that Spanish bookstore worker, who was also present on that day and identified himself formally as Antonio Serrano. Months later, he told me that he had lived for many years in Venezuela as an exile following the Spanish Civil War. The anarchist group I attended at the UCV later became the CAL."[179]

This is a great illustration of the older Iberian anarchists and the new generation in Venezuela meeting, and cooperating on anarchist initiatives.

In the House that Overcame the Shadows

Along with the libertarian experiments that were being spontaneously generated in the Caracas counterculture, there was another unfolding at the UCV, a collective with the name Nosotros. Among its members were Lenin Bandres, Lorena Almarza, Madera, and José Luís Colmena. There was also another group known as Los Autónomos in which the illustrator Eduardo de la Mano, better known by his pseudonym Coyote, his sweetheart Yuruani Rodríguez, John Jairo Marín, the brothers Piki and Ernesto Figueroa, Mafer, and Camilo participated. The Nosotros collective with help from other anarchists, put out the 'zine *La Gazeta*. One of its members, Eduardo de la Mano, created murals and pictures for the walls and hallways of the UCV, and also put out a small 'zine called *La Insumisión*.

Still another group was the Colectivo Libertarios Anarquistas which printed a bulletin of the same name which it distributed gratis in the halls of the university. One of its leading members was Héctor Gutiérrez. Still another disseminator of libertarian ideas at the UCV was professor José Luís Soldini, who for a while was imparting understanding to curious young people in the School of Social Work, helping them put out 'zines, texts, and all sorts of other things to help in deepening and understanding the ideas.

This practice continued until Bandera Roja and its student arm, in accord with its policies of forming fronts and and groups in leninist style, jealous of the anarchist activity in university halls and of the growing attraction of an increasing number of young revolutionaries toward anarchism, decided to pressure professor Soldini in several ways, which ended with him resigning from the UCV School of Social Work and going to work for to the College of Social Work at the Colegio Universitario de Caracas. From all of this the 'zine *Autogestión* sprang up in the College of Social Work, though only for a single issue.

The Colectivo Libertarios Anarquistas, back at UCV, defined its principles as follows:

> To obtain our objectives, we propose the complete emancipation of all oppressed people by themselves, through self-management and autonomy, direct action, mutual aid, and free agreement among equals. The collective has no intent of supplanting, managing, or subordinating popular autonomous movements.
>
> At the same time, we demand harmonious relations between human beings and their natural and social environment.
>
> We seek fraternal cooperation among all the oppressed people of the earth, no matter what their race, ethnicity, or culture, with the ends of their liberation from and self-defense against imperialism, exploitation, and ethnocentrism.
>
> We support the revolutionary struggle for the liberation of women.
>
> We combat the state and all of its forms of exploitation."[180]

Even though the anarchists were centered in the UCV, they didn't participate in the institutional channels for the student body, because they considered them at odds with their advocacy of direct action. Because of this, during the election campaign within the Federación de Centros Universitarios they decided to create the Colectivo del Burro and along with the activists of Desobediencia Popular nominated a burro as their candidate. The traditional political parties, which had their partisans within the university, considered this a dangerously provocative act. The climax came at a debate of the student candidates to which the Colectivo del Burro brought the animal after leading it across campus accompanied by a "happening," a type of street theater in which spectators participate. The event ended with verbal skirmishing.

* * *

In 1991, the Asamblea de Barrios de Caracas was created, a space for interchange of ideas, debate, and cooperation which gave birth from its roundtable to the Primer Encuentro Internacional de Rehabilitación de Barrios (First International Gathering on Rehabilitation of Barrios), which was held in the same year in the capital. In contrast with the neighborhood councils and other community organizations, the Asamblea was a space in which different political actors on the left were recognized, and who wanted to give political orientation to a type of creative space that until then had been categorized as "reformist." For this reason, some young anarchists participated in this community undertaking.

The writer and future vice-minister of Cordiplan (the government's planning office) Roland Denis Boulton, in his book, *Los fabricantes de la rebelión* (The Manufacturers of Rebellion) sums up the importance of this neighborhood organization: "The Asamblea de Barrios played a fundamental role as the center of the beginnings of social power in the country and as an articulator of popular struggles."[181] One example of this was that the Asamblea contributed to young libertarians being in contact with concrete collective struggles.

In the same year, 1991, there was an anecdotal event within the literary world when a handful of young anarchists burst into the headquarters of the Fundación del Centro de Estudios Latinoamericanos Rómulo Gallego in the Altamira neighborhood during a presentation of the [ludicrously titled] book *El Imperio Contracultural, del Rock a la Posmodernidad* (The Countercultural Empire, from Rock to Postmodernism) by professor Luis Britto García, armed with a manifesto criticizing the author's views about punk.

Another less reported event was the occupation of a vacant furniture store on the Avenida de Caracas by a group of young punks and anarchists from the Acacias and Valle areas with the intention of creating a self-managed social center, but for unknown reasons it soon disappeared.

At the same time as these events, in Caracas Emilio Tesoro published the magazine *Misceláneas Libertarias*, which produced several issues and also some newsletters all regarding anarchism. And Cappelletti published his book *Hechos y figuras del Anarquismo Hispanoamericano* (Events and Figures of Latin American Anarchism), which would serve as a prelude to his largest and most ambitious book, *El anarquismo en América Latina*.

* * *

On April 31, 1991, after suffering a painful bout of cancer, Salom Mesa Espinoza died in Caracas. He was one of the most fiery and picturesque figures in the world of Venezuelan anarchism. From a young age he considered himself an anarchist, but he participated in two political parties (AD and MEP). He considered himself an antiauthoritarian, but he was a deputy in the National Congress and revered the figure of Rómulo Betancourt, [and he had participated in armed struggle] but later condemned the guerrilla movement in the country. His life was filled with light and shadow, adventures and imprisonments, glory and shame, and uncertainties. His life was like few others. And it's one often forgotten in our national history.

His book *La vida me lo dijo, elogio a la anarquía* (Life told me this, elegy to anarchy) was a final goodbye from Mesa. In the book he gave us his reasons for, and his disillusion with, participating in party politics.

> I come from the social subsoil, and my ideas embrace political struggle. . . . to procure a revolutionary order, to leave behind justice for my equals; but the results of the political struggle in which I've been an actor haven't served these ends, but on the contrary have served turn me into an animal, to debase me, to corrupt and degrade the children of the people. And as an honest man—which I've always wanted people to see me as—I had to break with that which life itself showed to be evil. In my case, conventional [electoral] politics.

> The legal parties in which I participated were generous with me. The first, Acción Democrática, made me councilor for the Federal District and later a deputy to the Congress, and for it I spilled my blood. The second, Movimiento Electoral del Pueblo, made me a deputy for the Federal District three consecutive times, and the final time nominated me and secured my election while I was imprisoned. It conducted a vigorous and and valiant campaign for my freedom, and its president doctor Luís B. Prieto harshly criticized the government and vehemently demanded my release. I'm profoundly grateful to the MEP and Doctor Prieto, and I won't forget that.

> But for me social struggle makes sense [only] if it tends in the direction of human emancipation; and forty-four years of party militancy, surrounded in the vast majority by good people, has convinced me that through political action we'll never reach emancipation, that the children of the people, like me, should have nothing to do with politics nor with the government. And our mission is that of destroying the ruling political and social order so as to later construct a just order.

> With faith in human destiny, with resentment toward no one, I dedicate my remaining years to spreading libertarian socialist ideas in our country; their progress everywhere will perhaps offer humanity the possibility of living in a state of dignity worth of humanity's greatness.[182]

With the death of Mesa, the circle was closed on anarchists working within Acción Democrática and other social-democratic parties.

Hoodies and Repression

The period that ran from February 27, 1989 to May 20, 1992 was marked by political violence, protests, and disturbances, and many young anarchists took an active part in their places of study, fighting to preserve the "pasaje preferencial" (subsidized public transit). Around 50 young people were killed during marches and street protests, many of them connected with the Colectivo Rajatabla. Among them were José Gregorio Romero, better known by his pseudonym "Flecha" (Arrow) and Gonzalo Jaurena, who was detained and murdered by a police patrol. The bands 27F and Victimas de la Democracia held a tribute concert for Jaurena at the Universidad Simón Bolívar.

The 'zine *Caracas, Resiste y Ataka*, summed up these events:

Indignation, pain, rage, and a bitter resignation were what remained with us after the death of José Gregorio Romero Uzcategui, popularly known in the scene as "Flecha," who fell to the ground after being shot in the head . . . the event occurred at the culmination of a long day of protests and demonstration around the entire country against the economic measures introduced by the rotten government of Carlos Andrés Pérez, demanding the resignation of the same, and denouncing the increased repression unleashed all over the country the last few months . . .

With the death of Flecha, the afternoon of June 2, 1992 came to a close, delivering a blow to the face of those of us who had intended to deliver a low blow to them. Flecha, another victim of an unjust system, another reason to continue.[183]

Regarding the murder of Flecha, Eduardo de la Mano said:

When they killed Flecha some of us were there . . . the bullets whistled nearby; two people were wounded, Flecha was one of them, the other a kid from Desobedience Popular who wore a worker's overalls. They shot him from a tree by a tennis court . . . Flecha was shot throwing rocks and a Molotov . . . He was an anarchist, but his family were with the Bolivarians, who in those days had won over some of the punks . . .

Yes, [he was buried] as an anarchist. At the burial the Bolivarians shoved us aside, but we continued to sing . . . to us, he was a punk and so he was, and that's how they accepted us at the burial.[184]

When asked why "the Bolivarians" pushed them aside, de la Mano said: "Because they considered us filthy," which indicates a breech between the traditional marxist organizations and the university students.

These were times of political agitation, with the streets being epicenters of the struggle. Many young anarchists, or at least young people influenced by anarchism, took spontaneous part in the confrontations, the violent negation of established power, that was taking place in the streets and neighborhoods around the UCV and other centers of studies.

Regarding the clashes at the UCV and surrounding areas, de la Mano says:

> I remember that we joined with the people from Desobediencia Popular and other groups. Those days were difficult. The police shot at us and we defended ourselves. DISIP terrorized the students, and for that reason we wore hoodies.[185]

In December 1991, a situation developed that contributed in significant form to the radicalization of the [protesting] youths: an important bloc of mid-level cadres and university students from Bandera Roja decided to split from the party and to create the Coordinadora Nacional Revolucionaria, which joined with the young people of the Movimiento Juvenil Ezequiel Zamora (MJEZ) who continued with the agitation that BR had been doing in intermediate teaching centers.

Regarding the presence of anarchists in the MJEZ, musician and computer studies graduate Johnny Castro said, "There were kids from all over Caracas, and for the most part from student areas with leftist tendencies, including marxists and anarchists."[186]

Another form of libertarian expression at the time [which fit with the street protests] was graffiti. A few examples: "Against the frigidity of thought, the erection of creativity"; "It's not necessary to kill the tyrant but to kill tyranny"; and "Imagination versus power."

On January 23, 1992, UCV students and students from the Instituto Universitario Pedagógico de Caracas decided to hold a march called the National Day of Protest which would take the route from the Plaza de El Rectorado UCV to the center of the city. When the demonstrators arrived at the city center the Policia Metropólitana (PM—Metropolitan Police) threw tear gas, breaking up the march. The students congregated again at the UCV, where a squad of plain clothes municipal police entered the university district and arrested 13 students who supposedly had masks on hiding their faces. Among the arrested was the anarchist Julio Rojas Ávila.

Regarding these arrests, Eduardo de la Mano, who was present when they took place, said:

[I]t was a commando action like the Israelis do in the Gaza Strip. They arrived in a refrigerated truck and when [the students] were going to burn it, pure [police] types, masked, with pistols and submachineguns, came pouring out of the back to arrest several students . . .[187]

The following day, UCV rector Fuenmayor condemned the police incursion saying that "the university was raided by masked individuals, yes, but masked police hidden in [the truck's] refrigerated compartment."

The thirteen arrested students were sent to the headquarters of the PTJ. A group of UCV students descended on the place to demand the liberation of their comrades. After several hours of protest outside the PTJ, the then-president of the FCU-UCV (Federación de Centros Universitarias-UCV), Luis Figueroa, was permitted to come inside to talk with the arrested students and to verify that they hadn't been tortured. Upon leaving, he assured [the protesters] that their comrades were well and did not appear to have been beaten, but the protesters continued demanding the liberation of the prisoners.

Regarding these events, Eduardo de la Mano, says:

I also remember a protest in Caricuao to demand their liberation, where things turned red; there were several confrontations with the Guardia Nacional and Metropolitan Police. They attacked us again, using rifles and Uzis, but we defended ourselves by throwing rocks and Molotov cocktails . . . fighting for the liberty of the detainees.[188]

The national government stated that the detained students hadn't been tortured, and that, contrary to the comments of its rector, the UCV hadn't been raided—rather that the police had done their duty to protect public order. A government press release cited "vandalism" by "hooded individuals" that impeded "citizens' peace and the normal development of university activities," adding that the students "blocked" access to the University Hospital, "making impossible the delivery of medical services."[189]

This press release indicated that the government wouldn't give in to the demands of the students and would intimidate the student movement until it ceased protesting. This indication was reinforced when the 13 students were transferred to the Junquito prison and charged with the crime of obstructing public order while wearing hoods and for having injured Benjamin Pimentel, a member of the Policia Metropolitana.

This provoked new responses. The students decided to declare a hunger strike and sent a communique to the press holding the government responsible for whatever would happen. Johnny Castro, in later years the vocalist for the punk band Apatía-No, says that the students were released a little over a week after they were arrested.

One of the detainees, Julio Rojas Ávila, tells us of his odyssey after being detained by the forces of order:

> They arrested me during the raid on the UCV by the Metropolitan Police on January 23, 1992, when they found me protesting with other anarchists, punks, and anarcho-punks in a wide coalition of diverse political, social, and student collectives such as Movimiento 80, Desobediencia Popular, Bandera Roja, Colectivos Anarquistas de la UCV, among many other groups and individuals. We were protesting the privatization of the UCV, the neoliberal social and economic measures of he government of Carlos Andrés Pérez, the criminalization of protest, and the rise in the cost of student trasnport among other things.

> In the Puerta Tamanaco, the exit from the UCV to the plaza Venezuela, at the moment the Metropolitan Police assaulted barricades with tear gas, shotgun blasts, and small arms fire . . . a refrigerated truck with dozens of armed police hidden in the interior arrived. Using it as a Trojan horse, they entered the grounds of the university via the El Clínico entrance, saying they were transporting some wounded students to University Hospital so that they could be treated. The driver and the supposed "wounded students" sitting next to the driver, were in reality members of the Metropolitan Police, who evaded the vigilance of the UCV and [drove] to the center of the demonstration at the exit from the UCV to the Plaza Venezuela. The cops shot out of the truck and grabbed every demonstrator they could, detaining me, the only anarcho-punk in the group of socialist, communist, social activist, and student compañeros. Another comrade, Eduardo de la Mano, was able to escape.[190]

For participating in the protests around the UCV, several young anarchists earned short stays in the cells of various prisons. That was the case with Héctor Gutiérrez, who was arrested by DISIP in Bellas Artes and was held for two days in the dungeons of the Helicoide.

Other things were going on besides the street protests. One was the founding of the vegetarian restaurant Kai-Kashí in the chemistry building at the UCV. (Kai-Kashí means sun and moon in the Wayuunaiki language.) The restaurant was run as a self-managed cooperative. Among those participating were Omar "Vegetal" Rangel, Leonardo "Vampiro" Sánchez, Mayogiris Navas, Alicia, Lenín Bandres, and Aureliana. Kai-Kashí served breakfast and lunch, and the afternoons were dedicated to holding talks and meetings and showing films relating to anarchism and other social movements. It was a gathering place for anarchists and was known as such.

Regarding its activities, Julio Rojas said that in addition to providing healthy food as an alternative to "the industrial, capitalist" model based on "separation of producers and consumers, and economic profit to the detriment of the quality of the food," Kai-Kashi served as a model of "coexistence, [alternative] organization of work . . . based in egalitarianism, assemblies, communalism, and self-management, seasoned with a little indigenous Venezuelan cosmic perspective . . ."[191]

Another project at the time intended to facilitate both actions and ties between anarchists was the collective Patito Feo (Ugly Little Foot).

Julio Rojas comments on the collective's members and activities:

> Patito Feo was a project [started] by myself, Héctor el Morocho, and Eduardo De La Mano, based on the need to form an anarchist and anarcho-punk collective that would incorporate three strategic elements: anarchist propaganda via a magazine bearing the name of the collective; deepening [our understanding of] anarchist theory through reading and debate about anarchism's principles, and its place in the context of the local environment; and lastly the formation of a direct action group that would go beyond theoretical discussion and would do tangible, concrete libertarian things in communities, academia, labor [groups], ecology, education, and that would confront police repression, etc. I proposed the name Patito Feo because I thought people were prejudiced against anarchism, and because people would become involved in it and transform themselves, seeing how extraordinarily human, beautiful, and lofty anarchist ideals can be."[192]

Later in the year, the 500th anniversary of Columbus's "discovery" of the New World was a point of confluence for anti-statist rebels in the universities. They worked against the celebration through graffiti, concerts, and articles in the press (above all in *Correo A*) explaining that there was no "discovery," but rather conquest, a theft of lands and minerals by European countries. Therefore there was no reason to celebrate the arrival of Columbus in the Americas. The celebration was a farce put on by the forces of the status quo in continuance of deliberately ignoring the original peoples.

One example of Patito Feo's activities in this area was the spray painting of the words "Nobody discovered anybody, 500 years of shame" on the statue of Christopher Columbus in the Plaza Venezuela.

Anarchists were also participating in agricultural and labor struggles during this time. One example was the strike at the textile company HRH in Caracas and Los Teques in Miranda State. On September 7, 1992, 530 workers working for HRH and the affiliated companies Inversiones Monseny and

Confecciones Vertier began a labor dispute by disaffiliating from the Sindicato de Trabajadores de la ropa, hilo y tejido (Clothing, thread, and fabric workers union) of the Distrito Federal and Edo, Miranda, that was controlled by the attorney Germán Escarra, who was in clear collusion with the bosses. The workers decided to create a new union, from which was born the Unión de Trabajadores de la Industria Textil, which issued a list of grievances about the operators' noncompliance with the workers' contract. In reply, the bosses closed the factory and called in the Metropolitan Police. A strike ensued.

This break in the chain of production culminated in the firing of the 530 workers by the companies with the consent of the labor inspectors and judiciary in violation of labor laws and other guarantees. These events contributed to the radicalization of the young anarchists of the era, who saw the legal guarantees touted by the state and its devotees nakedly revealed in regard to the illegally fired workers. As well, these young radicals grew familiar with the work and union worlds, which some knew only by reference.

In parallel with what was happening in Caracas, in Barquisimeto another group of anarchist young people became active and started publishing things, including the 'zine *¿Qué hay de nuevo viejo?* (What's new old man?), which was put out by Daniel Ilorio, Enrique Luque, and Víctor Huelves, and the little periodical *El Provo*, which even though its content was quite varied, featured anarchist writers such as Rafael Uzcátegui [*author of Venezuela: Revolution as Spectacle*].

As well, and of vital importance, the Frente Ecológico de Liberación Animal arose in Barquisimeto, and even though it was ecological in nature, there were people in it who felt strong attraction to anarchism, social movements, and punk [culture and music].

The Barracks Uprising

On February 4, 1992, a group of mid-ranking military officers from MBR-200 attempted to overthrow the government of Carlos Andrés Pérez, but the coup attempt failed. The next day anarchists were the only ones to distribute flyers repudiating the attempted coup d'etat.

Five lieutenant colonels—Hugo Chávez, Francisco Arias Cárdenas, Yoel Acosta Chirinos, Jesús Urdaneta Hernández, and Miguel Ortiz Contreras—participated in the unsuccessful coup as its visible heads, followed by 135 lower-ranking officers, 166 noncommissioned officers, and 2,056 enlisted men from ten battalions forming part of the military garrisons in the states of Aragua, Carabobo, Miranda, Zulia, and the Distrito Federal.

This attempt began in the early morning hours when president Carlos Andrés Pérez returned from the World Economic Forum in Davos, Switzerland. The armed revolt intended to take by assault the presidential palace, Palacio Miraflores, as well as Fort Tiuna and Base Aérea Generalísimo Francisco de Miranda. There were major skirmishes with casualties on both sides in Zulia, Valencia, and Maracay, in which the plotters managed to obtain a precarious hold on power.

Even though the conspirators had held meetings with opposition parties and groups (Causa R, BR, Tercer Camino, LS, MEP and others) they carried out their military actions without wholehearted support from the civilian groups, with the sole exception of a group of students at the Universidad de Carabobo.

The adventure ended when a handful of mutineers decided to put down their arms upon seeing that their outlined objectives weren't being attained, and that they were not receiving immediate support from the people nor from other sectors of the armed forces.

Nonetheless, this event contributed to the radical transformation of Venezuelan politics, and introduced new actors to the scene, making the social panorama more complex and deepening the country's ungovernability crisis. At the end of this event, the soldiers returned to their barracks, and popular discontent continued to grow.

On this same day the Ministry of Interior Relations revealed that there had been over 50 deaths during the uprising, of which 17 were soldiers and the rest were civilians who had been casually shot during the revolt.

Here's what *Correo A* had to say about the military revolt:

The opposition to the present government, not only on economic grounds but also political, social, and moral, has had a dramatic manifestation: the rebellion of part of the armed forces . . .

The discontent with Carlos Andrés Pérez, the politicians, the bankers, and their [austerity] program is of such magnitude that it has given rise to a sentimental support for [the military uprising of February 4, 1989], which is a dangerous step backward in political conduct. If the infamous administration, which in three years has given us the worst conditions of alimentation, health, education, safety, standard of living, and services of all types in the entire democratic era, means that we're at the edge of the abyss, a military government would be a leap into the vacuum.

We say "vacuum" because we have no idea what they want to do, and neither do they want to make it known . . . We insist that we're not dealing with events in which discontented people used as their ultimate recourse the taking up of arms to correct an intolerable situation, but rather that a military group used popular discontent in an attempt to put themselves in power. It was an uprising with a vacuum at its center . . .

In the distant and recent history of Latin America, the army has without doubt been the guardian of the state. Never have the uniformed saviors brought anything other than bloody repression, redistribution but not elimination of corruption, [and] economic reverses for the majority . . . To support a coup is to renounce our collective right to control our own destiny.

There is only one route to positively construct the future: self-management in all areas of daily life; it's a way, with pain and hope, that we Venezuelans began to take to achieve what the social struggles on February 27, 1989 began. It's with direct action, without hierarchies nor vertical structures, at times slower than we want, but without loss of heart—that's how we'll gain the necessary confidence in ourselves, building with both correct decisions and errors the new edifice that we will choose to live in. No self-designated "savior of the country" can exercise this right in our name.

We will build the future! Nobody will give it to us!

For now and forever, self-management is the way![193]

But in contrast with other ideological currents, there was disagreement within anarchist groups about the coup attempt of February 4. In the youth groups, and especially those within the UCV, there was hidden support for the military uprising. Eduardo de la Mano says of this:

Correo A condemned the action, but the truth is that many didn't view it so unfavorably, perhaps because of naivete, lack of the will to succeed, or a bit of political expediency. Some supported the coup attempt with reservations. It's necessary to take into account that we were also part of the student movement and the Asamblea de Barrios, which brought us close to Desobediencia Popular, which did support it.[194]

The sentiments of Correo A were not shared by the traditional left. On the contrary, it viewed the uprising with hope and was no doubt rendering aid to the lieutenant colonel [Chávez] and his accomplices.

In February 1992, in the aftermath of the military uprising, there was the Primera Expoventa Alternativa (First Alternative Sales Expo) in the Casa de la Cultura Julio Garmendia in Barquisimeto. It featured anarchist and other alternative materials published in Venezuela, as well as films, videos, and other cultural presentations. The Grupo de Editores Alternativos (GEA—Group of Alternative Publishers) grew out of this event; it was a coordinating body for alternative, countercultural magazines, 'zines, and journals published in Barquisimeto, some of them anarchist influenced.

The GEA was composed of the publications *El Caleidoscopio, Caput Juves, ¿Qué hay de nuevo viejo?, El Provo, El Cavador, Igualdad, El Insulso, Utopía Realizable, Vía Subterránea, S.O.S, Mentes Abiertas, Anoche-ska, La Cuarta Hoja del Trébol* and *No Sumisión*. The members of the project included Rodrigo Acosta, Víctor Huelves, Enrique Luque, Joel Ochoa, Antonio Virguez, Marcial Ojeda, Alberto Garcia, Walter Falcon, Bragmario, Sonia Jaramillo "Mema," Maria Eugenia Da Silva, Rafael Uzcátegui, Renzo, Chaplin, and Daniel Iorio.

As well, the GEA had its own organ, *El Insulso* (Tasteless). And after several meetings, two alternative sales expos, and a film festival, the GEA decided to create a self-managed newsstand, where its members could sell their publications.

Meanwhile in Caracas, on June 4, 1992, in the School of Economic and Social Sciences at UCV, there was a concert by the anarcho-punk group Oktavo Pasajero, which was an outward sign of the antiauthoritarian tendency within this School.

And from December 16 to December 20 of that year in the School of Humanities and Education, there was a multi-day event, La A dentro del círculo (The A in the Circle), which included panel discussions, video conferences, art exhibitions featuring posters and ceramics, and sales of [printed] materials. Among the 'zines of the epoch with anarchist and marxist ideas were *Corrupción CAP, Anacreonte en horas muertas, Voz Sub-urbana, Antisumision, Arma Blanca, Venezuela Subterránea, Barri-K-Das Urbanas* and *Caracas resiste y ataka*. The event was sponsored by the Colectivo Círculo A and the Kai-Kashí collective to commemorate the fifth anniversary of publication of the first issue of *Correo A*, and an estimated 400 to 800 persons attended every day of the event.

Just before that event, on November 27, there was another unsuccessful coup. On this occasion, the insurrection was coordinated by a mixed group of civilians and military men under the name Movimiento Cívico-Militar 5 de Julio, involving high officials of all four branches of the military, leftist groups, and other groups opposing the government. The most notable officials involved were General Francisco Visconti Osorio and admirals Hernán Grüber Odremán and Luis Enrique Cabrera Aguirre.

Troops began to move at 11:00 pm on the night of the 26th, with the primary objective being the capture of Carlos Andrés Pérez and establishment of a civil-military junta as a transitional government. A secondary goal was to liberate Hugo Chávez and the other mutineers from the February uprising from the prison in Yare.

The public television station, Venezolana de Televisión, was taken by the rebels as were the repeaters of Radio Caracas Televisión and Venevisión, with the rebels having orders to transmit a recorded video by the leaders of the coup, in which they explained the reason for the rebellion and called on the armed forces to unite behind them. However, in place of that video another recorded previously by Hugo Chávez, who hadn't taken part in the coup planning, was broadcast, to the surprise of the principal plotters.

In the morning OV-10 Bronco planes piloted by mutineers from the Base Aérea Libertador in Maracay attacked objectives all over the country, including the presidential palace, Miraflores, Helicoide [intelligence services headquarters], the offices of the Policía de Sucre and the Base Aérea Generalísimo Francisco de Miranda, in Caracas. In the interior of the country there were firefights in the states of Aragua, Carabobo, Guárico, and Lara.

Civilians took an active part in this coup attempt including in the taking of the TV repeaters in Mecedores, in which a young punk tied to the Colectivo Rajatabla, Miguel "Culebra" Vivenes, was involved. He was subsequently sentenced to 14 years in prison. Upon his release [later in the year] he established ties with the Causa R leader Aristobulo Istúriz and later the Patria Para Todos (PPT) group, before dying under mysterious circumstances in Caracas. Ironically, 35 deserters from Grupo Zeta, the tactical squad from the Policia Metropolitana, who had taken part in many acts of repression against leftist groups at the UCV protests, also took part in the attempted coup.

Around 10:00 a.m. the leaders of the uprising realized that they had no chance of success, and by midday they had asked the Attorney General to mediate their terms of surrender. Meanwhile so many street demonstrations were happening in the 23 de Enero area and its surroundings, in the western part of Caracas, that military vehicles couldn't pass and people were asking the rebels for arms so they could join the uprising.

Despite all this the rebels surrendered between 3:30 and 4:00 pm in a message sent by the coup's military leaders to the Ministry of Defense. Admirals Grüber and Cabrera were taken to the headquarters of the Ministry of Defense.

But not all of the rebels surrendered. A group of 93 under the command of General Visconti left the air base Libertador in a C-130 and fled to Peru, and asked for asylum. Complicating things, diplomatic relations had been suspended following the April 5 "auto-coup" in which Peruvian president

Alberto Fujimori dissolved the Peruvian congress and assumed autocratic power.

On the day of the uprising Carlos Andrés Pérez called a cabinet meeting and decreed suspension of constitutional guarantees. The following day the government issued decree #2,669, which provided for an extraordinary judicial process for the rebel civilians and military men under Title 8, Book 1 of the Code of Military Justice, which created an Extraordinary Council of War.

In Caracas, government forces remained in the streets until the end of the week with the intent of reestablishing public order, especially in the western part of the city. The UCV was raided on the night of the 27th by the Guardia Nacional under the pretext of searching for arms and subversive materials on the grounds. Later, government forces would raid the schools of Agronomy and Veterinary Medicine at the Universidad Central in Maracay and the School of Medicine at the University of Carabobo, where they uncovered military firearms and uniforms, and subversive written materials.

The whole affair would end with 141 civilians and 29 military personnel dead. Direct financial costs were estimated at 800 million bolivars, but perhaps the most damaging economic cost was the financial jitters that caused the withdrawal of massive amounts of money from banking institutions that would eventually collapse.

The government did achieve military control, with a much stronger reaction than in the coup attempt in February. In contrast with that rebellion, this uprising was as much a political failure as a military failure. The violence of some actions, such as taking [the TV station] Channel 8; the image of the uprising as transmitted via its pronouncements; and the terror sown among the people by the warplane attacks generated reactions against the uprising and discredited those behind it.

Subsequently, 500 military officers and uncommissioned officers were arrested, along with 800 common soldiers and 40 civilians. Despite these large numbers, only 196 people were tried by the military tribunal, and that included those who had fled to Peru and were tried in absentia. In all only 97 were sentenced, within a few weeks the Supreme Court had overturned the sentences, and within a year all were once again at liberty.

An article by Armando Vergueiro in *Correo A* illustrates the impressions the Venezuelan anarchists had about the new military uprising:

Those who rose up assumed that militaristic messianism is the only valid way to respond to the discontent and the protest, the public being a type of Sleeping Beauty awaiting Prince Charming bearing the magic wand of TV and riding a

Bronco warplane. Now [the military plotters] want to mobilize us by decree, which most of us reject, not because of support for the kleptocracy of Pérez and company, but because they want us to take part in a fight that isn't ours, as on February 4.

The government, its empressarial leaches, the military high command, and the political party apparatus imposed with stunning vehemence that for which there was no reason: on the one hand a bloody repression more savage (executions in the street, a massacre of prisoners at the Catia prison, deliberately destructive raids at Universidad Central de Venezuela, Universidad de Oriente, and arrest of civilian opposition figures in no way tied to the coup attempt—and on the other a frenetic offensive of propaganda and manipulation of information to discredit as subversive and criminal all even moderately incisive adversaries and critics, with no justification other than cynical hypocrisy.

As part of this offensive they tried to make the failure of the coup into a miraculous remedy to save the wilting local and regional elections on December 6. The political parties, government, employers associations, and the rest of the gang in power have vigorously attempted to turn the election into "the occasion to demonstrate the undoubted legitimacy of the democratic system." Never have we Venezuelans felt such pressure to to vote . . .

And what success they had! . . . [A]lmost 60% of those eligible to vote abstained . . . As regards the minority who went to the polls, they were made to see that all of the crowing about unanimity, the impeccability of electoral politics, and democratic perfection were pure crap. . . .

Nonetheless, the crisis is going to grow worse in all of its dimensions. . . . At this time, popular alternatives are still weak, but in a country with massive electoral abstention, pot-and-pan-banging street demonstrations, military uprisings, and also the development of collective consciousness and action, we'll continue to affirm that it's more urgent than ever to advance toward the "impossible" utopia of self-management to defeat the intolerable present.[195]

The coup attempt on November 27 only served to worsen the climate of conflict in the nation. The obvious participation of civilians in this new uprising spurred the security and counterinsurgency organizations to turn their attention to radical circles and activists in the country, above all to those at the UCV.

Regarding the pre-insurrectional situation in November 1992, Nelson Méndez says this:

Those were very crazy days. We all expected the coup attempt. Two weeks before it, people from the UJR and BR went among us searching . . . to see if we as anarchists would be able to supply 20 people to participate in the military uprising, specifically to participate in the taking of the TV repeaters and antennas, with them supplying the arms . . . We weren't going to lend ourselves to such worse than shameful actions . . . all of which goes to show the magnitude of the irresponsibility of those who took part in the uprising . . .[196]

As for anarchist activities at the time, Ángel Cappelletti, put out *El Anarquismo en América Latina*, a well documented book which is filled with the lives and experiences of the anarchists in South and Central America. It was published by the Biblioteca Ayacucho de Venezuela. There were book presentations in Caracas and Barquisimeto, which was organized by the GEA.

Meanwhile in Guarenas, a group of young people created the Colectivo Expansión Libertaria, which published a magazine called *Contra Toda Autoridad* and had a show on Sundays featuring music and commentary on AM Radio Industrial.

In Caracas there was a high school bulletin called *Combate*, which appeared for four or five issues, and whose purpose was to coordinate Juventudes Libertarias groups. There were also other publications and projects such as the 'zine *Caracas, Resiste y Ataka* and the collective *Expansión Libertaria*, which stated it was formed to counter the "great amount of disinformation that exists" and to "spread libertarian ideas, to waken the struggle for liberty, for the elimination of inequality, to alert people to the manipulation in the media."[197]

At about the same time there was a project to bring libertarian education [the free school movement] to one of the poorest barrios in Caracas, the El Esfuerzo barrio in Nueva Tacagua. The project only lasted a short time, but provided useful experience to those who had carried it out with the aid of the Organización Comunitaria de Viviendas (Community Organization of Living Spaces). Participants included Zulma López, Madera, John Jairo Marín, Karol Guevara, Piki Figueroa, and Any Alarcón. According to Any Alarcón, the short-lived school was located in an abandoned building.

Another incident took place when the musical group Autogestión gave a concert on March 6, 1992, along with Grupo A, in the Auditorio del Pedagógico del Paraíso de Caracas. During the concert scuffling broke out in the audience when a group began to praise Hugo Chávez, leader of the February 24 coup attempt, as a revolutionary. Leonardo Sánchez, Autogestion's vocalist grabbed the mike and in the middle of the concert said, "I shit on CAP [Carlos Andrés Pérez] . . . and I also shit on Chávez."[198]

There were a lot of other anarchist-influenced bands in the period, including Allanamiento Moral, Palmeras Kanibales, and Los Residuos, whose members at first expressed anarchist principles not only in their lyrics but also in militant activism. It was composed of Freddy Ñáñez Chucho, David Dávila, Dennis Ranamax, and Beto, who were influenced by the Colombian "nadaísmo" movement, which stemmed from surrealism and dadaism. Los Residuos at this time had few but theatrical performance and were characterized by their poetic lyrics.

In Barquisimeto, on March 7, 1993, next to the Teatro Juárez de Barquisimeto on the Boulevard Tarmina Guevara, the GEA's Kiosco Alternativo opened its doors. It quickly became a libertarian and countercultural center and meeting place, featuring a mural with reproductions of magazine covers called Todos contra la pared (Up against the wall, everyone). The collective running the kiosk also devoted itself to cleaning up and reclaiming the street on which it was located, which was sunk in filth and crime.

Regarding this experience, Rafael Uzcategui, one of the collective members, in his book *Corazón de Tinta* (Heart of Ink) comments:

> On March 7, 1993, we were patching up parts of the kiosk. This day we were removing the dead earth from the planters and replacing it with fresh earth and fertilizer, and putting in new plants such as cayennes, and also washing the boulevard, declaring the place an "alternative space."
>
> During the following months we continued to repair the site. We put out garbage cans, painted a mural of periodical covers . . . put up two notice boards, put up posters and messages all over the place, and in general gave life to a formerly grey and cold site. In June we had a book fair and . . . [We did all this] in accord with our abilities and limitations and without asking anyone for a cent.[199]

While this was going on, from May 28 to May 30 the GEA held another well attended book fair in Barquisimeto, and an anarchist group in Caracas held a performance at the Auditorio Naranja at the UCV of the Living Theater-inspired Teatro Anarkista.

While the anarchists were busy engaging in projects such as the kiosk, the crisis that followed the Caracazo and that was constantly threatening the legitimacy of the government of Carlos Andrés Pérez would culminate following an accusation of embezzlement of public funds. On November 8, 1992, the journalist José Vicente Rangel charged that 250 million bolivars had been misappropriated, and the Congress initiated a long and complex investigation. The Attorney General filed charges against Andrés Pérez and two of his ministers, Alejandro Izaguirre and Reinaldo Figueroa, and on May 21, 1993 the Senate authorized the removal of Andrés Pérez from his post, and he was jailed in the Retén Judicial de El Junquito. The Supreme Court condemned him to two years and four months house arrest for embezzlement of public funds, and for the first time since 1958 a Venezuelan president did not finish the term to which he had been elected.

With the exit of the president, on June 4, Dr. Ramón J. Velásquez, was named to fill out Carlos Andrés Pérez's term. In his brief time in office, he instituted some [real] reforms [in contrast to the IMF austerity "reforms"], including a law regulating savings and lending; he returned a major amount of power from the federal government to the states; and in November 1993 he created the Fondo Intergubernamental para la Descentralización (Intergovernmental Fund for Decentralization).

.From mid-July through the first part of August, the Nosotros collective organized the Primer Encuentro de Juventudes Libertarias, in Nirgua, Lara state, on the ranch of CNT member Guillermo López. The gathering was timed to coincide with the visit of two "okupas" from Spain, who were part of a worldwide movement to occupy vacant buildings to turn them into [living spaces and] autonomous, anti-capitalist centers.

After that event Bandera Roja organized the Campamento Antiimperialista y Antifascista at the Universidad Simón Bolívar. Even though the attendees at the Nirgua gathering had agreed not to participate in the event because leninists controlled it, a group of young anarchists did attend it to represent the anarchist movement. They left before its conclusion [in all likelihood for reasons anyone familiar with leninists can guess].

At about the same time, there was a series of bombings in Caracas that would become known as "financial terrorism." A police investigation eventually revealed that the bombings were intended to destabilize Venezuela's stock market, and were carried out at the behest of speculators by DISIP agents tied to various killings, including the El Amparo and Yumare massacres. Even though those responsible were obvious, there was paranoid suspicion [by other anarchists] toward some UCV anarchists who had participated in direct actions, which made already deteriorating personal relationships even worse.

As a corollary of this, the Kiosco Alternativo in Barquisimeto was burned down on August 12, 1993 by unknown persons, and the same happened shortly after to the self-managed restaurant Kai-Kashí. These acts of sabotage, for which those culpable were never caught, contributed even further to the estrangement between anarchist individuals and groups. Later, both the

Kiosco Alternativo and Kai-Kashí would reopen their doors, although for only a short time.

Also on August 12, the publisher Editorial Hermanos Vadell issued Salom Mesa's posthumous work, *Cartas para Carlos* (Mesa's grandson), which was both an autobiography and an anarchist manifesto Mesa had written during the final days of his life.

In November, the Haximú massacre occurred in the extreme southern part of the country, perpetrated by a group of illegal miners [from Brazil], called in Portuguese, garimpeiros, against a Yanomami village. This was bitterly denounced by virtually all leftist Venezuelan groups, including the anarchists, who set up a meeting and teaching place in the Amazon region, in which Héctor Rodríguez and Jose Luis Soldini participated.

The presidential election on December 5, 1993, marked the end of the AD-COPEI domination of the electoral process. This time, Rafael Caldera, at 77 years of age, and not the COPEI candidate, won with the backing of several small and medium-size parties (MAS, MEP, PCV, etc.). The anarchists decided to take to the streets and to make calls for abstention via graffiti. The journalist Humberto Jaimes Quero noted that one of the slogans was "No Botes Votalos" (which translates very roughly to "No! Boot them out!"). Another common graffiti slogan of the time, especially around the UCV, was "CAP se fue ¿y?" (Carlos Andrés Pérez has gone. And now what?), which was a spur to Venezuelans to keep asking questions about the country's structural crisis.

In February 1994, a group of activists from the Colectivos Nosotros and Asamblea de Barrios, plus some individual libertarians, mounted a picket in front of the Mexican embassy in the El Rosal area of Caracas in solidarity with the Zapatista rebels in Chiapas. And on the 12th of the same month, the Frente Ecológico de Mérida organized an anti-bullfighting demonstration in the city of Mérida, in which anarchists from Caracas and other parts of Venezuela took part. On March 4, 11, and 18 there was also a series of video conferences in the Espacio Abierto (Open Space) of the cooperative Kai-Kashí, now in its second stage.

But the fall of Carlos Andrés Pérez didn't signify an improvement in the ongoing institutional disaster facing representative democracy in Venezuela. Street protests continued around various educational institutions such as the Liceo Fermín Toro and the UCV.

In one of these demonstrations in May at the Liceo Benito Juárez, Johnny Castro, at age 19, was arrested along with other demonstrators and held for three days, without their families being aware of their whereabouts. He recalls that the police recognized many of the individual demonstrators, despite their being hooded, and seemed to have something personal against them. After his arrest, he was carted around in the back of a jeep while handcuffed, being beaten [on the receiving end of "bambinazos"—a reference to Babe Ruth's slugging home runs] by the police. He also saw other students being badly beaten. He recalls:

> Truly the police made no distinction between common street criminals and students, and they were harder on the younger people. . . . When I spoke with various prisoners who had killed people, etc., and they asked me why I was there and I told them it was for being involved in the street protests, these people, not one of whom had taken part in the protests, told me I was crazy."

He adds:

> [A]s a way of pressuring us and causing public ridicule as well as to sow fear in the people, they had the idea of photographing us and showing us with hoods in the principal papers and TV stations. They showed my photo on TV, and said I'd been arrested for violating the Ley de Vagos and Maleantes (the Law of Bums and Evildoers—in other words, vagrancy). My mother saw this and since that day doesn't trust the communications media. . . .

> The police did evil things to us, psychological tortures that I won't comment on because it would take too long, but it was a very bad time.[200]

The detention of Johnny Castro, the irregularities in his brief imprisonment, at the margin of due process and respect for human rights, showed the pre-totalitarian, repressive state of that time of street protests and youthful revolt.

In the middle of September 1994 the self-managed vegetarian restaurant Kai-Kashí closed its doors for the last time.

After all of the lamentable events, the anarchist movement and punk scene were debilitated and for a time produced very few activities anywhere in the country. All they were able to do was to publish the 'zines *El Clandestino*, *Adoquín* (Cobblestone), *La Sedición*, of which only two issues appeared, and which was produced by young women from the circle of anarchists centered round the Plaza Altamira, *Apatía-No* edited by Johnny Castro, and *Realidad Hundida* (Sunken Reality) produced by Miguel Romero, which ran to six issues.

Also, the magazines *Correo A* and *La Gazeta* continued to appear, and *El Provo* put out the pamphlet *Cuadernillos de educación libertaria* (Manual of

Libertarian Education) and also managed to produce for a short time a radio program on 690 AM in Barquisimeto, organized by María Fernanda Barreto, an activist connected with the no longer active GEA.

In the same year, Venezuela experienced a banking crisis which affected nearly a third of the commercial banks, and which brought down many emblematic companies. The crisis began in February 1994 and extended into 1995, during which the state provided considerable financial help to the problematic banks; this led to their nationalization by the end of 1994. The most important of the banks were the Banco Latino, Banco Consolidado, Banco Metropolitano, and the Banco de Venezuela. The total aid rendered to the banks by the national government was approximately 1.272 trillion bolivars, the largest amount of aid ever provided to the banks during the country's republican period.

This banking crisis paved the way for the Caldera government to implement its economic "adjustment" plan known as the Agenda Venezuela, which was basically the implementation of [more] austerity measures recommended by the IMF as conditions of its loaning the government money. Among the economic "reforms" were the lifting of price controls on hydrocarbons (gasoline, oil, etc.) and public services, the imposition of a value-added tax, and privatization of some government enterprises. Some of the measures Caldera imposed were, of course, quite unpopular.

Amid spiraling inflation and economic austerity, in 1995 a new anarchist organization formed in Caracas, the Comité de Relaciones Anarquistas (CRA). It was founded by the Spanish CNT exiles Emilio Tesoro, Antonio Serrano, and Pablo Benaige, and young Venezuelans with backgrounds in the counterculture of the early 1990s, Rafael Uzcátegui, Víctor Huelves, José Antonio Cabrera, and Enrique Luque. There were CRA groups in Barquisimeto and San Cristóbal as well as Caracas, and the CRA undertook the publication of the magazine *El Libertario*, which had been abandoned years before by the CAL. At the start, the idea was to rotate the editing between the different groups, but that didn't work out, and the Caracas group was assigned the task. Thanks to its association with the Spanish CNT, the collective was accepted by the AIT/IWA (anarcho-syndicalist international) as Friends of the AIT (CRA-AIT).

The CRA-AIT, defined itself as follows:

It's an affinity group. It's manifested in a convergence of individual aspirations and interests, an identity of opinion about fundamental matters of theory and practice, a compatibility among diverse temperaments and ways of being, a mutual trust and friendship among all of its components. Being an affinity group, the CRA is a free association of individuals.

It's an egalitarian association. There aren't directors or managers, neither do we endorse the social division of work, as in capitalist societies. There's no submission of the will of the minority to the will of the majority, nor are the "interests" of the group nor the "will" of the group considered as abstractions, something disassociated and placed above the concrete aspirations, the wills of the individuals that comprise the group. The activities of the CRA are a consequence of freely realized agreements of all of the group's members, agreements that can be modified at any time.

The CRA is fully responsible for its actions (actions that result from internal accords or from pacts with other groups). The CRA is an autonomous association, constituted of autonomous individuals. The activities of the CRA do not necessarily involve the totality of the activities of each of its members. The individual is not bled dry by the group, just as the group is not bled dry in relation to or in coordination with other organizations.

The CRA is not a merely formal association. It's not in existence because its members regularly pay dues or periodically attend meetings. Its existence essentially manifests itself in the actions it takes: "If there is no anarchist practice, there is no anarchist group." Its principal goal is the propagation of anarchist ideas, because of which it issues a periodical called *El Libertario*, and also other media to spread the ideal. The same goes for propaganda by actions, a means of coordination and combination of individual efforts, a means of supporting practical actions of each of its members. It's a way to debate the most diverse questions that exist in the anarchist movement.

The CRA doesn't live in a marble tower. Its members can and do participate in accord with the method of direct action in the most diverse social struggles and participate, without managers, in the most diverse popular associations. Anarchism being a complete rejection of authoritarian society, the CRA is not a formal organization. It has no interest in participating in [electoral] democratic [politics].[201]

The first issue of the revived *El Libertario* appeared in the middle of October in 1995, with the printing made possible by contributions of individual CRA members and from [the old CNT members] Emilio Tesoro and Antonio Serrano, and from the proceeds of three anarcho-punk concerts held in El Junquito.

With time the Colectivo Nosotros dissolved itself and the Circle A collective joined the CRA, and with that stopped publishing its 'zine *La Gazeta* and the magazine *Correo A*.

The Colectivo Circulo A left an important legacy for libertarian ideas in Venezuela. They were the ones who did the most to raise local work to an international plane, maintaining contact with other overseas organizations such as the CNT, the AIT, the Industrial Workers of the World (IWW), the MLCE, and other anarchist groups in over 15 countries.

In February 1995, the CRA and several individuals participated along with the Red de Apoyo por la Justicia y la Paz (Mutual Aid Network for Justice and Peace), in the Vigilia por la Vida (Vigil for Life) held in the Plaza Bolívar in Caracas, with the intention of denouncing the humiliation and bullying of the people by the Policia Metropolitana and DISIP. On February 23, the CRA, along with the group Venezolanos Amigos de América (VENAMI) and other collectives demonstrated in front of the Mexican embassy in solidarity with the Zapatista uprising. And on March 16, anarchists participated in a march to the Congress in support of victims of [police and military] impunity. One other initiative took place on the Isla de Margarita, where Daniel Iorio created a theater group under the name of Teatro Libertario.

VENAMI—[a clever acronym, "ven ami" means "come friend"]—was a collective created at the UCV by individual anarchists, with the intention of creating a supportive place in solidarity with the popular struggles in Latin America. It defined itself in its bulletin as follows:

> We're a volunteer collective that recognizes in ourselves the struggle of the people of the Americas for social, economic, political, cultural, and spiritual emancipation. . . .

> We want to express our combative solidarity in actions that help people comprehend that in America there are two poles of social struggle: one representing oppression encompassing the autocrats, dictators, military, police, bourgeoisie, exploiters and other such specimens all over the continent; the other encompassing those with dreams of liberty of all the oppressed and exploited.

> We've decided to break the chains of silence and indifference, we want to be part of the future that's under construction, we want to express that the unity of the oppressed is the unstoppable force in our history. We're a collective open to all who want to participate and join forces regionally. VENAMI salutes your actions in solidarity.[202]

New Times

On November 25, 1995 the most outstanding anarchist thinker and writer in these lands died: Ángel Cappelletti, one of the indispensable intellectuals in the teaching of libertarians and philosophers in Venezuela. The CRA in a long and emotional editorial by Antonio Serrano, "¡Adios Compadre!", said a final goodbye to a uniquely knowledgeable man, a man like few others.

One day in 1970, in my place of work, Germinal Gracia (Víctor García) introduced me to a compañero who had just arrived from Argentina, Ángel J. Cappelletti. He wasn't tall, but he was strong, wide, square shouldered, with a grey beard—he looked like Bakunin. He had come to work at the Universidad Simón Bolívar as a professor of philosophy.

After meeting him, for many months we saw each other on Sunday afternoons in the house of Germinal Gracia, and would talk about the things of the world, at times putting our feet up, at others as a way of healing [old] wounds. But always [we had our] eyes open when Cappelletti initiated or contributed to a conversation, and with naturalness . . . peeling back leaf after leaf covering the fruit and leaving it free of defects, [peeling back the leaves covering] events throughout history that had been in the shadows, until they were totally [revealed].

His knowledge was almost without limits . . . [in] his works on ancient religions and history, the Renaissance . . . political philosophy, and economics . . . the flourishing [of philosophy] in France with Decartes, Montesquieu, Diderot . . . With much reason, one of [Cappelletti's] disciples, who's today a professor, has classified his knowledge as encyclopedic.

This knowledge was expressed in more than 80 books, including those that don't have anarchism as lodestar; [but it] is implicit in all of them that moral conduct should be the primary thing in human relations. . . . His philosophical output was recognized at long last when he . . . was awarded and accepted the National Essay Prize in 1995. . . .

Those of us who continue holding him as a compañero reaffirm that his ideals are ours . . .[203]

On July 12, 1996 a conference was held in memory of Cappelletti in the auditorium of the UCV School of the Humanities. After the conference anarchist activities continued at the UCV with the showing, a week later on July 19, of the documenary *¿Por qué perdimos la guerra?* (Why did we lose the [Spanish Civil] war?) on the 60th anniversary of the outbreak of the Spanish Revolution. The showing was organized by the Free Chair of the School of Engineering and Society with the help of the CRA.

Other activities included plastering the walls of the School of Sociology with posters about the May 1968 uprising in Paris, the IMF, and the anti G-7 campaign by members of the CRA and other anarchists. As well, there was a benefit concert at El Junquito by the anarcho-punk bands Risa (Laugh), Crisis Política and Época de Recluta (Epoch of the Recruit) to raise funds for *El Libertario*.

In October, the CRA also helped with a tour by the Canary Islands rock band Garrote Vil, with the tour being called "Alzados . . . contra el etnicidio" (Rise up against genocide [or ethnic cleansing]"; the tour included half-a-dozen stops in Caracas and appearances in La Guaira, San Cristóbal, and Barquisimeto.

In the same month there was a mural painting event in Barquisimeto sponsored by the Venezolanos Amigos de Cuba (VENAMICUBA), and the anarchist group CRA-Barquisimeto participated in it and painted an ecological and anti-militarist mural. Anarchists also participated in the demonstration in front of the French embassy to protest the French open-air nuclear tests on the island of Mururoa in the South Pacific.

As regards print media, at the beginning of 1996, Mercedes Medina presented her thesis, "Espacio Cultural Libertario, un acercamiento a la expresión juvenil urbana en Venezuela durante las décadas 1980-1990." This text was part of an exposition at the UCV School of Art, and was also published in *El Libertario*. On July 31, Antonio Serrano had an article in the daily paper *El Universal* in commemoration of the 60th anniversary of the Spanish Revolution. And in October of the same year, the intellectuals Arturo Uslar Pietri, and Manuel Caballero separately published articles in *El Universal* hailing [and explaining] anarchism as the most reliable and humane way to organize society.

In the longer-term, during the mid-1990s several anarchists began to be active in human rights groups, and the state responded with repression to try to frighten them into inactivity. Any Alarcón was one victim of the intimidation. She recalls:

> It was in December on Human Rights Day, and there was a film shown in the Plaza Balzac del Ateneo de Caracas. I was there with Julio "Amor", Yaruani,

and other people . . . After the film ended, many of them went to the UCV . . . and I left for Los Caobos. When I was on the way between the plaza and the Museum of Science, DIM (Military Intelligence Division) agents grabbed me and pushed me up against the fence . . . They grabbed my face and asked for my papers. Yuriani joined me so I wouldn't be all alone. . . . They didn't arrest me because a lot of people were just leaving the Cinematica Nacional, and among them was a journalist friend from *El Universal*, Roberto Gómez, who recognized me and identified himself [to the DIM agents], who after a while let me go. The DIM were political police, and this type of thing was common. They might have been after me because at the time I worked for the Red de Apoyo por la Justicia y la Paz (Support Network for Justice and Peace).[204]

Another, worse, act of repression the DIM committed against the young anarchists at the UCV was the seizure near the Municipio Sucre of John Jairo Marín. They arrested him, humiliated him, and beat him, for supposedly engaging in street fighting between anarchists and partisans of the extreme right-wing Nuevo Orden Republicano (NOR) in the Plaza Altamira. After a night of terror, they finally let the young activist go.

On October 31, 1996, the CRA tried to participate along with a conglomeration of activists of other stripes in a march of solidarity with the prisoners held at the Casa de Reeducación y Trabajo Artesanal del Paraíso, better known as La Planta. This action was intended to be in solidarity with the 25 prisoners who had died at the hands of the Guardia Nacional in that prison. But the police broke up the march before it even got started. The CRA also maintained contact with two non-anarchist prisoners in La Planta, Poveda Castillo and Jhon Richard, sharing with them the anarchist vision of abolishing prisons.

In 1996, on the initiative of Johnny Castro, the band Apatía-No formed. Its members were Johnny Castro (vocals), Oscar Moreno (bass), Arnaldo Morales (drums), and Carolina Guevara (guitar). This same group also started the self-managed record company Noseke Records.

[Almost alone among punk bands] Apatía-No had clearly defined anarchist principles [which they put in writing]. They included:

1. Spreading anarchist ideas . . . in all possible mediums . . .

2. Operating apart from authoritarian institutions . . .

3. Promoting horizontal structures . . .

4. Holding concerts at affordable prices [with transparent finances] . . .

5. Self-management of our recordings, cooperating and aiding other bands through Noseke Records and La Bruja Records [and charging affordable prices for materials and distribution] . . .

6. Operating without financial ends . . . with any excess funds going toward propaganda, equipment, recording . . . etc.

7. Aiding other projects . . . and all types of social entities in which the idea is to promote a more just and equitable world . . . [205]

In 1997, two new anarchist 'zines appeared, *El Ghetto* and *Subsuelo Insurgente*, which was edited by Roberto Valdivia and Robert Tirado, and in which other young libertarians participated, including Juan Miguel Pardo and Miguel Romero. Other countercultural and anarchist periodicals held, in Caracas's Plaza Las Tres Gracias, the Feria de Publicaciones Independientes, (Independent Publications Fair) which was intended as a means of spreading anarchist and counterculture ideals to the public.

At the same time, the number of protests called by leftist groups, and in which anarchists participated, lessened. As well, the weekly Friday demonstration held near the UCV diminished from being a constant to being sporadic, [in part due to] lack of proposals [about what to protest]. To this last we can add the surveillance of activists by DISIP. As evidence of this, one can cite the article by journalist Víctor Escalona, "Detectaron centro de espionaje en la UCV," in *El Universal*, regarding state surveillance of "nearly 100 members of the university [UCV] community . . . the majority identified as belonging to Bandera Roja, MBR-200, and Desobediencia Popular . . ."[206]

On May 27, 1997, administrators at UCV along with the rector and student groups conducted a poll with the intention of putting the brakes on the confrontations with the police, and on sabotage carried out by hooded demonstrators. The preliminary results showed that of the 16,922 members of the university who expressed an opinion, 94% supported confronting the hooded ones, 74% were in accord with arresting them, and 86% backed the UCV in organizing in peaceful and legal ways of defending [the goals of] the protests.

Here it's necessary to point out that the libertarian groups organized subsequent to 1994 rejected the cult of violence, as can be seen in a flyer the CRA distributed at the UCV. It reads in part:

Today, parodying Marx, one can say that specters are haunting the autonomous universities, pathetic jokes of specters who pretend to elevate themselves to the category of supreme revolutionary demons, as a way of organizing weekly gangs with Molotovs, rocks, shots, and tear gas, held with rigorous regularity and choreographed for the communications media and with the enthusiastic accompaniment of the police. Beneath the hoods is the residue of the extreme authoritarian left, well infiltrated by police bodies and common criminals. So that no one be confused, they are in absolutely no way an expression of popular discontent . . . [T]heir programmed vandalism on Friday afternoons has nothing to do with insurgency of the people or with direct collective action, but rather it's an incarnation of the "revolutionary vanguard" theory, which in all ages has been suspiciously close to police use of provocateurs. Similar street fights are sordid routines that are not only far from genuine collective demonstrations of popular exasperation . . . but have become an ideal pretext for police aggression against university communities . . . so as to persecute and destroy all budding expressions of genuine alternative opposition, in addition to being a way to distract public opinion from basic problems such as education. In fact, with no doubt whatsoever, we can say that if the hooded ones didn't exist, the state would have to invent them.

Besides, as everyone even halfway familiar with the university scene knows, the hooded ones espouse no ideology worthy of the name. They don't even bother with printing pamphlets or flyers to explain their motivations, and barely do anything more than produce graffiti that's grotesque ("viva la capucha"—"long live the hood") or unintentionally funny ("fuera Bill Clinton de la UCV"—"Bill Clinton get out of the UCV') . . . Neither is there any doubt that they practice fascist intimidation against those who have challenged them to debate . . . With stalinistic smugness, they declare themselves the "revolutionary vanguard," and others apathetic or traitors for not accompanying them on their criminal exploits. No one familiar with libertarian socialist positions should be surprised that television and the daily papers, out of ignorance or dishonesty, present their acts as an expression of "anarchy," a mindless desire for chaos. But anarchist history is full of examples of the anarchist struggle to differentiate anarchism from this sick cult, which our adversaries have used to libel us and to justify the repression from which we've always suffered. Our history also teaches that anarchists have never hesitated for an instant in participating in the most belligerent popular direct actions, but have never privileged violence as a means . . .

Even though the state and its minions ceaselessly put on the burlesque of their "concern about the matter [street violence] and ways of confronting it," in reality the hooded ones are truly only a problem for us—the much weakened Venezuelan radical movement inside and outside of the universities—in organizing collective struggle initiatives . . . This isn't an easy task, but if we don't undertake it we'll have to resign ourselves to being saddled with these ruffians and the police brutality for which they supply a pretext . . .[207]

While all this was going on, the CRA participated in the national march in defense of the Sierra de Imataca, denouncing the ecocide and mining in that environmental preserve. In April and May, the CRA in conjunction with activists and editors of underground publications, organized a series of periodical sales at the metro stop at the City University of the UCV on every Friday from 4:00 to 7:00 pm. And on June 14, the musical cooperative Renuencia Sónica (Sonic Reluctance) organized a concert promoting conscientious objection [to military "service"] in which several bands participated, Blanka Makinaria, Farándula Popular, Los Residuos and Crisis Política; anarchists also participated in the conscientious objector movement known as Elegimos la Paz (We Choose Peace). As well, CRA members started the online discussion list Anarqlat, with the intention of maintaining a wider channel of communication with other anarchist groups and individuals in Latin America.

During the year 1998, the CRA was very busy organizing cultural events, and toward the end of the year managed to rent an office. Among other things, it organized a concert titled Rock contra la comida basura (Rock Against Garbage Food) at the Plaza de las Tres Gracias at the UCV. Musical groups participating included Crisis Política, Renuencia, and Farándula Popular. Other anarchist-influenced bands of the period included Doña Maldad and Los Residuos.

The CRA also participated in the international anarchist conference Francia del 68—Bogota del 98 held in Bogota, Colombia. Participants included members of the Colectivo Ateneu Libertario Estell Negre from Spain, and Rafael Uzcátegui from the CRA's coordinating committee. At about the same time, the group Apatía-No toured Colombia sharing the bill with several other bands: IRA, Rechazo, Polikarpas, Anti-Todo and Resistencia. The CRA also participated in a march in Barquisimeto along with the Comunidad Chilena Democrática in support of the extradition of Chilean dictator Augusto Pinochet from Spain to Chile.

From July 14 to July 24, the CRA, with the support of the administration of the School of Sociology at the UCV, organized a series of events commemorating the Spanish Revolution of 1936. It placed a collection of 29 photographs in the halls by the Hungarian photographer Kati Horna; it held a workshop with CNT members Antonio Serrano and Emilio Tesoro; and it showed two films, *Bajo el Signo Libertario* and *Tierra y Libertad*.

On November 27, the CRA organized a colloquium in San Cristóbal on anarchist esthetics, including a discussion with professor Nelson Méndez and the showing of the film *Arte y Anarquía* produced by the CNT-affiliated Fundación Anselmo Lorenzo in Madrid.

As regards print activity, *El Libertario* continued to appear, and attorney Bruno Escatime's pamphlet *El Estado y la Contrarrevolución* appeared, which was a denunciation of the counter-revolutionary nature of all states, "no matter their populist coloring." There were also a lot of anarchist and anarchist-influenced 'zines: *Subsuelo Insurgente, Fuerza Kamejane, Juventud Rebelde, Apatiarlos,* produced by *Julia Araque, Gangster Skazine, Axioma, El Subte, El Alcornoque Subterraneo, El Clandestino, El Ghetto,* and *Amor Libre,* an anarcho-feminist 'zine produced by Maria Illymani Inojosa.

Alcornoque Subterráneo was a 'zine produced by Coromoto Jaraba, a student at USB; it appeared three or four times and was photocopied, as was common in the period. *Axioma* was the news organ of the Colectivo de Resistencia Libertaria based in Cúa in Miranda state; and that group was involved in the campesino struggle in the Valles del Tuy.

On November 22, 1998 the CRA, opened an office on Avenida El Cuartel in the Catai de Caracas area that it shared with other political groups with which it engaged in various political projects.

In the midst of all these anarchist projects, on December 6, 1998, new presidential elections took place, and Hugo Chávez won; he was the candidate of a conglomeration of center-left parties (PCV, MAS, MEP, PPT, etc.) as well as his own Movimiento Quinta Republica. The election of Chávez over his AD-COPEI rival, businessman Henríque Salas Römer, marked the definitive end to AD-COPEI domination of Venezuela's politics, a period known as the Fourth Republic [hence Chávez's Fifth Republic Movement].

Chávez's election marked the beginning of a new political, economic, and social process called Socialismo, which is still being played out.

[Anarchist activity in the Chávez/Maduro era deserves a book of it's own.] For now, this book is intended as a legacy for future generations of anarchists, social rebels, and antiauthoritarians, intended to give them heart in a future that holds as much authoritarianism and social and economic inequality as in the year of Venezuela's founding in 1811.

Epílogue

"Some burn out, others persevere, but they are always few. Now it's necessary to prepare the ground for a future, no matter how remote from the miserable present. I won't see it, but my blood burns with emotion for those who will."

—Domingo Alberto Rangel

We're finished with this voyage of anecdotes, experiences, and expressions of Venezuela's anarchist movement. A whirlwind of events and portraits, of rebels, guerrillas, academics, writers, congressional deputies, painters, workers, unionists, ethnologists, musicians, students, heroes, and poets: men and women of all stripes who fought for radical transformation of Venezuelan society from the bottom up.

As we can see, anarchist ideas have always been present in national affairs, anarchism's partisans at times promoting those ideas under other names while committing heroic political deeds and making important socials demands. This is why the principles espoused by Venezuela's anarchists have been intertwined with the most fervent desires of the Venezuelan people: liberty, gender and class equality, overcoming petroleum dependence, sustainable production, self-management, federalism, direct democracy, antimilitarism, recognition of labor rights, and struggle against all types of monopolies and dictators; these are some of the desires of a movement that has always been composed of those excluded from the banquet of the rich and the petroleum bureaucrats.

Regarding this book, every reader will take from it what they consider pertinent. But it's necessary to point out that the events and matters related here are an incomplete history, as there are undoubtedly persons and events that have vanished without a trace, or near to it. The experiences of the dispossessed classes, and especially of those who live on the border of legality, have not been generously recorded for posterity. The periodicals, judicial archives, police reports, memoirs all serve as documentation. But what has been lost? How much has been taken to the grave?

Conscious of this, it's also true that the historical facts outlined here are real and undeniable. We've found sources that support in capital letters what we've narrated here; tomorrow others will find more. Having said that, we've had to weave our narrative through many subjective accounts, judgments, and histories that either coincide or are contradictory.

We insist on rescuing anarchist history from being seen as a mere antiquarian exercise. It's much more than that. Our forerunners have cleared the path for those who find themselves on the margins of the state, the military, and capital on the road to human and social liberation. Of course, material and social conditions, as well as the state, have changed significantly. But they retain their essence, and the lessons to be learned from this book will enrich our practice. We hope that this book will serve those compañeros and compañeras who reflect upon these matters.

Today, the libertarian movement in this region is divided. With good reasons at times, with futile and infantile reasons at others, people supposedly pursuing the same ends have engaged in defamation, bitter feuds, and excommunications. Because of this, it's necessary to turn our gaze back to the path trodden, and to contrast it with our current situation and conceptions; in the past there were also divergencies and splits within a movement that faced the most daunting challenges in the field of ideology. For example, it's worth debating the opportunism of some anarchists in making and retaining ties with populist governments that spouted revolutionary rhetoric, but in practice pillaged the people. It's necessary to criticize to satiety the employment of the methods of representative democracy to achieve the vision of liberation in an arena wholly antagonistic to anarchism's seditious project. As well, it's necessary to ponder academic intellectualism disconnected from our national problems, and that lacks concrete programs and projects to put into action. All of this points to why anarchism at present won't reach national relevance [without significant changes].

Summing up, this book presents mechanisms and actions that we ought to rescue from oblivion: such things as resolute participation in the centers of national production against all types of totalitarianism, and more involvement in the unions. Ones to reject are construction of electoral platforms and support of populist political parties, things which left a bitter taste of failure on the palates of some anarchists. The theoretical bases and principals of anarchism have been outlined here, and also the portraits of anarchist militants and their exploits and failures in Venezuela.

The past is ours. Now we need to create the future. From here on, let's not write history, let's make it.

ENDNOTES

CHAPTER 1

1 BANDINI, Ángelo María (1948). *Vida y cartas de Américo Vespucio.* Editorial P.T.C.M. p. 57.
2 VÁZQUEZ DE ESPINOSA, Antonio (1948). *Compendio y descripción de las Indias Occidentales.* Dirección de Cultura. p.23.
3. GRAEBER, David (2011). *Fragmentos de antropología anarquista.* Virus Editorial, Barcelona., p. 27.
4. ARANGO, Luis y SANCHEZ, Enrique (2004). *Los pueblos indígenas de Colombia en el umbral del nuevo milenio.* Bogotá: DNP, pp. 360-362.
5. MONTAIGNE, Michele (1981) *Essais.* Réimpression en facsimilé de l´Exemplaire de Bordeaux, par Fortunat Strowski, 1906-33 en 5 vol. Hildesheim-Nueva York, Ed. Geog Olms, 3 vol.

CHAPTER 2

6. GIL FORTOUL, José (1967). *Historia Constitucional de Venezuela.* Caracas, Librería Piñango, p.225.
7. PARRA PÉREZ, Caracciolo. (1992) *Historia de la Primera República de Venezuela.* Biblioteca Ayacucho.
8. RANGEL, Domingo Alberto (29 de enero 2010). *Coto Paúl, el olvidado 1810.* Semanario Quinto Día.
9. USLAR PIETRI, Juan (1962). *Historia de la rebelión popular de 1814.* Editorial Edime, p.137.
10. MIER HOFFMAN, Jorge (2008). *Bolívar y la Anarquía.* Recuperado de: http://www.simon-bolivar.org/bolivar/ven_y_la_anarquia.html#inicio
11. CABALLERO, Manuel (2007). *Ni dios, ni federación.* Editorial Planeta. p.109.
12. MIER HOFFMAN, Jorge (2008). *Bolívar y la Anarquía.* Op cit.
13. NARVAJA DE ARNOUX (2008). *El Discurso Latinoamericano de Hugo Chávez.* Argentina. Editorial Biblos. p. 71.
14. ROJAS, Aristides (1891). *Leyendas históricas de Venezuela.* Caracas. Segunda Serie. Imprenta y litografía del Gobierno Nacional. p. 44.
15. *Boletín de la Academia Nacional de la Historia,* Caracas, Venezuela, octubre de 1921. Documento fechado en 1915, es pieza sustantiva de cualquier expediente político e histórico que se haga de Boves.
16. LEON, José Javier (2008). *El Demócrata.* Recuperado de: http://josejavierleon.blog.com.es/2008/11/20/eldemocrata-5071784/
17. BRITO FIGUEROA, Federico (1996). *Historia Económica y Social de Venezuela.* Tomo IV. Ediciones de la Biblioteca UCV, p. 13065. p. 1306.
18. SALCEDO BASTARDO, José Luis (1993). *Historia Fundamental de Venezuela.* Ediciones de la UniversidadCentral de Venezuela, p. 89.
19. LOVERA DE SOLA, Roberto J (2009). *Un Zamora Chavista.* Recuperado de: http://www.analitica.com/va/ sociedad/articulos/3378370. asp
20. PALMA, Douglas A (1997). *150 biografías de los personajes notables de Venezuela.* Editorial Panapo. p. 126.
21. GONZÁLEZ, Juan Vicente (1846). *Diario de la tarde,* n° 94, Caracas. 15 de septiembre y n° 114, 8 de octubre de 1846, cf. Presidencia de la Republica, Pensamiento Político Venezolano del Siglo XIX, textos para estudios, vol. 3, t. II, pp. 104 y 105, Caracas, Editorial Arte. 1961, p. 45.
22. PALMA, Douglas (1997). Op. cit, p. 126.
23. BRADFORD, José (2 de noviembre de 1846). Correspondencia. Caracas, Venezuela.
24. SHIKES, Ralph (1986). "Pissarro's political philosophy and his art," from *Studies on Camille Pissarro.* Edited by Christopher Lloyd. London and New York: Routledge & Kegan Paul. p 54.
25. POTENZIANI BIGELLI, Julio (Enero-Marzo 2012). *Camille Pissarro y Venezuela, una huella que duraría toda una vida.* Vitae Nro. 49. Academia Biomédica Digital.
26. MATHEWS, Robert. *Violencia rural en Venezuela 1840/1858.* Monte Ávila Editores, p. 3120
27. Ibid.
28. *Opúsculo.* p. 83-84.
29. Ibid.
30. HOBSBAWM, Eric (2001). *Bandidos.* Barcelona. Crítica. p. 33.
31. DÍAZ SÁNCHEZ, Ramón (1950). *Guzmán, elipse de una ambición de poder.* Caracas. p. 377.
32. ALVARADO, Lisandro (1856). *Historia de la revolución federal en Venezuela.* Obras Completas, Vol V. Caracas Ministerio de Educación.
33. BRITO FIGUEROA, Federico (1951). *Historia económica y social de Venezuela.* Tomo IV. Ediciones de la Biblioteca Central de Venezuela. p. 178.
34. BRITO FIGUEROA Federico (1951). *Ezequiel Zamora, un capítulo de la Historia Nacional.* Editorial Ávila Grafica. Caracas. p.56.
35. LOVERA DE SOLA, Roberto J (2009). *Un Zamora Chavista.* http://www.analitica.com/va/sociedad/articulos/3378370.asp

36. UGALDE, Luis (1978). *Venezuela Republicana Siglo XIX*. Curso de formación sociopolítico.

37. GONZALEZ, Juan Vicente (14 de diciembre de 1859). *Guerra Social*. El Heraldo. Nº 48.

38. RODRIGUEZ, Adolfo. *El Fuego sagrado*. Caracas. Ipasme. p. 107.

39. PARDO, Miguel Eduardo (1981). *Todo un Pueblo*. Caracas, Monte Ávila. p. 44.

40. BRANDT, Carlos (1936). *El problema económico-social.Rosario-Argentina*. Ediciones Símbolo. p.10.

41. SERRANO, Antonio (18 de octubre de 1998). *Apuntes sobre Anarquismo en Venezuela*. Suplemento Cultural Últimas Noticias. Caracas,

42. URQUIJO, José Ignacio (2000). *El movimiento obrero en Venezuela*. OIT-UCAB.

43. ÁLVAREZ, Ernesto /2 de mayo de 1892). *El Primero de Mayo para los Anarquistas*. El Fonógrafo.

44. FARIAS, Eduardo (1990). *1928, responden los protagonistas*. Caracas. Fondo Editorial Tropykos.

45. GODIO, Julio (1980). *Historia del movimiento obrero latinoamericano*. México. Editorial Nueva Imagen,

46. RAMA, Carlos M (1976). *Historia del movimiento obrero y social latinoamericano contemporáneo*. Barcelona. Ediciones de Bolsillo. Editorial Laia.

47. SALCEDO BASTARDO, José Luis (1993). *Historia Fundamental de Venezuela*. Ediciones de la Universidad Central de Venezuela. p. 339.

48. ALVAREZ DE ESCALONA, Sandra (1993). *Evolución del Derecho Laboral en Venezuela*. Academia de Ciencias Políticas y Sociales.

49. VILLANUEVA MARTÍNEZ, Orlando y otros (1992). *Biofilo Panclasta, el eterno prisionero*. Bogotá, Colombia. Editorial CODICE LTDA. p.230.

50. Ibid. p. 231.

51. ENZO, David (2007). *Carlos Brandt y el Misterioso Almirante*. Recuperado de: http://enzodavid.wordpress.com/2007/05/12/carlos-brandt-y-el-misterioso-almirante-que-nos-descubrio/

52. LOPEZ CONTRERAS, Eleazar (1949). *El triunfo de la verdad*. Edición Genio Latino.

53. ZAMBRANO, Luis Eduardo. *El intento de magnicidio de Cipriano Castro*. Diario La Nación. Recuperado de: http://www.lanacion.com.ve/noticias.php?IdArticulo=113745&XR=2

54. NOGALES MÉNDEZ, Rafael (1991). *Memorias*. Biblioteca Ayacucho. p.155-160.

55. Ibid. p. 161

56. Ibid.

57. BRANDT, Carlos (1947). *La época del terror en el país de Gómez*. Editorial Pentalfa.

58. MECHE (2011). *Las andanzas de Rafael Bolívar Coronado*. Recuperado de: http://cuentaelabuelo.blogspot.com/2011/03/las-andanzas-de-rafael-bolivar-coronado.html

59. MATA, Celestino (1985). *Historia Sindical de Venezuela*. Editores Urbina y Fuente asociados, Caracas, Venezuela.

60. QUINTERO, Rodolfo. "Historia del Movimiento Obrero en Venezuela," en P. Gonzáles Casanova, *Historia del Movimiento Obrero en América Latina*.

61. FARIAS, Eduardo. Op. cit. p. 49.

62. RANGEL, Domingo Alberto (2004). *Un Socialismo para el Siglo XXI*. Caracas, Venezuela. Editores Mérida.

63. SERRANO, Antonio. (20 de mayo de 2006). Entrevista. Caracas, Venezuela.

64. Mensajes que el Dr. Victorino Márquez Bustillo, Presidente Provisional de Venezuela presenta al Congreso Nacional, mensajes presidenciales, Tomo IV, 1910-1939, Caracas, 1971. p. 102-103.

65. PELLEGRINO, Adela (1989). *Historia de la inmigración en Venezuela, siglos XIX y XX*. Academia Nacional de Ciencias Económicas. p 151.

66. GODIO, Julio. Op. cit. p.112.

67. Ibid.

68. RODRÍGUEZ, Leonardo (1988). *La clase obrera en el tiempo de Gómez 1908-1935*. Publicaciones El Pueblo.

69. *El Obrero* (9 de diciembre de 1920), Caracas.

70. *El Obrero* (19 de septiembre de 1920), Caracas.

71. LARES, Fermín. *El movimiento sindical y la lucha política en Venezuela 1936–59*. Monte Ávila e Instituto Nacional de Altos Estudios Sindicales, INAESINO.

72. V.V.A.A (1984). *Pío Tamayo. Un combate por la vida*. Ediciones UCV.

73. *Compañero* (Mayo de 1976). Nro 2,

74. RANGEL, Domingo Alberto (2013). *Alzado contra todo, memoria y desmemoria*. Caracas. Editores Hermanos Vadell y Editores Mérida. p. 118.

75. MESA, Salom (1987). *La Vida me lo dijo, elogio a la anarquía*. Valencia, Venezuela. Editorial Hermanos Vadell. p. 18.

76. LARES, Fermín. op.cit.

77. QUINTERO, Rodolfo. "Historia del Movimiento Obrero en Venezuela," en P. Gonzáles Casanova, *Historia del Movimiento Obrero en América Latina*.

78. AGUDO FREITES, Raúl (1969). *Pío Tamayo y la Vanguardia*. Ediciones UCV.

79. SOTO PRIETO, Jesús. *La lucha obrera por nuestro petróleo*. p. 37.

80. Ibid. p. 39.

81. PÉREZ SALINAS, Bernardo. *Tras las huellas del sindicalismo*. Cuadernos Obreros de Acción Democrática..

82. SOTO PRIETO, Jesús. Op. cit. p. 17.

83. RODRÍGUEZ Leonardo (1988). *La Clase Obrera en el tiempo de Gómez, 1908–1935*. Op. cit. p. 24.

84. BOLIVAR, Rafael (1919). *Las grandes figuras del bolcheviquismo. El sindicalismo en acción. Lenine*. Biblioteca Véritas. p. 133.

85. Ibid. p. 134.

86. CASTELLANOS, RAFAEL, RAMÓN. *Un hombre con más de 600 nombres*.

87. FERNANDEZ, Frank (2000). *Anarquismo en Cuba*. Madrid. Fundación Anselmo Lorenzo. p. 64.

88. OTERO SILVA, Miguel (2004). *Cuando quiero llorar, no lloro*. Caracas. Editorial CEC, S.A. p. 77.

89. SOSA ARTURO, Legrand Eloi (1981). *Del Garibaldismo estudiantil a la Izquierda Criolla.* Caracas, Venezuela. Ediciones Centauro. p.37.
90. CABALLERO, Manuel (1998). *La crisis de la Venezuela contemporánea (1903-1992).* Ediciones Alfadil. p. 65.
91. FARIAS Eduardo. Op cit. p. 44.
92. V.V.A.A (1984). *Pío Tamayo, un combate por la vida.* Op. cit. p.14.
93. FARIAS, Eduardo. Op. cit. p. 85.
94. AGUDO FREITES, Raúl. Op. cit. p. 30.
95. FARIAS, Eduardo. Op. cit. p. 35.
96. Ibid.
97. Ibid.
98. AGUDO FREITES, Rafael. Op. cit. p. 40.
99. QUINTERO, Rodolfo. *Sindicalismo y cambio social en Venezuela.*
100. ALBA, Víctor (1964). *Historia del Movimiento Obrero en América Latina.* México D.F. Editorial Limusa Wiley. S.A. p. 54
101. CABALLERO, Manuel (2004). *Rómulo Betancourt, político de nación.* Editorial Alfadil, Fondo de Cultura Económica. 2ª Edición.
102. MESA, Salom (1987). *La Vida me lo dijo, elogio a la anarquía.* Op. cit. p. 47.
103. OLIVO, Libertad (1997). *Francisco Olivo, un hombre, una vida, una escuela.* Caracas, Venezuela. Instituto Municipal de Publicaciones. p. 27.
104. Ibid. p. 32.
105. MESA, Salom (1978). *Por un caballo y una mujer (Memorias).* Op. cit. p. 72.
106. MESA, Salom. *Cartas para Carlos.* Valencia. Hermanos Vadell Editores. p. 194.
107. MESA, Salom (1987). *La Vida me lo dijo, elogio a la anarquía.* Editorial Hermanos Vadell. Valencia.
108. Ibid. p. 22.
109. SANIN, Rómulo. *Los adecos en el poder.* Colección Criterios. Venezuela. p 27-28.
110. DÍAZ RANGEL, Eleazar (1998). *El 14 de febrero y otros relatos.* Monte Ávila Editores. p.23.
111. CABALLERO, Manuel. *Rómulo Betancourt, político de nación.* Editorial Alfadil, Fondo de Cultura Económica. 2ª Edición.
112. CABALLERO, Manuel. *Ni dios, ni federación.* Editorial Planeta. p.285.
113. PRATO BARBOSA, Nelson. *Desobediencia Social en Venezuela.* Colección José Agustín Silva Michelena. APUCV.
114. BRANDT, Carlos (1936). *El problema económico-social.*Op. cit. p. 89.
115. Ibid.
116. SOSA, Arturo (1994). *El programa nacionalista izquierda y modernización (1937-1939).* Caracas, Venezuela. Editorial Fundación Rómulo Betancourt.
117. QUINTERO, Rodolfo (1967). *La huelga petrolera 1936-1937.* Folleto publicado en Barranquilla en 1937 y reeditado en Venezuela por el Departamento de Reproducción de FACES.
118. OLIVO Libertad (1997). Op. cit. p. 49.

Chapter 4

119. RANGEL, Domingo Alberto. *Alzado contra todo, memoria y desmemoria.* Editores Hermanos Vadell y Editores Mérida. Caracas. Marzo de 2013. p. 118.
120. VELASQUEZ Ramón J (1976). *Venezuela Moderna. Medio siglo de historia.* Caracas, Venezuela. Fundación Eugenio Mendoza. p. 97.
121. INIGUEZ Miguel (2001). *Esbozo de una Enciclopedia Histórica del Anarquismo Español.* Fundación Anselmo Lorenzo.
122. RANGEL, Domingo Alberto (2004). *Un socialismo para el siglo veintiuno.* Editores Mérida. Caracas. Venezuela. Febrero.
123. CATALAN, José Agustín (1983). *Venezuela, bajo el signo del terror.* Libro Negro 1952. Caracas, Venezuela. Ediciones Centauro. p. 110.
124. IÑIGUEZ Miguel (2001). *Esbozo de una Enciclopedia Histórica del Anarquismo Español.* Fundación Anselmo Lorenzo. p. 382.
125. MOLEIRO, Moisés (1979). *El Partido del Pueblo, crónica de un fraude.* Editores Hermanos Vadell. Valencia.
126. MESA, Salom (1978). *Por un caballo y una mujer.* Op. cit. p. 124.
127. DAGER, Jorge (1979). *Testigo de Excepción, en las trincheras de la resistencia 1948-1955.* Caracas, Venezuela. Ediciones Centauro. p. 78-79.
128. *La Esfera* (13 de octubre 1951). Tiraron una Bomba al paso de la Junta de Gobierno.
129. *La Esfera* (27 de julio 1951) . Asalto al puesto de emergencia: Pistola en mano se llevaron al doctor Alberto Carnevali.
130. CONSALVI Simón Alberto (1980). *Alberto Carnevali, vida y acción política.* Caracas, Venezuela. Ediciones Centauro. p. 255-256.
131. *La Primera Internacional y el debate entre Marx-Bakunin.*
132. CATALÁ, Jose Agustín (1983). *Venezuela, bajo el signo del terror.* Libro Negro 1952. Ediciones Centauro. Caracas.
133. ACUÑA, Guido. *Pérez Jiménez, un gendarme innecesario.* Editorial Poradise S.A. pp. 170, 172.
134. CATALÁ, José Agustín.. *Venezuela, bajo el signo del terror.* Libro Negro 1952. Op. cit. p. 272.
135. PENELAS, Carlos (2004). *Ácratas y crotos. Informes del sur, cuadernos de investigación.* Ediciones BP. Prosa.
136. CHRISTIE, Stuart (2005). *La resistencia libertaria al franquismo.* Recuperado de: http://www.alasbarricadas.org/noticias/?q=node/1730
137. SERRANO, Antonio. (20 de mayo 2006). Entrevista. Caracas, Venezuela.
138. ESCAMILLA, Francisco (2002). *Pablo Vila y el Exilio Español.* Revista Bibliográfica de Geografía y Ciencias Sociales. Universidad de Barcelona. Vol. VII. Nro. 409.
139. MESA, Salom (1978). *Por un caballo y una mujer.* Op. cit. p. 63.
140. SERRANO, Antonio. (24 de junio de 2004). Entrevista. Caracas, Venezuela.
141. ALBEROLA, Octavio (17 de febrero 2009). Cuestionario enviado por internet.
142. RICO, Francisco (1969). *Asalto al Santa María.* Editorial Esfuerzo. p40.
143. *Crisol Juvenil.* n° 8.
144. DIAZ, Carlos. *Víctor García, el Marco Polo del anarquismo.* Madre Tierra.
145. Ibid.
146. HERNANDEZ PARRA, Pablo (14 de enero 2013). Entrevista. Caracas, Venezuela.
147. FERNANDEZ, Frank. Op. cit. p. 59.
148. SERRANO, Antonio (20 de mayo 2006). Entrevista. Caracas, Venezuela.

149. BRANDT, Carlos (1927). *Filosofía del Vegetarianismo.* Barcelona (España). Editorial Francisco Sintes.
150. SERRANO, Antonio (Mayo/Junio 1999). Hace 35 años. Periódico *El Libertario.* Año 3, Nro. 14.
151. MESA, Salom (1964). *AD y el Problema Universitario.* Publicaciones de la Secretaría Nacional de Propaganda. Caracas.
152. MENDEZ, Nelson (28 de mayo 2005). Entrevista. Caracas, Venezuela.
153. DE CARLI, Humberto (17 de febrero 2005). Entrevista. Caracas, Venezuela.
154. MÚJICA, Héctor (1970). *Co-gobernabilidad: Balance de un Año de Renovación Académica.* Caracas. Cantaclaro.
155. ROMERO, Miguel y otros (2010). *Así se iniciaron nuestras luchas. Testimonios de la consecuencia revolucionaria del movimiento estudiantil de los años 60 y 70.* Caracas, Venezuela. Colección Alfredo Maneiro. Serie de Testimonios. p. 41.
156. UZCATEGUI, Rafael (2001). *Corazón de Tinta.* Bogotá, Colombia. Náufrago de Itaca Ediciones. p.22.
157. DE LA CRUZ, Rafael (1988). *Venezuela en busca de un nuevo pacto social.* Alfadil/Trópicos. pp.109-110.
158. LOVERA DE SOLA, Roberto (2009). *40 años de la Renovación en Letras.* Recuperado de: http://literanova.eduardocasanova.com/index.php/2009/05/12/40-anos-de-la-renovacion-en-letras-ucv-1-1969
159. SERRANO, Antonio (1998). *Apuntes sobre Anarquismo en Venezuela.* Op. cit.
160. MESA Salom. *Por un caballo y una mujer.* Op. cit. p. 92..
161. OLIVO, Libertad. Op. cit. p. 59.
162. DÍAZ, Carlos. Op. cit. p. 112.
163. OLIVO, Libertad. Op. cit. p. 167.
164. MESA, Salom. *Por un caballo y una mujer.* Op. cit. p. 149.
165. OLIVO, Libertad . Op. cit. p. 168.
166. PARRA HERNANDEZ, Pablo (14 de enero 2013). Entrevista, Caracas, Venezuela.
167. Ibid.

CHAPTER 5

168. MESA, Salom (1987). *La Vida me lo dijo, elogio a la anarquía.* Op. cit. p. 17.
169. *El Zuliano* (29 de mayo 1983). "En la calle Papeles Anárquicos, nuevo órgano de difusión cultural."
170. SERRANO, Antonio (12 de julio 1985). "El anarquismo, Sr. Betancourt, no es lo que usted así denomina." *El Nacional.*
171. LÓPEZ MAYA, Margarita (2005). *Del Viernes Negro al Referendo Revocatorio.* Colección Hogueras. Venezuela profunda. Alfa Grupo Editorial. p. 57.
172. VERGUEIRO, Armando. *Sobre el Caracazo.* Recuperado de: http://samizdata.host.sk/CAFebrero27.txt
173. DE LA MANO, Eduardo (1 de abril 2013). Cuestionario enviado por internet.
174. ROJAS AVILA, Julio (10 de mayo 2013). Cuestionario enviado por internet.
175. HEREDIA, Claudia (24 de mayo 2012). Cuestionario enviado por internet. Caracas, Venezuela.
176. TARAZONA, Félix (22 de maro 2013). Cuestionario enviado online.
177. UZCATEGUI, Rafael (2012). "Victimas de la Democracia, concierto en el Julius Pub." Recuperado de: http://exiliointeriorzine.blogspot.com/2012/08/victimas-de-la-democracia-en-concierto.html
178. BODOUTCHIAN, Jessica. Érase una vez el punk pero tuve que matarlo, entrevista a Elías Yanez. Revista Plátano Verde. p.24.
179. Entrevista online realizada el 10 de mayo de 2013.
180. Extraído del Boletín del Colectivo..
181. DENIS BOULTON, Roland (2001). *Los fabricantes de la rebelión, movimiento popular, chavismo y sociedad en los años 90.* Editorial Nueva Línea. Editorial Nuevo Sur. Caracas. Venezuela.
182. MESA, Salom (1987) *La Vida me lo dijo, elogio a la anarquía.* Op. cit. p. 49.
183. *Caracas, resiste y ataka* (1992). "Otra Victima más del gobierno asesino. Mayo-Junio,. nro 3. año 2."
184. DE LA MANO, Eduardo. Op cit.
185. DE LA MANO, Eduardo (22 de marzo 2013). Cuestionario enviado online.
186. CASTRO, Johnny (19 de mayo 2013). Cuestionario enviado online.
187. DE LA MANO, Eduardo (04 de abril 2013). Entrevista enviada online.
188. DE LA MANO, Eduardo (30 de marzo 2013). Entrevista enviada online.
189. *El Nacional.* "El gobierno nacional niega allanamiento de la UCV." Caracas 25 de enero de 1995.
190. ROJAS AVILA, Julio (15 de mayo 2013). Entrevista enviada online.
191. Ibid.
192. ROJAS AVILA, Julio (10 de mayo 2013). Entrevista enviada online.
193. Correo A (1992). Recuperado de: http://samizdata.host.sk/CAGolpes.txt
194. DE LA MANO, Eduardo (8 de abril 2013). Cuestionario enviado online.
195. VERGUEIRO, Armando (1992). "Golpe, video y mentira." Correo A.
196. MENDEZ, Nelson (22 de abril 2013). Entrevista. Caracas, Venezuela.
197. *Caracas, resiste y ataka* (1992). "Otra Victima más del gobierno asesino." Mayo–Junio, Nro 3. año 2.
198. CASTRO, Johnny (12 de febrero 2010). Entrevista. Caracas, Venezuela.
199. UZCATEGUI, Rafael (2001). *Corazón de tinta.* Op. cit. p. 24.
200. CASTRO, Johnny (19 de mayo 2013). Cuestionario enviado por internet.
201. CRA. "¿Quienes somos?" Recuperado de: http://www.nodo50.org/ellibertario/tripaquienessomos.htm
202. VENAMI (1995). *Declaración de VENAMI.* Boletín nº 1. Caracas. Venezuela. Abril.
203. CRA. Editorial: "¡Adiós Compañero!" Año 1, n° 3.
204. ALARCON, Any (22 de febrero 2013). Cuestionario enviado por internet.
205. APATIA NO. "¿Qué somos?" Recuperado de: http://www.geocities.com/apatiano
206. ESCALONA, Víctor (6 de enero de 1997). "Detectaron centro de espionaje en la UCV." *El Universal.*
207. CRA (1997). "Encapuchados: Un show sin gracia en 'Las 3 Gracias.'"

BIBLIOGRAPHY

ACUÑA, Guido. *Pérez Jiménez, un gendarme innecesario*. Editorial PoradiseS.A.

AGUDO FREITES, Raúl (1969). *Pío Tamayo y la Vanguardia*. EdicionesUCV.

AIZPÚRUA, Jon (2010). *Carlos Brandt*. http://www.maestre.org/f%20Carlos%20Brandt.html

ALBA, Víctor (1964). *Historia del Movimiento Obrero en América Latina*. Editorial Limusa Wiley. S.A. México. D.F. México.

ALCIBIADES Mirla (2010). *Carlos Brandt*. Biblioteca Biográfica Venezolana. El Nacional.

ALVARADO, Lisandro (1856). *Historia de la revolución federal en Venezuela*. Obras Completas, Vol V. Caracas Ministerio de Educación.

ALVAREZ DE ESCALONA, Sandra (1993). *Evolución del Derecho Laboral en Venezuela*. Academia de Ciencias Políticas y Sociales.

ÁLVAREZ, Ernesto. "El Primero de Mayo para los Anarquistas," *El Fonógrafo*, 2 de mayo de 1892

APATIA NO. *¿Qué somos?* http://www.geocities.com/apatiano

AREVALO GONZALEZ, Rafael. *Una Vida Rotunda*. http://doctorpolitico.com/wp-content/uploads/2013/08/Memorias-R.-Are%CC%81valo-G.pdf

Archivo General de la Administración del Estado (AGA)-Alcalá de Henares, Sección "Asuntos Exteriores", Caja 11831

ARRIETA ALVAREZ, José Ignacio (1995). *El movimiento sindical en Venezuela*. Fundación Centro Gumilla.

Amnistía Internacional. Documento - UA 203/92 - *Venezuela: possible extrajudicial execution: Rommer Figueroa Lizardi, Pedro Jose Vasquez, Jose Gregorio Romero Uzcategui; victims of torture: Omar Uribe, Arnel Rodriguez, Jose Antonio Briceno, Julio Cesar Vera, Oswaldo Rodriguez.*

ARANGO, Luis y SANCHEZ, Enrique (2004). *Los pueblos indígenas de Colombia en el umbral del nuevo milenio*. Bogotá: DNP.

ARELLANO MORENO, Arturo (1974). *Breve Historia de Venezuela (1492-1958)*. Italgrafica, SRL. Caracas, Venezuela.

ARMAS CHITTY, José Antonio (1969). *Vida política de Caracas en el siglo XIX*. Caracas.

AVRICH, Paul (1971). *The Russian Anarchists*. Princeton University Press.

AVRICH, Paul (1991. *Kronstadt 1921*. Princeton University Press.

BAKUNIN, Mikhail (1970). *God and the State*. New York, Dover.

BAKUNIN, Mikhail (2004). *Marxism, Freedom and the State*. London, Freedom Press.

BARRETO, Morela (1980). *La prensa obrera artesanal en el siglo XIX*. Caracas, FACES, UCV.

BANDINI, Ángelo María (1948). *Vida y cartas de Américo Vespucio*. Editorial P.T.C.M.

BANKO, Catalina (1996). *Las luchas federalistas en Venezuela*. Monte Avila Editores - CELARG. Caracas. Venezuela.

BAYER, Oswaldo. *Severino Di Giovanni, el idealista de la violencia*. Editorial Planeta.

BERKMAN, Alexander (2003). *What Is Anarchism?* Oakland, AK Press.

BIBLIOGRAPHY ♦ 206

BERKMAN, Alexander (1989). *The Bolshevik Myth*. London, Pluto Press.

BERKMAN, Alexander (1986). *The Russian Tragedy*. London, Phoenix Press.

BERROES, Manuel. *Historia de Venezuela*. Fundación de empresas Polar.

BLANCO MUÑOZ, Agustín. "Habla el General Marcos Pérez Jiménez." UCV. Caracas. *Boletín de la Academia Nacional de la Historia*, Caracas, Venezuela, octubre de 1921. Documento fechado en 1915, es pieza sustantiva de cualquier expediente político e histórico que se haga de Boves.

BOLIVAR, Rafael (1919). *Las grandes figuras del bolcheviquismo. El sindicalismo en acción*. Lenine. Biblioteca Véritas.

BOLLOTEN, Burnett (1961). *The Grand Camouflage*. New York, Praeger.

BOLLOTEN, Burnett (1979). *The Spanish Civil War*. Chapel Hill, University of North Carolina Press.

BOOKCHIN, Murray (2001). *The Spanish Anarchists: The Heroic Years (1868-1936)*. Oakland, AK Press.

BOSCH, Juan. *Bolívar y la Guerra Social*. http://www.simon-bolivar.org/Principal/bolivar/bylgs2_10.html

BODOUTCHIAN, Jessica. "Érase una vez el punk pero tuve que matarlo, entrevista a Elias Yanez." *Revista Plátano Verde*. p.24.

BRANDT, Carlos (1936). *El problema económico-social*. Ediciones Símbolo, Rosario. Argentina.

BRANDT, Carlos (1947). *La época del terror en el país de Gómez*. Editorial Pentalfa.

BRINTON, Maurice (2004). *For Workers Control*. Oakland, AK Press.

BRITO FIGUEROA, Federico (1996). *Historia Económica y Social de Venezuela*. Tomo IV. Ediciones de la Biblioteca UCV.

BRITO FIGUEROA, Federico (1981). *En tiempos de Ezequiel Zamora*. Ediciones Biblioteca UCV. Caracas.

CABALLERO, Manuel (2007). *Ni dios, ni federación*. Editorial Planeta.

CABALLERO, Manuel. *Rómulo Betancourt, político de nación*. Editorial Alfadil, Fondo de Cultura Económica. 2ª

CABALLERO, Manuel (1998). *La crisis de la Venezuela contemporánea (1903-1992)*. Ediciones Alfadil.

CAPPELLETTI Ángel (1990). *Anarquismo en América Latina*. Biblioteca Ayacucho.

Caracas, resiste y ataka (1992). Otra Victima más del gobierno asesino. Mayo-Junio. n° 3. año 2.

CARRERA DAMA, Gérman (1969). *Temas de historia social y de las ideas*. Universidad Central de Venezuela. Caracas.

CATALA, José Agustín (1983). *Venezuela, bajo el signo del terror*. Libro Negro 1952. Ediciones Centauro. Caracas.

CHRISTIE, Stuart (2005). *La resistencia libertaria al franquismo*. http://www.alasbarricadas.org/noticias/?q=node/1730

CIENFUEGOS, Leo (1992). *Conociendo a Daniel De León*. Correo A, Nro. 19.

CLAUDIO, Iván (1970). *Radiografía presupuestaria de la UCV*. Caracas. Italgráfica.

CRA (1997). *Encapuchados: Un show sin gracia en "Las 3 Gracias"*. (1995) Editorial: ¡Adiós Compañero! Año 1, n° 3.¿Quienes somos? http://www.nodo50.org/ellibertario/tripaquienessomos.htm

Crisol Juvenil. n° 8

CODAZZI, Agustín (1840). *Atlas Físico y Político de la República de Venezuela*. París. Litographie de Thierry Fréres.

COLECTIVO ALAS DE XUE. *Una historia del anarquismo en Colombia, crónicas de utopía*. Queimada.

Compañero. N° 2, mayo 1976

CONSALVI, Simón Alberto (1980). *Alberto Carnevali, vida y acción política*. Ediciones Centauro. Caracas. Venezuela. 1980.

DAGER, Jorge (1979). *Testigo de Excepción, en las trincheras de la resistencia 1948-1955*. Ediciones Centauro. Caracas, Venezuela.

DE LA CRUZ, Rafael (1988). *Venezuela en busca de un nuevo pacto social*. Alfadil/Trópicos

DENIS BOULTON, Rolan (2001). *Los fabricantes de la rebelión, movimiento popular, chavismo y sociedad en los años 90*. Editorial Nueva Línea. Editorial Nuevo Sur. Caracas. Venezuela.

DELLA PERUTA, F (1954). *La banda del Matese e il fallimento della teoria anarchica della moderna Jacquerie in Italia.* Movimiento Operaio.

DELACOURT, Frédéric (2000). *L'Affaire bande à Bonnot.* De Vecchi. Colec. Grands procés de l'histoire.

DÍAZ RANGEL, Eleazar (1998). *El 14 de febrero y otros relatos.* Monte Ávila Editores.

DÍAZ SÁNCHEZ, Ramón (1950). *Guzmán, elipse de una ambición de poder.* Caracas.

DÍAZ, Carlos (1993). *Víctor García. El Marco Polo del anarquismo.* Ediciones Madre Tierra.

DOLGOFF, Sam (1974). *Collectives in the Spanish Revolution.* New York: Free Life Editions.

DUKAKIS, Michael (1977). Proclamation by Gov. Michael S. Dukakis of Nicola Sacco and Bartolomeo Vanzetti Memorial Day.

ELLNER, Steve. (1995). *El Sindicalismo en Venezuela, en el contexto democrático (1958-1994).* Fondo Editorial Tropykos. Universidad de Oriente.

ENZO, David (2007). *Carlos Brandt y el Misterioso Almirante.* http://enzodavid.wordpress. com/2007/05/12/carlos-brandt-y-el-misteriosoalmirante- que-nos-descubrio/

ESCAMILLA, Francisco (2002). "Pablo Vila y el Exilio Español," *Revista Bibliográfica de Geografía y Ciencias Sociales.* Universidad de Barcelona. Vol. VII. Nro. 409.

ESCALONA, Víctor (1997). "Detectaron centro de espionaje en la UCV. 6 de enero."

El Zuliano (1983). "En la calle Papeles Anárquicos, nuevo órgano de difusión cultural." 29 de mayo.

El Nacional (1945). "Rota las relaciones entre Venezuela y Franco." 2 de noviembre.

El Nacional (1952). "Grupo armado de civiles penetro en Boca del Rió." 6 de mayo.

El Nacional (1995) "El gobierno nacional niega allanamiento de la UCV." Caracas 25 de enero.

FABBRI, Luigi. *Bourgeois Influences on Anarchism.* Alberta, Canada: Thoughtcrime Ink.

FARIAS Eduardo (1990). *1928, responden los protagonistas.* Fondo Editorial Tropykos. Caracas.

FERNANDEZ, Frank (2000). *El anarquismo en Cuba.* Fundación Anselmo Lorenzo. Madrid.

FERNANDEZ, Frank (2001). *Cuban Anarchism: The History of a Movement.* Tucson: See Sharp Press.

FONTANILLAS, Antonia. *Germinal Gracia y el valor de la amistad.* Mayo 25 de 1992.

FLORES, Rodrigo (1991). "Orígenes de la Palabra Anarquía en Venezuela." *Revista Correo A,* Año V, N° 17, noviembre.

FLORES MAGÓN, Ricardo (2005). *Dreams of Freedom.* Oakland: AK Press.

FLORES MAGÓN, Ricardo (1984). *Discursos.* Mexico DF, Ediciones Antorcha.

FOMBONA BLANCO, Rufino (1915). *La lámpara de Aladino.* Editorial Renacimiento.

GARCIA, María Yolanda (1992). "Estudiantes lograron su cometido se hicieron sentir." *El Diario de Caracas.* Caracas, 25 de enero.

(1992). "Ucevistas presos se declararon en huelga de hambre." *El Diario de Caracas.* 29 de enero.

GARCÍA SALAZAR, Pantaleón. *Apuntes para la Historia del Movimiento Sindical Zuliano*

GIL FORTUE, José (1967). *Historia Constitucional de Venezuela.* Caracas, Librería Piñango.

GODIO Julio (1980). *Historia del movimiento obrero latinoamericano.* Editorial Nueva Imagen, México. (1980).

GODIO, Julio (1980). *El Movimiento Obrero en Venezuela 1850-1944.* Editorial Ateneo de Caracas.

GOLDMAN, Emma (2003). *My Disillusionment in Russia.* New York: Dover.

GOLDMAN, Emma (2003). *My Further Disillusionment in Russia.* New York: Dover.

GÓMEZ CASAS, Juan (1986). *Anarchist Organization: The History of the FAI.* Montreal, Black Rose.

GÓMEZ PICÓN, Alirio (1978). *Páez, fundador del Estado venezolano.* Ediciones Tercer Mundo, Caracas.

GÓMEZ, Carlos Alarico (2007). *El poder andino: De Cipriano Castro a Medina Angarita.* Los Libros del Nacional. Caracas, Venezuela.

GONZÁLEZ, Juan Vicente (1846). Diario de la tarde, n° 94, Caracas. 15 de septiembre y n° 114, 8 de octubre de 1846, cf. Presidencia de la Republica, *Pensamiento Político Venezolano del Siglo XIX, textos para estudios,* vol. 3, t. II, pp. 104 y 105, Caracas, Editorial Arte. 1961

GONZALEZ, Juan Vicente (1859). *Guerra Social.* El Heraldo. N° 48. 14 de diciembre.

GRAEBER, David (2004). *Fragments of Anarchist Antropologist.* Prickly Paradigm Press, Chicago.

HEREDIA José Francisco (1895). *Memorias sobre las Revoluciones de Venezuela.* Edit. Garnier. París.

HERRERA LUQUE, Francisco (1985). *Boves el Urogallo.* España: Editorial Pomaire.

HOBSBAWM, Eric (2010). *Rebeldes Primitivos.* Critica.

HOBSBAWM, Eric (2001). *Bandidos.* Critica. Barcelona.

IÑIGUEZ Miguel (2001). *Esbozo de una Enciclopedia Histórica del Anarquismo Español.* Fundación Anselmo Lorenzo.

JIMENEZ, Iván (1996). *Los golpes de Estado desde Castro hasta Caldera.* Centralca, Caracas.

KROPOTKIN, Pyotr (1974). *Fields, Factories, and Workshops Tomorrow.* New York: Harper.

KROPOTKIN, Pyotr (1987). *Mutual Aid.* Boston: Porter-Sargent.

La Esfera. "Asalto al puesto de emergencia. Pistola en mano se llevaron al doctor Alberto Carnevali."

LANDATE ROSALES, Manuel (1907). *Recepciones hechas en Caracas a personajes notables.* Caracas. Imprenta Bolívar.

LARES, Fermín. *El movimiento sindical y la lucha política en Venezuela 1936-59.* Monte Ávila e Instituto Nacional de Altos Estudios Sindicales, INAESINO.

LEAL, Lilia (2011). *En la rebelión del 27N no estaba previsto el asesinato de Carlos Andrés Pérez.* Correo del Orinoco. Consultado el 1 de agosto.

LONDRES, Albert (1927). *L'homme qui s'évada.* Ed. Albin Michel. Paris, Francia.

LEON, José Javier (2008). *El Demócrata.* http://josejavierleon.blog.com.es/2008/11/20/el-democrata-5071784/

LEVAL, Gaston (1975). *Collectives in the Spanish Revolution.* London: Freedom Press.

LÓPEZ MAYA, Margarita (2005). *Del Viernes Negro al Referendo Revocatorio.* Colección Hogueras. Venezuela profunda. Alfa Grupo Editorial.

LOVERA DE SOLA, Roberto J (2009). *Un Zamora Chavista.* http://www. analitica.com/va/sociedad/articulos/3378370.asp

LOVERA DE SOLA, Roberto J (2009). *40 años de la Renovación en Letras.* http://literanova eduardocasanova. com/index.php/2009/05/12/40-anos-de-la-renovacionen-letras-ucv-1-1969

LUCA, Gerardo (1998). *La Industrialización Pionera en Venezuela (1820–1936).* Universidad Católica Andrés Bello.

MARSHALL, Peter (2010). *Demanding the Impossible: A History of Anarchism.* Oakland: PM Press.

MARTÍNEZ, Ibsen (2010). *El divino fracaso. Caracas, Venezuela.* http://ibsenmartinez.com/archives/1200

MARTURE MEDINA, Carolina (2003). *Gobierno de Isaías Medina Angarita, un régimen de libertades que duro cuatro años.* Mención Periodismo Impreso. Universidad Católica Andrés Bello.

MATA, Celestino (1985). *Historia Sindical de Venezuela.* Editores Urbina y Fuente Asociados, Caracas.

MATHEWS, Robert. *Violencia rural en Venezuela 1840/1858.* Monte Ávila Editores.

MAXIMOFF, G.P. (1979). *The Guillotine at Work: The Leninist Counter-Revolution. Sanday, Scotland,* Cienfuegos Press.

MECHE (2011). *Las andanzas de Rafael Bolívar Coronado.* http://cuentaelabuelo. blogspot.com/2011/03/las-andanzas-de-rafael-bolivar-coronado. html

MENDEZ, Nelson (1995). *Érase una vez el futuro. Una indagación sociohistórica sobre la Renovación Universitaria en la Escuela de Ingeniería de la UCV.*

MESA, Sálom (1987). *La Vida me lo dijo, elogio a la anarquía.* Editorial Hermanos Vadell.,Valencia.

MESA, Sálom (1978). *Por un caballo y una mujer (Memorias).* Hermanos Vadell Editores.Valencia.

MESA, Sálom (1978). Cartas para Carlos. Hermanos Vadell Editores. Valencia.

MESA, Sálom (1969). *El gallo de Machillanda(Relato).* Imprenta Nueva. Caracas, Venezuela.

MESA, Sálom (1964). *AD y el Problema Universitario.* Publicaciones de la Secretaria Nacional de Propaganda. Caracas. Frente al Consejo de Guerra Permanente de Caracas.

MIER HOFFMAN, Jorge (2008). *Bolívar y la Anarquía.* http://www.simonbolivar.org/bolivar/ven_y_la_anarquia.html#inicio

MIJARES, Silvia (1980). Organizaciones políticas de 1936, su importancia en la socialización política del venezolano. Biblioteca de la Academia Nacional de la Historia. Caracas, Venezuela.

MINTZ, Frank. Anarchism and Workers Self-Management in Revolutionary Spain. Oakland, AK Press.

MOLEIRO, Moisés (1979). *El Partido del Pueblo, crónica de un fraude.* Editores Hermanos Vadell. Valencia.

MONTAIGNE, Michele (1981) *Essais. Réimpression en facsimilé de l´Exemplaire de Bordeaux, par Fortunat Strowski, 1906-33 en 5 vol.* Hildesheim-Nueva York, Ed. Geog Olms, 3 vol

MUDIE SPENCER, James. *The land of Bolivar; Or, War, Peace and Adventure in the Republic of Venezuela.*

MÚJICA, Héctor (1970). *Co-gobernabilidad: Balance de un Año de Renovación Académica.* Caracas. Cantaclaro.

NAVAJA DE ARNOUX (2008). *El Discurso Latinoamericano de Hugo Chávez.* Editorial Biblos. Argentina.

NOGALES MÉNDEZ, Rafael (1991). *Memorias.* Biblioteca Ayacucho.

NÚÑEZ TENORIO, José Rafael (1977). *Reencarnar el espíritu de Bolívar.* Editorial Panapo. Caracas, Venezuela.

OLIVO, Libertad (1997). *Francisco Olivo, un hombre, una vida, una escuela.* Instituto Municipal de Publicaciones. Caracas, Venezuela.

OTERO SILVA, Miguel (2004). *Cuando quiero llorar, no lloro.* Editorial CEC, S.A. Caracas.

OTERO SILVA, Miguel (1961). *Fiebre.* Biblioteca Popular de Venezuela. Caracas.

OVALLES, Lenin (2006). *Caracas resiste y ataka.* N° 5. Caracas.

OVERING, Joanna (1988). *Los Wothuha, Aborígenes de Venezuela.* Fundación La Salle.

PANNEKOEK, Anton (2002). *Workers' Councils.* Oakland, AK Press.

PARDO, Miguel Eduardo (1981). *Todo un Pueblo.* Caracas, Monte Ávila.

PALMA, Douglas A (1997). *150 biografías de los personajes notables de Venezuela.* Editorial Panapo.

PARRA PÉREZ, Caracciolo. (1992) *Historia de la Primera República de Venezuela.* Biblioteca Ayacucho.

PEIRATS, José (1987). Anarchists in the Spanish Revolution. London, Freedom Press.

PELLEGRINO, Adela (1989). *Historia de la inmigración en Venezuela, siglos XIX y XX.* Academia Nacional de Ciencias Económicas.

PENELAS, Carlos (2004). *Ácratas y crotos. Informes del sur, cuadernos de investigación.* Ediciones BP. Prosa.

PEÑALOSA, Carlos (2001). *La poderosa Mafia Garibaldi.* http://www.analitica.com/va/economia/opinion/4207838.asp

PÉREZ, Francisco Javier (2010). *Julio Cesar Salas.* Biblioteca Biográfica Venezolana. Editora El Nacional. Caracas, Venezuela.

PÉREZ SALINAS, Bernardo. *Tras las huellas del sindicalismo.* Cuadernos Obreros de Acción Democrática.

POTENZIANI BIGELLI, Julio (2012). "Camille Pissarro y Venezuela, una huella que duraría toda una vida," Vitae Nro. 49. Academia Biomédica Digital. Enero-Marzo.

PLAZA OLARTE, Guillermo (2008). "Los Llaneros en la Independencia (1ra Parte)." *Revista de las Fuerzas Armadas.* Vol. XLIII-Nro. 129. 21 de Julio. Colombia.

PRATO BARBOSA, Nelson. *Desobediencia Social en Venezuela.* Colección José Agustín Silva Michelena. APUCV.

QUERO, Humberto Jaimes (2003). *Mentalidades, discurso y espacio en la Caracas de finales del siglo XX.* Fundación para la Cultura Urbana. Caracas.

QUINTERO, Rodolfo (1967). *La huelga petrolera 1936-1937.* Folleto publicado en Barranquilla en 1937 y reeditado en Venezuela por el Departamento

QUINTERO Rodolfo (1955). *La vida y las luchas del revolucionario Daniel De Leon*, México DF.

QUINTERO, Rodolfo. *Sindicalismo y cambio social en Venezuela*.

RADA ARANGOL, Yasmín y CONTRERAS Orlando José (2010). *Protesta estudiantil y represión en Venezuela 1983-1993*. Archivo General de la Nación. Centro Nacional de Historia. Caracas.

RAMA, Carlos M (1976). *Historia del movimiento obrero y social latinoamericano contemporáneo*. Ediciones de Bolsillo. Editorial Laia. Barcelona.

RANGEL, Domingo Alberto (2013). *Alzado contra todo, memoria y desmemoria*. Editores Hermanos Vadell y Editores Mérida. Caracas.

RANGEL, Domingo Alberto (2010). "Coto Paúl, el olvidado 1810." Semanario Quinto Día. 29 de enero.

RANGEL, Domingo Alberto (2004). *Un socialismo para el siglo veintiuno*. Editores Mérida. Caracas. Venezuela. Febrero

RESZLER, André (2006). "La estética anarquista. Libros de la Araucania." *Revista Opúsculo*. Biblioteca Nacional de Venezuela.

ROCKER, Rudolph (1988). *Anarchism and Anarcho-Syndicalism*. London, Freedom Press.

ROCKER, Rudolph (2004). *Anarcho-Syndicalism: Theory and Practice*. Oakland, AK Press.

RODRIGUEZ, Alonzo. *El Fuego sangrado*.

RODRIGUEZ Leonardo. *Primer Congreso Obrero de Venezuela*. 1896. Publicaciones El Pueblo.

RODRÍGUEZ, Leonardo (1988). *La clase obrera en el tiempo de Gómez1908-1935*. Publicaciones El Pueblo.

RODRIGUEZ, Manuel Alfredo. *El Capitolio de Caracas, un siglo de historia de Venezuela*. Ediciones del Congreso de la República.

ROJAS, Aristide (1891). *Leyendas históricas de Venezuela*. Segunda Serie. Imprenta y litografía del Gobierno Nacional. Caracas.

SALCEDO BASTARDO, José .Luis (1993). *Historia Fundamental de Venezuela*. Ediciones de la Universidad Central de Venezuela

SANIN. *Los adecos en el poder*. Colección Criterios. Venezuela.

SANZ, Víctor (1985). *El Exilio español en Venezuela*. Casa de España.

SANOJA HERNÁNDEZ JESUS (2001). *Crímenes políticos en Venezuela*. Colección Ares. Los Libros del Nacional. Caracas, Venezuela.

SERRANO, Antonio (1998). "Apuntes sobre Anarquismo en Venezuela." Suplemento Cultural *Últimas Noticias*. Caracas, 18 de Octubre.

SERRANO, Antonio (1999). "Hace 35 años." *El Libertario*. Año 3, numero 14. Mayo/Junio.

SERRANO, Antonio (1996). "Gracias a Caballero." Periódico *El Universal*. 5 de octubre

SERRANO, Antonio (1985). "El anarquismo, Sr. Betancourt, no es lo que usted así denomina." *El Nacional*, Viernes 12 de Julio.

SHIKES, Ralph (1986). *Pissarro's political philosophy and his art, from Studies on Camille Pissarro*. Edited by Christopher Lloyd. London and New York: Routledge & Kegan Paul.

STRAKA Tomas (2009). *Contra Bolívar*. Editorial Libros Marcados.

SOSA ARTURO, Legrand Eloi (1994). *El programa nacionalista izquierda y modernización (1937-1939)*. Editorial Fundación Rómulo Betancourt. Caracas.

SOSA ARTURO, Legrand Eloi (1981). *Del Garibaldismo estudiantil a la Izquierda Criolla*. Ediciones Centauro. Caracas, Venezuela.

SOTO PRIETO, Jesús. *La lucha obrera por nuestro petróleo*.

THOMSON, Fred and BEKKEN, Jon (2006). *The Industrial Workers of the World. Its First 100 Years*. Chicago, IWW.

TROCONIS GUERRERO, Luis (1962). *La cuestión agraria en la Historia Nacional*. Biblioteca de Autores y Temas Tachirenses. Tribuna Popular. Caracas. Febrero 1977.

UGALDE, Luis (1978). *Venezuela Republicana Siglo XIX*. Curso de formación sociopolítico.

ULACIO, Sandy (2007). *27N, la historia de un baño de sangre.* Seminario Versión Final.

URQUIJO José Ignacio (2000). *El movimiento obrero en Venezuela.* OITUCAB

USLAR PIETRI, Juan (1962). *Historia de la rebelión popular de 1814.* Editorial Edime.

UZCATEGUI, Rafael (2012). *Victimas de la Democracia, concierto en el Julius*Pub. http:// exiliointeriorzine.blogspot.com/2012/08/victimas-de-lademocracia-en-concierto.html

UZCATEGUI, Rafael (2001). *Corazón de tinta.* Naufrago de Ítaca Ediciones.

UZCATEGUI, Rafael (2010). *Venezuela: Revolution as Spectacle.* Tucson, See Sharp Press.

VÁZQUEZ DE ESPINOSA, Antonio (1948). *Compendio y descripción de las Indias Occidentales.* Dirección de Cultura.

VELASQUEZ Ramón J (1976). *Venezuela Moderna. Medio siglo de historia.* Fundación Eugenio Mendoza. Caracas 1976.

VENAMI (1995). Declaración de VENAMI. Boletín nº 1. Caracas. Venezuela, Abril.

VERGUEIRO, Armando (1992). *Así de golpe, no.* Caracas, Correo A.

VILLANUEVA MARTÍNEZ, Orlando y otros (1992). *Biofilo Panclasta, el eterno prisionero.* Editorial CODICE LTDA. Bogota, Colombia.

VILLEGAS, Luis Enrique (1988). *La huelga petrolera 50 años (1936-1986).* Publicaciones El Pueblo, Caracas, Venezuela.

VINOGRADOFF, Ludmila (1993). "Un tribunal militar condena a 97 golpistas en Venezuela." *El País.* 14 de enero.

VOLINE (1974). *The Unknown Revolution.* Detroit, Black & Red.

V.V.A.A (1984). *Pío Tamayo. Un combate por la vida.* Ediciones UCV.

WARD, Colin (2002). *About Anarchism.* London, Freedom, Press.

WARD, Colin (1992). *Anarchy in Action.* London, Freedom Press.

ZAMBRANO, Luis Eduardo. "El intento de magnicidio de Cipriano Castro. Diario La Nación." http:// www.lanacion.com.ve/noticias. php?IdArticulo=113745&XR=2